MW01063482

SPIKED

HOW CHAIN MANAGEMENT
CORRUPTED
AMERICA'S OLDEST NEWSPAPER.

By
ANDREW KREIG

TROC

PEREGRINE PRESS, Publishers
Old Saybrook, Connecticut

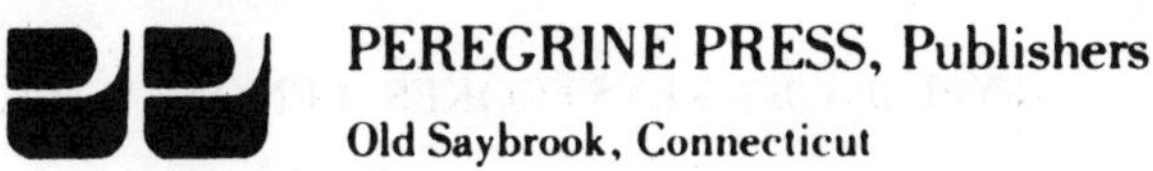

PUBLISHED BY PEREGRINE PRESS
(203) 388-0285
P.O. BOX 751
OLD SAYBROOK, CT 06475

Grateful acknowledgment is made to the following publishing houses and creators for permission to reprint material from their copyrighted works:

To Alfred A. Knopf, Inc. for quotations from *The Powers That Be* by David Halberstam (Knopf 1979);

To John Morgan for quotations from *Noah Webster* by John Morgan (Mason/Charter 1975);

To Robert Gottlieb and Irene Wolt for quotations from *Thinking Big* by Robert Gottlieb and Irene Wolt (Putnam 1977);

To the *Hartford Courant* and Bob Englehart for his editorial page cartoon first published in the *Courant* on May 6, 1983.

MANUFACTURED IN THE UNITED STATES

Library of Congress Catalogue Number 87-061691

ISBN 0-933614-27-6

COVER DESIGNS BY CORTLANDT TROC HULL

TYPESET BY KEYSTROKES, LENOX, MASS.

To my parents Margaret and Albert and grandmother Gladys for their love and force of example.

CONTENTS

CONTENTS

PREFACE

NEW YORK TIMES writer Sydney Schanberg was near the top of his profession in 1985 when he pushed his luck to the limit. Earlier, he had won a Pulitzer Prize for his courageous war coverage in staying at his post while Communists overran Cambodia. *The Killing Fields*, nominated for the "best-picture" Academy Award, portrayed his experiences. In 1981, Schanberg began writing a public affairs column, a position at his paper reputed to confer almost lifetime security. "A *Times* column," wrote one commentator, "has historically been the journalistic equivalent of a Supreme Court judgeship."

So the *Times'* former metropolitan editor seemed safe when he used his forum one day to criticize the city's newspapers. While not identifying his targets by name, he disparaged coverage of a controversial project called Westway. The plan was to build a major highway along Manhattan's West Side and fill in some two hundred acres of river water for luxury housing. Its pricetag was estimated at between four and fifteen billion dollars. Westway was strongly supported by New York politicians, developers and the *Times* itself. It was opposed by community and environmental groups. "Our newspapers, oddly, can't seem to find space for

Westway and its scandal," Schanberg alleged, adding, "As a public works project, the Westway plan may be this generation's largest suggested misuse of scarce public funds . . . ."

The publisher of the *Times* abruptly reassigned the twenty-six-year veteran of the paper to unspecified duties, ending the urban affairs column.

With his Vandyke beard and big, sad eyes, Schanberg looked stoical, rather like a worldly wise El Greco figure. He resigned from the *Times* during much speculation about the reasons for his demise. No meaningful comment came from the newspaper. When Schanberg finally provided his own assessment, he used a phrase that has long been known to working journalists around the country: "The Afghanistan Theory." This is the concept that newspapers "believe in vigorous coverage of anything that happens in distant lands such as Afghanistan," Schanberg told one interviewer. "But a sea change takes place when the same vigorous standards are applied at home."

Nothing is more "at home" than a news organization's internal affairs. Revelations might puncture the image of dignity, infallibility and altruism that the news media construct as eagerly as any Supreme Court justice. And if the *Times* cannot endure criticism from within, what about the news organizations with less lofty standards? "Newspapers write about other newspapers with circumspection," said the late *New Yorker* commentator A. J. Liebling. "They write about themselves with awe, and only after mature reflection."

Historic changes have been occurring during the 1980s in the ownership and operation of the news media. Most public attention has focused on press lord Rupert Murdoch's expanding empire, on group acquisition of such noted independent voices as the *New Yorker* and on battles for control of the three major television networks. An untold story—and one I believe is extremely important—concerns changes at our regionally dominant newspapers. Many of these are in monopoly markets. Most operate with no real scrutiny by other media. These newspapers have tremendous impact on the public. Their judgments are often echoed by broadcasters and smaller newspapers in their areas, thus setting the public affairs agenda for entire regions.

Since 1985 chains have bought such respected locally-owned papers as the *Des Moines Register* and *Tribune*, *Detroit News*, *Louisville Courier-Journal* and *Times*, *Houston Chronicle*, *Arkansas Gazette*, and *Baltimore Sun* and *Evening Sun*. "In 1971, fifty percent of all U.S. dailies were owned by groups," said an industry spokesman. "Today, over seventy percent of all dailies are group-owned. We feel that by 1995, about eighty-five percent of all U.S. dailies will be group-owned." His prediction may be conservative.

The Los Angeles-based media conglomerate Times Mirror is especially intriguing. Experts generally regard it and Knight-Ridder of Miami, Fla. as the best of the chains. Times Mirror, though, has more firepower in the country's major media and governmental centers. Its flagship paper, the *Los Angeles Times*, dominates Southern California. At the other end of the continent, Times Mirror's *Newsday* is expanding into Manhattan from its solid base on New York's Long Island. The 1986 acquisitions of the highly respected Baltimore papers and of the Washington-based *National Journal* solidified Times Mirror's capitol region clout, which had already been strong because of its high-profile Washington bureaus and Los Angeles Times-Washington Post Wire Service. The wire service provides stories to client papers around the country. The Los Angeles chain also has had outlets in substantial mid-size markets, including Denver, Dallas and Hartford, Conn. Overall, Times Mirror was the country's seventy-ninth largest industrial firm in net income before its $600 million purchase of the Baltimore papers and $110 million sale of the *Dallas Times Herald*.

More than other newspaper chains, Times Mirror has repeatedly sought recognition for providing thoughtful public service. It underlined its leadership role in the industry by its large-scale advertising campaign, "The People & The Press." Full-page advertisements in newspapers and national magazines promulgated the firm's findings on public attitudes as revealed in a specially-commissioned Gallup poll: "There is no credibility crisis for the nation's news media."

Press analyst Ben Bagdikian presented a more troubling assessment during a panel discussion in Washington, D.C. of "The Merger and Acquisition Frenzy in the News Business: Where Will It all End?" Bagdikian was the dean of the Graduate School of Journalism at the University of California at Berkeley. But he confessed to his audience (mostly chain executives) that he was "the skunk at the garden party" because of his message: "In the long run, in general, chains are not going to be good for journalism." He provided four reasons:

> —*Reductions of news coverage to enhance profits.* "Most major chains are in the race for expansion and acquisitions on a national and even international scale . . . . And newspapers, especially monopoly newspapers, are especially easy to squeeze for surplus profits by cheapening content." [By using more advertisements, and less locally reported news.]
>
> —*Conflicts of interests between newspaper management and the national industries and financial institutions they cover.* "There is seldom a memorandum that goes up on the bulletin board saying, 'When the parent firm's other interests are involved we will handle it differently.' You don't need to do that in most operations."
>
> —*Increased bureaucracy and demands for uniformity.* "The MBAs are moving into the newsrooms."
>
> —*Too much concentrated power.* "It isn't enough, I think, to say that the power is there, but it'll never be used. Power will always be used if the stakes are high enough."

"[The] 'chains people' are always saying that some chains have improved papers," continued the silver-haired former *Washington Post* ombudsman. "I agree and have always said so. Chains have also worsened papers, and I don't hear that said so often." Conceding that criticisms like his were apt to be disregarded because he no longer works in a newsroom, he challenged newspaper editors to do their own studies. "If that were done—an honest, careful survey—and I turned out to be wrong, I promise personally to sell *USA TODAY* [the Gannett chain's national newspaper] for one hour at high noon on the corner."

In the hotel lobby just after his speech, he encountered Norman Isaacs, the retired newspaper publisher who headed the National News Council (a watchdog group) for seven years. Poking their fingers onto each others' chests to emphasize their points, the two eminent press analysts agreed that the flagship papers of Times Mirror and Knight-Ridder were excellent—but the quality didn't necessarily extend elsewhere. The *Los Angeles Times*, *Philadelphia Inquirer* and a few other papers, they seemed to be saying, were like the flashy convertibles in auto showroom windows—displays primped and polished to lure customers for lesser products.

My original intention was to write a magazine article describing Times Mirror's transformation of one of its papers, the regionally dominant *Hartford Courant* in Connecticut. But as I pursued the research about the paper where I had worked fourteen years, I came to believe the story had wider significance.

No single case history, of course, has universal implications. There are nearly 1,660 daily newspapers in the country, ranging from elite giants such as the *New York Times* to tiny community organs. Yet the *Courant* has an archetypal quality. It inflamed one of the thirteen original colonies with news of the Boston Tea Party and the Declaration of Independence. During the Revolutionary War, it was by far the country's largest newspaper and one of the strongest voices for independence. By publishing Noah Webster's books, it helped shape a distinctly American language. After criticizing President Thomas Jefferson, its owners were sentenced to prison—and then won acquittal in the first press freedom case to reach the U.S. Supreme Court.

Under local ownership in the 1970s, the paper reported the news in an independent, responsible manner that largely satisfied its readers and staff. Its management was ingrown, however, and it implemented new ideas sluggishly. Times Mirror bought the paper in 1979 for the then-record price of $105.6 million, and twice transformed editorial operations from top to bottom. In the 1980s, the paper has mounted lavish investigations. Also, it has been in the vanguard of some of its industry's more innovative ideas in advertising, magazine style, photography and graphics. The results have reaped high profits and bushel baskets full of journalism prizes. Michael Davies, recruited from Kansas City to be publisher of the paper, was 1985 president of one of the most important trade groups in journalism, Associated Press Managing Editors. He boasted to his staff that their newspaper was increasingly recognized as one of the top twenty in the country, and might soon begin to crack "Top Ten" lists.

Yet there is also evidence that hidden corporate imperatives and taboos thwarted the newspaper's mission of truth-telling. The chain conferred power onto fiercely loyal, ruthlessly ambitious executives brought in from afar. By controlling the region's dominant information source as tightly as they did, the chieftains were free to bungle and lie, and to suppress inconvenient facts and ideas. The manipulators were so arrogant that they made repeated efforts to win journalism's highest honor, the Pulitzer Prize, with highly deceptive entries. Far from being the "public service" they purported to be, these efforts grossly distorted public perceptions on important issues. They wasted taxpayer money and devastated individuals who were without means to contest the paper's inaccuracies.

One of many observers willing to discuss this dark side was former business writer John Tarpey, even though he had a rapid series of promotions under Times Mirror before he became a writer and editor at *Business Week*. "It boggles the mind," said Tarpey, his voice rising with a note of wonderment, "what they tried to do, and the lives they ruined."

Part of my goal is to reveal news-management trends during the era of merger mania. Part is to portray the life of a contemporary newspaper reporter, much as Scott Turow's blunt, detailed account of his law student experiences in *One L* illuminated legal education. Like him, I make no claim that my reactions are universal. Also, I concede at the outset that it's impossible to prove irrebuttably that every incident I describe was caused by the nature of my newspaper's ownership. All newsrooms have internal alliances, power plays and critics. Yet the sudden, pervasive onslaught of abusive practices in Hartford suggests an overall cause-and-effect relationship. And even if some of the mismanagement could have occurred in either a chain or independent operation, it's still worth learning how little scrutiny the parent chain and other major institutions provided.

Under Times Mirror, I received the most exotic assignments of my career: magazine editor, full-time writer covering the Boston Celtics, company-salaried student at Yale Law School; and investigative reporter on one of the most ambitious projects ever undertaken by the paper—a ten-month probe of some of the country's biggest manufacturers and insurers.

I suffered serious reverses, as well. And I watched powerlessly as capable co-workers were humiliated in arbitrary ways that had counterparts in actions directed against the public. I felt my own ethical values under serious assault even though the paper's public relations machine was creating an ever-growing national reputation.

My 1984 resignation put me among the 106 reporters and editors who left during a two-year span. Those departing included Times Mirror's first *Courant* publisher, along with the real-life model for TV's "Lou Grant" plus nine of the paper's other top fourteen supervisory news executives. All the departed executives had arrived or received their titles during the first wave of chain appointments. And as the newspaper lost much of its institutional memory, the next wave of executives could manipulate or suppress information with impunity. Suspicious of tradition and ideas, the newspaper's new managers used their power again and again to co-opt, intimidate and punish critics of the corporate agenda. While most such tactics were so deft that only those directly involved could detect them, some general patterns were clear to outsiders.

The transformation of the *Hartford Courant* is "a classic example" of nationwide changes, commented Maureen Croteau, head of the journalism department at the University of Connecticut and former financial editor of the *Providence Journal Bulletin* in Rhode Island. "Hartford is an example of the kinds of newspapers that have come and gone. You had two independent dailies. Then the PM newspaper went out of business. Then you had one independent AM paper. Then one chain-owned paper. And that's the story of newspapers across the United States."

"I was making nothing at the *Hartford Times*," the professor recalled of her reporting days during the early 1970s in the city. "It was absolutely crazy and, of course, everybody grumbled about money from time to time. But still, it was a mission. That's changed as competition has lessened. If ten, fifteen years ago, you had told someone in a newsroom, 'This is our product,' they would have looked at you like you were nuts. Products were shoes. But now newspapers are thought of as products, marketed as products. It's a different philosophy. And when you change the shape of an industry like that, you're going to have terrible discontent—legitimate discontent—among the people who have been in it."

From time to time in my research, I have heard the question, "Why should anyone outside of Connecticut care what happened to the *Hartford Courant* and its readers?" The economic forces that created the situation in Connecticut are nationwide. Times Mirror's Los Angeles and New York executives and their counterparts in other chains are pulling strings all over the country. In his apt and pioneering book *The Media Monopoly*, Bagdikian in 1983 surveyed conglomerate control of the media. Critics writing in the *New York Times* and in the *Columbia Journalism Review* attacked him for not providing, in the words of one reviewer, "more elaboration and documentation." My book provides concrete examples of the problems Bagdikian identified. I describe a newspaper and its internal scandals that happen to be in Connecticut. They could be anywhere.

The *Courant*'s experience holds implications beyond journalism. Conglomerates in the mid-1980s were taking over and transforming local businesses of all sizes and types. Factories, farms, banks, airlines and even community hospitals were all part of a shakeout having enormous impact on everyday life.

Where can the public look for a frank appraisal of these developments? The media? The media is part of it. The government? The Justice Department's Antitrust Division has increasingly tended to applaud rather than critique the process. "Takeovers," argued Acting Antitrust Chief Charles Rule, "are an efficient means of ousting managements that are incompetent or are more interested in their own comfort than in enhancing their shareholders' wealth." His justifiications are noteworthy. To cut expenses, the chain-operated *Courant* reduced news coverage of communities with low buying power, which were unattractive to advertisers. Newspapers, of course, have an important role in sustaining democratic values. Can "efficiency" be the standard for measuring the performance of newspapers? If not, what is?

Times Mirror controls not only newspapers, but television and radio stations, plus magazine and book publishing subsidiaries. In addition, it wields considerable influence over university and professional organizations affiliated with the field of journalism. So I am deeply grateful to the whistleblowers who made this book possible by telling what they knew. In commenting on *Spiked* as he neared his ninety-seventh birthday, the venerable press muckraker George Seldes told me that he had never before seen journalists say such strong things about their own news organization. My debt is especially strong to the first few who risked their careers by violating the Afghanistan Theory and talking on-the-record about the profession they love. They had no guarantee others would speak up.

Also, I thank the Fund for Investigative Journalism, its board of directors and Executive Director Howard Bray. Their encouragement meant much to my spirits. *Connecticut Magazine* has kindly allowed me to reprint parts of my investigative articles it published from 1985 to 1987. The magazine research involved hundreds of interviews that deepened my understanding of some of the major public events in the region. Finally, I thank the financial supporters and the helpful staffs of a number of libraries, especially those at the Connecticut State Library and Yale University.

The story here unfolds rather like a novel—except that the hero is an idea, not any one person. The American idea of a free and fair press is old and somewhat battered by now. It is occasionally ludicrous in its pretensions. It is resilient, though. And its adventures and tribulations command attention—not for its sake, but for ours.

A.K.
June 1987
Hartford, Conn.

PART I

Setting the Stage

CHAPTER 1

Disaster

INTERSTATE 95, the central artery along the Atlantic Coast, winds from southern Florida to the Canadian border, passing through Washington, D.C., New York City and Boston along the way. The six-lane section on Connecticut's shoreline is one of the most heavily traveled highways in New England because it accommodates New York commuters as well as long-haul drivers.

In the early morning darkness of June 28, 1983, a recently married Georgian named David Pace, aged twenty-seven, guided his tractor-trailer northeast on the last miles of a trip that had begun in Indiana. His wife, Helen, slept beside him in the Mack cab, which pulled 26,000 pounds of beer bottles intended for recycling.

In passing through the Connecticut suburb of Greenwich at 1:30 a.m., Pace suddenly saw a black chasm looming before him. All three northbound lanes of the highway had just collapsed, leaving a gap of a hundred feet before the pavement resumed. He had time only to push a pillow at his wife and shout for her to cover up before the cab sailed over the edge. It dropped seventy feet and splashed into the Mianus River. Water gushed in through the broken windows.

Pace, overcoming his pain from a fractured back, reached for his wife. He couldn't find her, and he began panicking. Finally, he felt her fingertips. He pulled her to him and carried her up to a corner of the cab not yet filled with water. They grabbed a deep breath. "Hold on!" the trucker told her in his deep, Southern voice. He got his arms around her, and carried her to the surface. "And, thank God!" he later recalled. "There was people there in a boat, a man and his son, who were there to help us out."

Two other drivers and a passenger died from falls that night when their vehicles plunged into the river or its bank. A college student survived, but was partially paralyzed. Someone else skidded to a stop near the brink. Desperately waving his hands, he flagged other oncoming drivers to a halt.

The survivors—all with broken spines and other extensive injuries—endured a grim recuperation. Amazingly enough, they faced the strong possibility that they might never be compensated for the accident because of legal technicalities. Connecticut had a narrow doctrine of government liability for highway accidents. The state of Connecticut was immune from damages if anyone else shared in even a small part of the blame for a traffic accident. In the Mianus River Bridge case, the precedents suggested that the victims might get nothing. The state needed to show only that the bridge design by outside engineers was a factor causing the collapse.

The David Pace family, quickly exhausting its private insurance coverage, faced medical costs, living expenses and the uncertainties of litigation with minimal resources. Pace had worked for a small trucking company with inadequate insurance. By mid-1985, he could walk around on his parents' farm in Georgia without showing pain. But he could no longer work as a truck driver, a job that is notoriously hard on the lower back. He and his family remained out of work. They lived mainly on the charity of his parents, both of whom had cancer.

It would be well over two years before Connecticut's largest newspaper noticed what the state attorney general called "a scandalous situation"—that the innocent victims of such a horrifying accident might never be compensated. It's not uncommon, of course, for newspapers and broadcasters to cover accidents exhaustively when they occur, then forget about them. But this was different. The *Hartford Courant*'s new chief executive officer was Michael Davies—a tall, dark-haired native of England whose polished, low-key manner obscured his ambition. He arrived in Hartford two months after the disaster. For a while, he was preoccupied with consolidating his power. But he ultimately decided to make the bridge collapse a showcase for the newspaper's ability to provide in-depth news coverage.

How then, could his paper have missed such a compelling story as that of the survivors' money problems? Probably it was an oversight. But perhaps it occurred also because Davies had a blind spot for that type of story. He liked to say that the American legal system (which uses juries in civil cases, unlike Great Britain's judge-dominated system) makes it too easy for people bringing lawsuits to collect obscenely large sums. Whatever the case, he orchestrated other Mianus Bridge follow-ups that (as he correctly predicted in a staff meeting) would "really shake up the state."

Chief among these was a plan patterned after his previous successes at Midwestern newspapers. It would use the drama of a disaster, in this case a bridge collapse, as a "news peg" for a thorough-going investigation of state Department of Transportation (DOT) safety inspectors. The purpose? To show that they were incompetent, lazy and larcenous on a grand scale—and that the newspaper was protecting the public by the revelations.

Davies brought in editors from the *Kansas City Star* who zealously applied the same methods that had brought them journalism prizes at the *Star:* assigning reporters and photographers to spy on government inspectors. The intention was to go beyond the acknowledged problems of bridge design, budgets and maintenance—and to target individuals, thus making lively reading. After one of the most costly investigations in the paper's long history, the paper published a series in June 1984 to coincide with the anniversary of the collapse of the Mianus River Bridge. The stories were typified by the first-day headline, "FRAUD, LAXITY MAR DOT PROGRAM." They reverberated in the paper and in the regional media for much of the next year.

The project went on to become the biggest award-winner in the newspaper's history. Among other things, it garnered first-place prizes for public service in both of the main New England journalism contests, which are run by the Associated Press and United Press International for their member newspapers. Nationally, the Scripps Howard Foundation awarded the *Courant* its first-place public service award for the bridge series. Although the stories fell short of a Pulitzer, Davies was later installed as chairman of a Pulitzer judging committee.

The lavish display accorded the bridge inspection exposé bothered me at the time of publication. As an employee of the paper, I knew more than the ordinary reader or contest judge about the stories' zealous preparation and weaknesses.

But because of all the accolades the series had won, I treated it in positive fashion in a magazine article I was drafting in December 1984 on changes in the newspaper business. I did not undertake real detective work on the series until I spoke the next month with Charles Towne, who had been one of my first bosses at the *Courant*. Dignified and soft-spoken, the white-haired man had retired as the editorial page editor in 1977 after forty-seven years with the paper. His devotion to the institution was so great that for four decades he maintained a private log of its history and of the news events it chronicled. A part-time journalism professor at the University of Connecticut before his health failed, Towne nonetheless kept at his record-keeping for several hours a day. It was a labor of love.

We arranged to meet on the steps of Connecticut's Supreme Court and State Library, a huge granite structure across the street from the State Capitol. The words chiseled in stone fifty feet over our heads, "KNOWLEDGE, HISTORY, JUSTICE," seemed an auspicious beginning for the interview. In it, Towne would entrust me with the loan of his records compiled through the decades.

As we sat at a long table in an empty conference room, he surprised me when I asked his opinion of the bridge inspection series. I knew of his conservative temperament, and suspected he was not likely to have much sympathy for malingering inspectors. For another thing, he had no inside information about the exposé. Neither of us knew at the time that Connecticut's chief state's attorney had privately concluded that the series was riddled with factual mistakes and unwarranted assumptions that discredited its thesis. Charles Towne knew only the "facts" that the paper's editors chose to present.

"That was the biggest disgrace," he said, "that I've seen in Connecticut journalism since I started."

"Really? Why?"

"They did a wonderful job of investigating. But they didn't *find* anything. When that happens, you pack it up and call it a day."

Honor or disgrace? The question popped up again and again as I surveyed the range of the newspaper's operations. It was too much to describe in a magazine article. Even *Courant* staffers often had difficulty tracing the abusive practices around them. Only a book-length treatment could lay it all out.

Close scrutiny unearthed three highly deceptive efforts by the *Courant*'s top editors to win Pulitzer Prizes. Other news crusades stood revealed as having smeared leading institutions without just cause. The targets included: the Hartford police department, the chief state's attorney and some of Connecticut's top judges, including a retired chief justice of the Supreme Court. In addition, the paper goaded Connecticut's legislature and governor into a number of dubious measures, some of them enormously expensive. While the newspaper always advocated these projects in terms of public need, they actually stemmed in large part from the news executives' personal career or political agendas.

None of these deceptions were ever revealed even years after they occurred. As late as the *Miami Herald*'s 1987 surveillance of Gary Hart that drove him out of the Presidential race, the *Courant*'s opinion writers were free to publish pieties condemning both Hart's sexual morals and the *Herald*'s "sloppy" surveillance.

The best way to examine such varied developments is chronologically, beginning with a description of the newspaper before chain acquisition. In due course, the bridge investigation will show the new journalistic standards in force. The bridge series, in fact, was pivotal. If it had not been such an overwhelming success with other media, contest judges and trusting readers, some of the newspaper's other efforts might have been presented in more balanced fashion. As it was, the bridge series and similar efforts became models held up for emulation by journalists elsewhere.

It is helpful to describe at the outset the process news organizations use to decide if a specific idea is worthy of publication. Every story requires three things: 1) a writer; 2) "newsmakers" in the community who provide facts, perspective and quotations; and 3) editors. Anyone can initiate a story idea. Ultimately, however, all three elements—the writer, the public and the editors—must contribute.

Baseball is a useful analogy. Every baseball team needs hitting, pitching and fielding in each game. Yet some teams are characterized for only one of these qualities. The 1927 Yankees, with the famous "Murderers Row" that included Ruth and Gehrig, were a "hitters team." The 1954 Cleveland Indians of Bob Lemon and Bob Feller were a "pitchers team." And so on. Similarly, the public element was predominant in the pre-Times Mirror *Courant*. Most reporters fanned out across the circulation area to learn the thinking of community figures. It became a writer's newspaper in 1981 after Times Mirror installed a crew of editors from Los Angeles nicknamed "The Beach Boys" because of their laid-back style. Writers had considerable freedom to devise themes, although ultimately the ideas had to be supported by facts and quotations, then pass muster with editors. Under the so-called "Kansas City Chiefs" Davies brought in after 1983, editors tended to originate major projects. Reporters then found supporting data from public sources.

There is another useful analogy between baseball and newspapers. The value of a team franchise cannot be computed by adding up its bats, balls and players under contract. The team's worth is largely comprised of an intangible—the affection and loyalty of its fans. So it is with newspapers. Charles Towne's mentor John Reitemeyer put it well. "A newspaper's greatest asset," the longtime *Courant* publisher told stockholders in the 1950s, "is not its building, its equipment, or the money in the bank or the bonds in its vault. A newspaper's greatest asset is public confidence, public belief in its fairness, in its honesty, in its integrity."

This confidence can be won either by actual performance or by adroit use of public relations. The *Wall Street Journal* tried to explore these matters in a 1985 article headlined, "TIMES MIRROR ZIGZAGS BRING STAFF, COMMUNITY PROBLEMS." Lacking adequate sources, the *Journal* writer treated such things as the *Courant* bridge series simply as the triumphs they purported to be. The *Journal* story was notable also for the comments of David Laventhol, the New York-based Times Mirror vice president overseeing the *Courant*. Laventhol, who would go on to become president of the chain, said that his firm had learned a lesson from its first transformations in Hartford. "If you change a newspaper, change it carefully," he said. "Newspapers are a lot like old shoes. Some people would rather wear old shoes than the shiny new ones you offer them."

Yet newspapers have a more important mission than shoe factories. And it's one that arouses even fiercer loyalties.

CHAPTER 2

America's Oldest Newspaper

"Was it not for the Prefs, we fhould be left almoft intirely ignorant of all thofe noble Sentiments which the Antients were endow'd with."

—from the *Courant*'s first issue in 1764
(with original "f" for "s" spellings)

FRESH FROM AN EDITORSHIP at Cornell University's student newspaper, I was commissioned with a new pair of scissors as I began my duties as a $120-a-week *Courant* reporter on June 15, 1970. I was sent to a desk in the last row in the huge, unwalled city room. The chamber's yellowish ceiling was high. Its checker-patterned tiled floors were grimy. The desks were cluttered with old newspapers and documents, and even older manual typewriters. The flat, gray Underwoods had been built at the firm's world headquarters, a half mile to the southwest of the newspaper. The black ones came from the Royal typewriter plant a short distance farther away.

Next to the water fountain at the back of the newsroom, a plastic box hung on the wall to dispense salt tablets to employees who became heat-afflicted on stifling summer days. Cigarette smoke overhung the room, and there was a continuous clatter from the teletype machines bringing in news from the paper's bureaus and wire services. The racket became especially loud when an editor turned up the police radio to monitor a crime or fire in progress, or when the staff crowded around a teletype machine to follow a major breaking news event out-of-state. It was, in other words, a typical newsroom of its day—and far different from the carpeted, air-conditioned, fern-decorated, computerized office environment that existed by the mid-1980s.

Mine was the standard beginner's job, "obits," which largely involved transcribing telephone dictation from funeral directors. Obituary-writing was the first assignment because any errors were immediately spotted by irate relatives whose complaints would help the city editor sniff out careless reporters. In one such case, a reporter reprinted a woman's death notice directly from the rival *Hartford Times* without checking it with a funeral home. The city editor personally wrote the headline for the correction: "SHE'S ALIVE, WE'RE MORTIFIED."

I was intent enough on trying to make good so that I didn't persist in trying to strike up a conversation with the aloof reporter whose desk adjoined mine, William Cockerham, a slender young man with a deep tan and piercing blue-gray eyes. After my second day of work I located a neighborhood tap room called The Press Box. I saw Cockerham sitting at the bar talking to three or four other reporters. Joining them, I was surprised to hear him describing my newsroom arrival, or, more precisely, that of my scissors. He spoke of the injustice of the situation: that he, one of the top journalists in the city, could not obtain scissors but a newcomer was issued them without even asking. He noticed me, and announced that he had already confiscated my pair for his own use. Put on the spot by the hazing, I replied that he could keep them.

Later, I was to learn that he was, in fact, one of the ace reporters, and like many of them, had an all-consuming passion for getting "the story," whatever it might be. An Army veteran, he'd skipped the traditional cub reporting stints on obits and local news by telling his editors the day he was hired in 1968 that the Ku Klux Klan was secretly resurgent in Connecticut—and he could infiltrate it. Cockerham developed contacts in the Klan, submitted to blindfolding and passed muster at open-air, clandestine meetings lit up in the woods by a flaming cross. Although he told the Klansmen from the start that he was a newspaper employee, he pretended to be sympathetic to the group. He played the role so effectively that when he finally told his Klan sponsor that he was going to expose the organization, the bewildered bigot could only blurt out, "Does this mean you're not coming to the meeting Friday night?" Cockerham's newspaper stories caused the Connecticut Klan to disband and its leaders to leave the state. He went on to develop a host of tipsters in the underworld and among law enforcers.

During the 1970s, the frugal, tradition-bound *Courant* was undergoing a remarkable transition into modern journalism. Early on, I began collecting random notes on the changes. Later, I unearthed Revolutionary War-era accomplishments that hardened my resolve to reveal the paper's 1980s scandal, no matter what the difficulties. "This is, after all, America's oldest newspaper still in business," Cockerham would encourage me in 1985, eyes flashing. "It was here before the First Amendment!"

"Courant" (pronounced like the berry) comes from a Dutch word meaning "newspaper." In 1764, the first front page provided an essay on the value of printing. "It lays open to View," the first editor wrote, using old-style spellings, "the Manners, Genius and Policy of all Nations and Countries and faithfully tranfmits them to Pofterity." As one of four Connecticut papers, the *Courant* fanned the Revolution by publishing highly colored accounts of the Boston Tea Party, the Battle of Lexington and the Declaration of Independence. The paper boasted of 8,000 copies per issue in 1778, giving it by far the largest circulation in the colonies. That level was more than double the size of the second biggest, a Loyalist (pro-British) organ in New York.

The newspaper's success after the Revolution stemmed partly from a young *Courant* correspondent who became one of the most influential scholars in American history. Noah Webster, the future dictionary-maker, began his career as an author by writing a spelling book. He sought endorsements from leading figures of the day, including George Washington and Benjamin Franklin. They turned him down, as did all the publishers he approached.

When the *Courant*'s owners, Barzillai Hudson and George Goodwin, finally printed the speller in 1783, its first 5,000 copies sold out in nine months. Until well into the twentieth century, it ranked next to the Bible as the all-time American best-seller. *The Blue-Backed Speller*, as it came to be known, sold between sixty million and a hundred million copies.

Webster adroitly combined patriotism with the ABCs. He also simplified the American language by favoring the ending *-or* over the English *-our* in *color*, *honor*, *error*. He chose *-er* over *-re* in *center* and *theater*. Our present-day spellings of *jail*, *plow* and *draft* were Websterized from the English *gaol*, *plough* and *draught*. "New England's speech became a general standard for the nation" because of Webster, wrote a biographer. "Thanks largely to Webster's speller, Americans' speech habits are fixed despite the wide geographic diversity of the nation and the un-English background of many of its inhabitants. Until television and radio pervaded the consciousness of the world's people, national unity in written and spoken speech among large nations existed only in America." Although most of these copies were printed by others (many through pirated editions or franchise agreements) the income from the speller and Bible-publishing provided a healthy cushion for Hudson and Goodwin while their newspaper sales slackened because of increased competition.

A *Courant* attack on President Thomas Jefferson led to a U.S. Supreme Court decision establishing that the federal government must operate under written law when it accuses people of crime. The square-off began after Congress secretly appropriated two million dollars in a complex plan in 1806 to buy western Florida from Spain. France, the dominant power on the Continent, was assisting the United States in the negotiations but wanted to extort money for itself out of the transaction. These events triggered New England phobias of France and Jefferson. The *Courant* told its readers in 1806 that a United States ship had sailed for France with "sixty tons of precious silver" to pay for the acquisition of Florida. "Reader, bear in mind," the newspaper warned, "that this vessel is bound not for Spain, to whom the Floridas *belong*, but for France...." The implication was that Jefferson's government was squandering money.

Jefferson's administration was so outraged by the *Courant* story that it obtained a federal indictment of the owners for seditious libel. That crime was derived from Anglo-American common law, the unwritten legal customs of the two nations. The *Courant*'s publishers were convicted at trial and sentenced to prison. A Supreme Court decision in 1812 saved them by saying that no one can be federally prosecuted under common law or executive order. Crime, in other words, must be defined by statutes passed by Congress. That protected not only the *Courant* publishers, but other Americans who might otherwise have been subject to arbitrary prosecutions. Specific written law is much easier to obey, after all, than amorphous custom. The decision terminated federal seditious libel prosecutions until the World War I era. Bit by bit, the Supreme Court thereafter broadened free speech and free press protections of the First Amendment, but did not confirm the major advances until the 1960s.

The *Courant*'s owners amicably dissolved their partnership in 1815, with Goodwin continuing to publish the paper. Peter Parley, a best-selling author, assessed the company as:

> A firm then known all over this hemisphere as publishers of the Bible, Webster's Spelling-book, and the Connecticut *Courant*. They were, in the popular mind, regarded as the bulwarks of religion, education, and federalism.

"It is very seldom," Parley dryly concluded, "that plodding industry rises so high."

A few snapshots suffice to trace the paper's modernization. Mark Twain, who unsuccessfully tried to buy a share of the *Courant* in 1869, developed a close friendship with Editor Charles Dudley Warner, who frequently contributed to the nation's leading magazines. Warner coined the expressions "Everybody talks about the weather but nobody does anything about it" and "Politics makes strange bedfellows." Twain, Warner and novelist Harriet Beecher Stowe lived in a world-famous literary colony called Nook Farm, which was a cluster of ornate red brick homes on a wooded knoll overlooking Hartford's Park River.

Col. John Reitemeyer, a tall, decisive man with a high-pitched nasal voice, led the paper into contemporary times. He began as city editor in 1925 and continued as publisher into the late 1960s. The newspaper generally backed conservative Republican policy. But it was fairly liberal on free speech issues. For example, it defended the right of actor Paul Robeson, an outspoken pro-Stalin Communist, to perform at a Hartford school in 1952 during the fierce pressures of the McCarthy Era. When a local theater barred a newspaper critic because of his adverse reviews of performances, Reitemeyer decried "the growing, nationwide tendency to muzzle the press." The real issue, the publisher argued, "is the right of the people to know and the right of the press to tell them. It is part of the fight for freedom of information throughout the world."

Nonetheless, the paper during the 1950s and 1960s had the typical shortcomings of newspapers during that period, including 1) undue deference to major retail advertisers and 2) low-paid journalists who accepted junkets and Christmas gifts of liquor from outsiders. A major embarrassment was the paper's timid mid-1960s coverage of the financial scandals that drove Connecticut's senior U.S. Senator, Democrat Thomas Dodd, into censure and oblivion. The facts were revealed by the syndicated Washington columnists Drew Pearson and Jack Anderson. "The Hartford papers took no notice of the columns until Dodd began to issue denials," recalled Anderson. "This required some explanation, of course, of what he was denying."

Neither of the paper's two senior political writers, each of whom had been with the paper more than three decades, had the skeptical attitude about entrenched power that typified many journalists coming of age during the Vietnam War and Watergate. "I believe," explained political columnist Jack Zaiman, "in the legal principle that a person is innocent until proven guilty." Yet critics of the affable pundit were not asking him to act like a prosecutor or a judge, only like a modern journalist.

Almost all the major executives had been at the paper their entire careers. At the top was Reitemeyer's successor, President Edmund Downes. A pipe-smoker with a benign, friendly manner, Downes had worked his way up from a clerkship in the paper's accounting office. He was close to Hartford's business community. But he respected the newsroom's independence. After he assumed day-to-day control of the company in 1968, he virtually never interfered in decisions made by the newsroom. "There were good people running it," Downes would say, "and so there was no need for me to become involved."

This, then, was the environment I entered in 1970. The newspaper was housed in a former factory building two blocks from the State Capitol. Advertising, circulation and production workers largely kept to themselves on the bottom two floors of the building. Journalists worked on the third floor.

Executives saw little need for security at the newsroom door. Celebrities, small town officials, concerned citizens and cranks were free to wander in unannounced looking for coverage. News stories were shoehorned into drab-looking pages divided into eight columns. (Most non-tabloids, including today's *Courant*, have become six columns because that width of type is easier to read.) Photographs received scant display, rarely more than three columns wide. The management's theory was that readers wanted, above all, facts.

My progression as a reporter was typical. After two days on obituaries, my next assignment was to provide town news stories that would appear seven days a week. I went to a 20,000-population town called Glastonbury, a community-spirited place in the New England tradition. It had a big annual Grange Fair and a volunteer fire department, and was dependent on the newspapers for civic information.

After nine months there as a cub reporter I was promoted to night police reporting in Hartford, a dramatically different kind of job. It put me at more murder scenes than the city's average homicide detective. My work carried a great deal of freedom. In the tradition of "police beat" reporters before me, I often cruised the city or even visited bistros while half-listening to my hand-held police radio. I was expected to race to the scene of any significant crime or fire, especially upon hearing the spine- chilling code phrases: "10-0" (officer in trouble) or "10-89, with a 10-83, active" (a homicide with a gun, in progress).

Reporters should be able to bridge social chasms, and this was a region of marked contrasts. From the farmlands of Glastonbury, one could see Hartford's tall buildings fixed on the skyline like the Land of Oz. Those sleek, modern buildings showed the financial clout of what is known as "The Insurance City." Hartford, however, was also packed with the bulk of the region's minority population and much of its poor. Nearly half the city's school children were on welfare, a figure that would rise during the decade. Along with the city welfare moms and the button-down, suburban insurance executives, there existed the real driving wheel of the region's economy: the many thousands of skilled factory workers, especially those who crafted precision metal products such as jet engines. This industrial base (though fading in the early 1970s with the complete shutdown of the typewriter industry) helped keep average family income in the area among the highest in the country.

The paper devoted vast resources to coverage of local news. There was daily coverage of ninety-one of Connecticut's 169 towns. Much of this was dry fare: advance stories on town school board meetings and the like. But if something important happened, the *Courant* was there. The newspaper continued blanket coverage after most metro newspapers cut it back, partly because of Connecticut's unique structure of government. Since colonial days, the major regional decisions have been made at the level of town, not county, government. That gives news of local affairs more immediacy. Just a few determined citizens, armed with advance knowledge of issues, can have considerable impact at, say, a school board meeting in a 20,000-person town. The newspaper was intended to appeal to these concerned citizens, and there were enough of them around so that it succeeded economically.

It's worth a moment to reflect on the vanishing "newspaper of record." Its encyclopedic treatment of zoning issues, legislation and litigation contrasts markedly with the magazine-style of the more modern newspaper. There were many routine stories in the old days, and reporters disliked doing them. But the stories served the community in a manner impossible for television or news magazines, or for flashy newspaper wrap-ups. The impact of the old newspaper tradition is reflected in the quality of life in Connecticut, which I believe is better than that in comparable regions. "It's much harder to get people aware of a local issue without newspaper coverage," commented consumer activist Ralph Nader, who grew up reading the *Courant* in the northwestern Connecticut city of Winsted. Times Mirror cut off the paper's regular coverage of such outlying areas in 1981. The ostensible reason was because there was not enough news in those communities. But many within the state believe it was because the chain wanted to pare costs and increase profits.

During the early 1970s, the *Courant* undertook more investigative reports, usually because of reporters' initiative. Several of these efforts rebut the notion that locally owned newspapers will not challenge the regional power structure. The first such effort I saw was the paper's long-running probe of the International Telephone and Telegraph Co., which was making the then-largest acquisition in world history. In 1968, ITT sought to buy the Hartford Fire Insurance Co., the city's oldest insurance company (and one that the *Courant*'s own Hudson & Goodwin had helped found in 1810). Connecticut Insurance Commissioner William Cotter forbade the merger in December 1969 on legal grounds. He reversed himself five months later after some changes in the proposal and intense lobbying by Hartford's business and political leaders. Among the inducements: Hartford Fire shareholders would reap windfall profits and ITT's Sheraton subsidiary would build a twenty-two story hotel to help the city's downtown revitalization project. Cotter privately complained that on a typical afternoon he would receive more than two score telephone calls by local businessmen advocating the merger.

The *Courant* could have been swept along in the general enthusiasm. Instead, the newspaper followed up on leads provided by Nader and by career officials in the U.S. Justice Department and the U.S. Securities and Exchange Commission. The published stories laid out an enormous amount of information embarrassing to ITT, Hartford Fire, the insurance commissioner and others. The stories were prominently displayed on the front pages over a span of years. Even so, the newspaper's fear of seeming unfair or manipulative caused it to postpone a major story until after the 1970 elections—provoking a classic debate about press responsibility.

By late October 1970, Joseph O'Brien, the reporter on the story, had verified that federal authorities were investigating such "irregularities" as: 1) attempts to influence Cotter by ITT's secret lobbyist, Attorney Joseph Fazzano; and 2) deft speculation in stocks by well-connected Hartford area residents shortly before the key rulings by Cotter, who happened to be readying his candidacy for the vacant Congressional seat in Hartford. The newspaper had a firm policy against publishing last-minute controversy during local election campaigns. Although the paper's top executives were stalwart Republicans, they postponed the veteran reporter's story over his protests because they believed the timing would be unfair to the Democrat Cotter. The Democrat squeezed into the House seat by a margin of just 1,165 votes over the Republican mayor of Hartford—whom the newspaper had been supporting on the editorial page.

On the Sunday after the election, the front page hammered at the merger with a copyrighted story: TWO AGENCIES PROBING ITT MERGER/COURANT GIVES INFORMATION. The newspaper received strong criticism from both sides. The defeated Republican argued that the news should have been published as soon as it was in hand. Cotter fumed that the newspaper had been unfair by writing such a strong story. The two probes, in fact, dissolved without any formal accusations of wrongdoing against the firm or anyone else. The first Congressional election is usually the toughest, and Cotter, true to the pattern, was reelected until his death in 1981.

"Pretty good" was the assessment Ralph Nader gave of the newspaper's overall coverage of the suspicious merger. "They made the effort, a greater effort than the comparable governmental institutions." Washington columnist Jack Anderson ultimately found the so-called smoking gun that made the merger a major national scandal. A tipster gave Anderson a top-secret ITT internal memo. The note to an ITT vice president revealed a far more sinister version of the back-room, wheeler-dealing that had received a trial run in Hartford. ITT secretly paid up to $400,000 to help finance the 1972 Republican National Convention. In a scandal that foreshadowed Watergate, ITT apparently spent the money hoping it would induce the Attorney General to shepherd the merger past his hostile Antitrust Division.

While there were some other major investigative stories, it would be a mistake to focus on them. The newsroom's main goal was to scoop the afternoon *Hartford Times* in daily news coverage. Reporters and editors were acutely conscious of which newspaper broke a story first. Even so, the afternoon *Times* was quite different from the *Courant*. The Gannett chain's paper had a crisp and eye-catching layout. It played up national and foreign news more than my newspaper did. Its strength was the *Courant*'s weakness. The *Times* had a number of excellent columnists, and its editorial pages and "women's section" (as it was then known) were much more contemporary than its competition's.

"The *Hartford Times* (circulation 124,501) is everything a modern, by-the-book newspaper should be," said a 1973 book by thirteen journalism experts entitled, *Evaluating the Press: The New England Newspaper Survey.* "It is all very attractive and immensely readable and enjoyable—and, one is tempted to speculate, irrelevant. Reading the *Times* is like filling up with snack food: when you're finished you're still hungry." The book described the *Courant*, on the other hand, as "a triumph of content over form."

> It's an old-fashioned, overstuffed grab bag of a newspaper into which an astonishing amount of information is crammed. In this age of instant communications, of bite-sized news that can be digested quickly, the *Courant* practically defies the reader to read it.
>
> Yet for all of that, the *Courant* . . . is alert to, and reports on, the changing life styles of America, and its readers; restlessly probes beyond the obvious and the official to the truth that may be obscured; in the past twelve years has seen its circulation rise from 112,000 to 169,664, or fifty percent.

"In short," the book's editors concluded, "the *Hartford Courant* is a good newspaper, a successful newspaper, that with drawbacks or not, is answering the needs and the interests of a growing number of readers."

The *Times* closed in 1976. Part of its magnificently colonnaded, gray marble headquarters would become a bar. The *Courant*, suddenly, loomed much more powerful and much more attractive to outside interests.

CHAPTER 3

Playing Monopoly

THE *Courant*'s directors— Edmund Downes and eight other prominent local businessmen or professionals—realized that the paper was too ingrown and too parochial for its growing public responsibilities. In 1976, they chose Richard Mooney of the *New York Times* to lead the newsroom as executive editor and vice president. The tall, tweedy Mooney was new blood and, for newspaper circles, blue blood. A Yale College graduate who attended Harvard University as a Nieman Fellow, he had worked at the *Times* almost all his career. At the time of his *Courant* appointment, he was forty-nine and the editor of the *Times* Sunday financial section. Friendly and relaxed, the new editor was soon "Dick" to his staff in Hartford. He expanded business coverage, changed the "women's pages" into a contemporary life/style section and made editorial writing much sharper.

But larger forces were at work elsewhere. During the 1970s, nationwide chains were swallowing locally owned media outlets with an ever-growing hunger. In 1910, there were thirteen American newspaper chains. In 1980, there were 155. From 1910 to 1980, the percentage of chain-owned newspapers increased from three to more than sixty-five percent. During the process, Times

Mirror President Robert Erburu approached the *Courant* in early 1976. At the confidential meeting, Downes said the paper was not for sale. Erburu replied that the chain had a "sincere interest" in it "whenever it might be welcome and appropriate."

There was scant indication it would be soon. The paper had long been owned by employees, retirees and their heirs, with small blocks also controlled by two Hartford-based insurers, Aetna Life and Casualty Co. and Travelers Insurance Companies. In patriarchal fashion, the paper paid low salaries, but otherwise treated employees well. The restricted ownership and easy-going management style tended to keep the paper more traditional and less sophisticated than it should have been. But it also maintained control by those trained in journalism.

There is no substantial evidence that news stories during the 1970s were unduly influenced by powerful figures within the local business or political communities. Nothing of the sort happened to my work during the five years I spent as the paper's reporter covering federal courts and bureaucracies. I often wrote about businesses on that beat, much of it hard-edged reporting on criminal investigations and lawsuits. Others support my perception.

"One of the weaknesses of the *Hartford Courant*," retired Aetna Chairman Olcott Smith told me while complaining about business coverage during the 1970s, "was that the view of the management always was that the board of directors of a newspaper should have nothing to do with the editorial policy of the paper." Smith had been Connecticut's most important financial leader in his day, and a man intimately involved with the newspaper located just a few hundred yards from Aetna's huge, red-brick, colonial-style world headquarters. He had begun his career as a private attorney in 1932. The *Courant* and Aetna numbered among his corporate clients. In 1947, he devised a stock ownership plan for the newspaper that forbade individual shareholders from selling to outsiders. The purpose was to keep the paper locally owned unless directors and trustees approved a sale. Smith, who served as a *Courant* director for two decades, explained the board's fears: "We always saw a lot of burglars under the bed who'd like to take the newspaper over." In 1962, he left his law practice to join Aetna as vice chairman. As chairman, he led a series of Aetna expansions into mutual funds, real estate development and commercial finance. By the time of his retirement in 1972, the firm ranked as the country's sixteenth largest corporation in assets.

Despite Smith's criticisms of the paper, he was committed to local ownership. But some shareholders were restless over the low value their stock brought in the restricted market. One of these was Director Michael Sudarsky, a Hartford attorney whose late father had owned the newspaper's largest single block of shares. His main ally was Director Millard Pryor, a blunt-speaking, action-oriented entrepreneur who ran Lydall Inc., a manufacturer of shoe parts and industrial components. Pryor, an Ohioan who came to Connecticut in 1972, thought that the paper was boring; that it lacked an agenda to improve the community; and that it earned poor profits, given its potential. And he feared that Mooney might not overcome these problems.

"I've never been in an organization where there was less worry about the fact they weren't doing as well as they could," Pryor would say. "The critical job that Ed Downes and his minions felt was to preserve the culture and the environment. As a businessman, I've always been worried about shareholders. They're the ones that pay the dues. I really got appalled over this. I made a lot of waves." But there was little Pryor could do, either to rectify news judgments he didn't like or to bring in new management. "It was very bad form to criticize the handling of an affair during a board meeting," he recalled. "And directors don't go around selling their companies. That's not 'stewardship.'"

In 1976, the death of an editorial page editor who had owned 4.3 percent of the stock unraveled the protections against outside acquisition. The editor's executors complained about the low appraisal of the shares. To cooperate, the newspaper set up easy credit terms to encourage employees to pay higher prices, first at $33 and then at $36 per share. Some of us invested our savings, with considerable trepidation. The staff knew the stock had cost just $12.50 a share during the early 1970s.

For a time, the stock sale worked exactly as intended. It boosted prices and broadened the employee base of ownership. I invested all of my savings, some $5,600, which brought me three/ten-thousandths of the company's stock. As the certificates sold, however, the number of shareholders nudged over a magic number, five hundred. At that point, the newspaper had to file a financial statement with the U.S. Securities and Exchange Commission. Until that time, industry analysts had no solid numbers about the newspaper's profits. "An hour after the papers got to the SEC," said one observer, "there were six newspaper brokers Xeroxing away." They saw that the paper's net operating revenue had risen from $29.2 million in 1974 to $47.5 million in 1977. Not bad. Profits had zoomed from $1.7 million to $5.6 million. Not bad at all.

The shadow of aggressive profiteers first fell on the community Aug. 28, 1978. Management announced that Capital Cities Communications Inc. of New York City wanted to buy the newspaper for seventy million dollars. The sum far exceeded the paper's assessed value. Industry analysts regarded "Cap Cities" as one of the most ruthless of the nation's media groups, though not at the absolute bottom in terms of community service.

The chain's top officials secretly met with a *Courant* committee of directors. These Cap Cities officers included Chairman Thomas Murphy, who would superintend the chain's phenomenal growth that by 1985 would include the takeover of ABC-TV. Also attending was Cap Cities Director William Casey, a former SEC chairman. Casey went on to direct Ronald Reagan's 1980 Presidential campaign and, later, the U.S. Central Intelligence Agency.

"Why are you willing to pay so much more for this newspaper than we think it's worth?" Sudarsky asked them.

Someone from the Cap Cities contingent just mumbled in response, not really addressing the question.

Olcott Smith had a theory, but he kept it to himself that day. "An out-of-towner can offer the advantages of mass buying—and can raise the advertising rates with less fear." Later, Smith chuckled softly as he talked about why local owners would never squeeze advertisers that hard. "The local newspaper executives would hear the howls of their friends who had to pay."

In a meeting after the Capital Cities proposal, seven of the nine *Courant* directors voted to reject the offer and to end any negotiations with Capital Cities. Sudarsky, a dissenter along with Pryor, wanted, at the minimum, for stockholders to be able to learn the newspaper's worth on the open market.

The seven directors in the majority signed an emphatic group statement that the region would be better off if the paper remained locally owned. At the time, the directors were already putting the vast bulk of increased revenue into better news gathering. Spending on it rose from $16.2 million to $30 million from 1974 through 1977.

Downes and some others on the board had a deep commitment to the concept of local ownership even though their personal financial incentives seemed to point toward a sale. Downes, for example, earned just $59,285 in 1977 to run a newspaper that made $5.6 million in profits. He and the other directors had substantial stock holdings that could be converted into cash in a sale. In such buy-outs, local executives also can often arrange comfortable guaranteed salaries for years after they have stopped working. "He could have been offered all the money in the world and he still would have opposed the sale," Sudarsky said of Downes. Sudarsky discounted my devil's-advocate suggestion that Downes and other directors opposed the sale out of reluctance to give up their positions of community power and prestige. "I don't think that was it. Really, it was a matter of philosophy—a feeling that the *Hartford Courant* had been an independent newspaper since before the country was founded, and that they were custodians of a trust. The *Courant* was regarded by many people as a family. They believed it wouldn't last under chain ownership."

Reporters, like police officers, tend to get jaded by looking so much at the underside of life. But I was touched by what Sudarsky had to say.

Downes and his allies had to be concerned, however, about acting too independently. They faced the possibility of a lawsuit if they failed to act in the shareholders' financial interests. Times Mirror's offer of $105.6 million in 1979 broke the resistance. In recommending sale, Downes and the others emphasized that Times Mirror was an outstanding newspaper chain that promised to recognize community concerns and to guarantee employee benefits at least at existing levels.

The future seemed bright. We believed Times Mirror was different from the notorious profiteering chains. It was, after all, the publisher of one of the most respected newspapers in the country, the *Los Angeles Times*. Most of us in the newsroom thought the editorial product would become much better with the help of such a sophisticated organization. As for the price, the offer of $200 a share was six times what many people had paid for stock in the last big sale. The paper's directors and trustees approved the transaction, as did the overwhelming majority of shareholders. Naively, I, too, voted for it.

PART II

The House of Mirror

CHAPTER 4

Tinseltown and Television

THE SALE brought the nation's oldest newspaper into a remarkably successful conglomerate whose revenues had more than doubled in the previous five years, reaching $1.6 billion in 1979. Everything about Times Mirror was larger than life, beginning with its six-foot three, brawny-chested, square-jawed chairman, Otis Chandler, a world-class athlete at Stanford who in middle age continued to sport a slim waist, chiselled features and a towering blond pompadour. He was the scion of California's leading family. "Its power and reach and role in Southern California," wrote David Halberstam in *The Powers That Be*, "are beyond the comprehension of Easterners, no Easterner can understand what it has meant in California to be a Chandler, for no single family dominates any major region of this country as the Chandlers have dominated California." Halberstam continued:

> They did not so much foster the growth of Southern California as, more simply, invent it. There is water because they went and stole water. The city is horizontal instead of vertical because they were rich in land, and horizontal span was good for them, good for real estate.

> There is a port because they dreamed of a port. They had settled in a garden of nature, and where nature failed they and their friends provided.

The dynasty's founder, Gen. Harrison Gray Otis, began building his communications empire in Los Angeles in 1882. He bought shares in a nearly bankrupt newspaper, the *Times*, and a related advertising sheet, the *Mirror.* The family prospered through the years with aggressive commercial practices and with journalism that supported a conservative political agenda. The morning *Times* became the city's most influential newspaper. But experts regarded it as having poor professional standards during the 1940s and 1950s.

Otis Chandler (the great-grandson of the founder) became *Times* publisher in 1960. "Otis's first desire was to be acknowledged as the great publisher of the best newspaper of the United States, and failing that, the publisher of the second best newspaper after the *New York Times*," wrote two biographers in their book, *Thinking Big.* Infusions of capital and talent improved the paper and brought it nearly the recognition the publisher sought. The corporation also broadened its financial base by acquiring properties in related fields: forest products, books, magazines, radio and television stations, and cable television franchises. The single most important enterprise, however, remained newspapers.

"The track record was uneven," commented *Thinking Big* coauthor Robert Gottlieb, a professor of urban planning at the University of California at Los Angeles. "At the *Dallas Times Herald* they took a very, very bad paper and made it better. With *Newsday*, they took a very good newspaper, and the modest attempts at intervention they made were resisted, creating quite a bit of tension."

In acquiring media properties in Connecticut, Times Mirror reenacted the kind of wheeler-dealing that Halberstam had described in California. It began with the secret negotiations to buy the *Courant* and two other newspapers. Next, high-level officials of the chain sought to acquire cable television franchises.

To do so, they tried to manipulate Connecticut's public utilities regulators. The matter prompted a nationally important test case of the power of state officials to control cable television franchises.

The *Courant*, not surprisingly, provided limited coverage of these developments. Even working in the newsroom, I did not know the case's overall significance until I attended Yale Law School in 1983 and one of my professors focused on it as a lecture topic. Later, I was startled by a classmate's term paper. It concluded that the chain's top management had intentionally deceived state regulators. Ultimately, I followed up by examining legal documents on file at various government offices. It's a fascinating story.

Times Mirror's goal in the late 1970s was to acquire newspapers and cable franchises in the Connecticut market. When the chain failed in its secret 1976 attempt to purchase the *Courant*, it proceeded elsewhere. In 1977, it spent $21 million to buy the *Advocate* of Stamford and the *Greenwich Time*, two family- owned dailies in Fairfield County near New York.

During the summer of 1978, Times Mirror asked Connecticut utilities regulators for permission to buy from local ownership two television cable franchises. At that time, the enormous potential of cable television for delivering entertainment, news and advertising to the public was just being realized. The Federal Communications Commission's (FCC) regulations had forbidden cable stations from competing freely with broadcasters in movies and sports programming. The FCC's position was that its restrictions protected consumers by preserving nearly all the best shows for free broadcast. Critics believed that its real reason for stifling cable television development was to protect the three politically influential networks: CBS, NBC and ABC.

In a landmark 1977 decision, a federal appeals court threw out the entire FCC scheme of cable regulation. The judges (who included the distinguished jurist J. Skelly Wright) also attacked secret lobbying at the FCC. Like other regulatory agencies, the FCC was supposed to reach its decisions on the basis of open testimony and documents available for public inspection. Yet the

FCC commissioners and staff also heard lobbyists in private.

"Wright went crazy when he saw a legal brief describing all these contacts," Yale Law School lecturer Stuart Robinowitz later told students in my class. A prominent New York attorney in the law of electronic media, Robinowitz had represented Home Box Office, the successful cable plaintiffs. He said of that case:

> This was a blatant example of what had been going on at the FCC for decades, like when it stopped subscription TV dead in its tracks.
>
> The stench of this record—a foot-high volume of secret communications, most from networks—so colored the court's perception that it no longer was willing to accept the FCC's predictions and rationales. The court was saying to the FCC, in effect, "We're sick and tired of regulations where you're trying to restrain new technology to protect vested interests."

This court decision would benefit tens of millions of families across the country. Cable systems quickly used their new freedom to provide attractive shows. Movie channels such as Home Box Office flourished, as did sports cable services. Times Mirror, owners of network-affiliated television stations in several states, sought a piece of these profits by developing its own cable movie system, Spotlight. Times Mirror also bought up local cable franchises around the country.

One franchise the chain sought in 1978 was in Meriden, a small city on the southern fringe of the *Courant*'s circulation area. An even more attractive prize was the cable franchise for Hartford and its suburbs. It had been owned by investors, not builders. When the franchise became valuable the investors were happy to sell to a conglomerate that could string the cable and provide services.

First, though, Times Mirror had to win approval of the sale from Connecticut's utilities regulators. They worried that Times Mirror might gain too much media control in Connecticut. The fear was a farsighted prediction of what might happen. It was not an existing problem. The Stamford and Greenwich newspapers' circulations did not overlap with cable franchise areas in the central part of the state. The commissioners in 1978 had no idea that Times Mirror two years previously had approached the *Courant*, or that Times Mirror had been collecting data on Hartford area advertising markets for a possible newspaper purchase.

The 1978 sworn statement of Ralph Swett, president of Times Mirror's cable subsidiary, misled the commission, "I would say, in general," he testified, "the Connecticut markets being the size they are, are not the target for Times Mirror in television and/or newspapers, and they would have hoped to get into a larger market." The commissioners approved Times Mirror's acquisition of the two cable firms exactly a week later. In explaining the rationale, the commissioners' written decision said, "Times Mirror does not own or control any newspaper, radio or television stations in the franchise areas." The commissioners, however, ordered Times Mirror to inform them "of any and all contemplated acquisitions of Connecticut media."

Roughly a year later, after many months of confidential negotiations with *Courant* executives, Times Mirror announced its agreement to buy the state's largest newspaper. The chain did not bother to inform Connecticut utilities regulators until two days after its press release announcing the purchase.

The utilities commissioners opened hearings to reexamine the cable TV sale. Robert Erburu, president of Times Mirror under Chairman Otis Chandler, took the witness stand. He endorsed all of his company's statements made in the hearings the previous year—including Swett's remark that Connecticut media were too small to interest the parent firm. Times Mirror maintained throughout the hearings that "contemplate" had a special meaning in legal circles, and therefore the company had no obligation to inform regulators of its negotiations in Connecticut until the deal was consummated. Moreover, it said regulators should not disrupt the cable acquisition unless experience showed abusive trends by Times Mirror's joint control of the newspaper and cable franchises.

But Connecticut's consumer counsel, Barry Zitser, emphatically disagreed. He pointed to *Black's Law Dictionary* and other legal sources to show that "contemplate" has the same meaning in law as in ordinary usage: "To view or consider with continued attention." He charged that Times Mirror's failure to notify regulators of its contemplated acquisition by the end of October 1978 "was inexcusable"—especially in light of its earlier statement that Connecticut was not a fit market for further acquisitions. Zitser accused Times Mirror of other misconduct during the hearing process. He cited secret contacts between it and the commission's staff rather similar to the back-door lobbying that the federal judges in Washington had criticized so harshly at the FCC. "Such *ex parte* contacts," Zitser said, "were certainly improper if not illegal."

The commissioners' decision in March 1980 ignored Zitser's allegations of improprieties, which were denied by Times Mirror. But the commissioners adopted essentially intact his main argument: that cross-ownership was a public menace that could stifle competition between the *Courant* and cable television.

Zitser maintained that the great danger of cross-ownership was stunted development of cable services (both advertising and news) to help the newspaper. "Advertising is the life-blood of a newspaper but a cable company can always ask for a rate increase," he argued. "Times Mirror is looking for a 15.7 percent return on its investment in the *Courant*. Currently, the return is a mere four percent. In addition to wanting to quadruple the *Courant*'s present profits, Times Mirror also desires to 'double earnings per share every six years. . . .' It is folly to believe that Times Mirror would let its [cable] systems compete with and cut into the profits of the *Courant* now or in the future."

In Times Mirror's testimony rebutting the allegations, its president maintained that Times Mirror's policy of "autonomous subsidiaries" prevented problems for the public. He claimed that

Times Mirror operated its subsidiaries independently, with minimal interference from the parent firm.

The commissioners were skeptical about whether these neatly separate corporate identities were meaningful in the real world. "A parent company," the commissioners wrote, "may encourage a subsidiary to maintain a separate image but of more significance are the unseen reins that are placed upon a subsidiary by a parent." The commission ordered Times Mirror to sell either the newspaper or the cable systems within thirteen months.

Times Mirror held onto the contested properties while it appealed the decision. Connecticut's Supreme Court unanimously ruled that states have the right to regulate cable television. While litigation on related issues proceded, opposing attorneys achieved an out-of-court compromise. Times Mirror agreed to sell its Hartford cable franchise. It kept the one in Meriden, subject to restrictions forbidding collusive operations between the newspaper and cable franchise. After intensive lobbying inspired in part by the Connecticut litigation, Congress in 1984 transferred cross-ownership disputes from state regulators to the FCC. The Great Connecticut Cable War faded away. Times Mirror sold the franchise for $61.5 million to another cable firm that owned no newspapers.

On the whole, the *Courant*'s coverage of these developments was perfunctory and in line with the dire prediction by the utilities commission: "Certainly, unsparing criticism by a subsidiary of a position taken by the parent cannot be expected." To be sure, the *Courant* usually ran a story after a major news event such as a court hearing or a legal decision. Often the stories were on the front page, usually with a two-column-wide headline.

Yet the paper did not once run an in-depth news story on the case—its considerable implications for Connecticut consumers, and for businesses and consumers affected by similar situations elsewhere in the nation. These implications were clear to many legal and business experts with other sources of information—not so for the ordinary subscriber to the paper. Their television choices were directly affected by the controversy. Yet it took a leap of imagination for many readers to understand the potential effects of the new technology, especially before cable became generally available in their own neighborhoods.

The *Courant*'s news coverage faltered even on ordinary reporting, much less enterprise work. Typical was the handling of Zitser's revelations that Times Mirror had been secretly trying to buy the *Courant* since 1976 while publicly professing no interest in "Connecticut markets." Zitser's allegation was a centerpiece to his theme that Times Mirror could not be trusted to own too large a share of Connecticut's media. The secret negotiations were mentioned only once in the paper. That was in the last paragraph of a story in December 1979. The reporter disclosed the negotiations matter-of-factly, failing to note that they were part of the consumer counsel's evidence of Times Mirror's duplicity.

The paper's editorial board for years declined to write anything at all about the controversy or about the abysmal service the cable company was providing the public. Its rationale, expressed to me privately by one board member, was that criticism of Times Mirror would be disloyal—and support of the parent firm's cable efforts would look suspicious to the public. The rationalization was exactly the type of self-censorship that regulators had feared from cross-ownership.

CHAPTER 5

The Beach Boys

IN THE LATE 1970s, retired *Courant* messenger Joseph Vetrano would walk into the newsroom about 7 p.m. each night. The octogenerian (born in 1894) would find a quiet corner and read his newspapers, the *National Enquirer* and New York *Daily News.* Often he would light up a cigar. Invariably, he would be wearing a fedora, a tie and suit, usually blue or grey. Although he had never been a reporter, he looked like one from his favorite era, the Twenties.

When the managing editor left for the day, Vetrano would install himself in the glass-walled office to watch the television set. Some nights the old man wandered out to chat with journalists if things were slow. We called him "The Professor" because of his inflexible opinions. He waxed sentimental on vaudeville's glory and held forth on his extreme right-wing politics. Sometimes we would see him stand up and salute when Richard Nixon appeared on television.

Vetrano would often fall asleep with head rocked back, his mouth half-open and his hat pulled low over his forehead. He slept in the managing editor's chair until morning, leaving before the first arrival of daytime staff. The lifelong bachelor went home to change before starting again on his daily rounds that put him in the Hartford Public Library most of the day, listening to records. Why did he sleep at the newspaper after his retirement in 1966? He preferred the newsroom to his shabby hotel.

His presence showed that even after acquisition by Times Mirror the newspaper retained some of its paternal aspects. The relations with the community were similar. Many small "inefficiencies"—blanket coverage of crime news, the courts and zoning disputes, for example—were continued under the theory that a newspaper had a different mission than a shoe factory.

The strengths of the paper were: 1) "credibilty" and 2) day-to-day news coverage. "If it moved, the *Courant* knew about it" was an aphorism of Tom Condon, a blond, barrel-chested Vietnam veteran who was the paper's most honored reporter.

There were weaknesses, as well. The sports editor repeatedly sought funds without success to hire a larger, better-trained staff. The greatest backwater was the photo department, which until 1975 sought to hire only Connecticut residents who were inexperienced and without college educations. "My observation is that guys like that don't move," explained a former photo editor. He held the quaint belief that the *Courant*'s brand of on-the-job photo training was so valuable that the paper couldn't afford to lose anyone who had received it. While no other part of the paper was nearly so ingrown, there was throughout a resistance to innovations, even worthwhile ones.

The paper's single most impressive investigation in recent decades, even more than the ITT probe, began in 1980. A reporter tipped off his boss that one of Connecticut's most illustrious attorneys was an ominous presence within the mansion of an heiress named Ethel Donaghue. Once a glamorous society figure noted for her wit and independence, the spinster by 1980 was mentally helpless and had no close relatives. Greedy attorneys and household servants were feuding and secretly stalking her $36 million fortune. The abuses included neglecting her health, looting her luxurious furnishings and coaxing her into signing a revised will. The emotional barrage upon the eighty-four-year-old included repeated warnings to her that someone might smother her at night. "The theme," commented one of the few friends allowed to see her, "was the same, night after night—that her life was in danger."

Longtime court reporter Dennie Williams and youthful Mark Stillman were assigned to the story. A big, vehement, black-haired Irishman, Williams was a street-savvy idealist who had been my predecessor on the federal court beat. As Williams had led me around on my introductory tour of the courts in 1976, a prosecutor had warned me with a rubbery smile, "Remember in your reporting, the government is always right!" I took it partly as a joke, but partly as a subtle suggestion of the kind often made to reporters: Go along, get along. Later, at the end of the introductions to the courthouse personnel, Williams took me aside in a gray-marbled corridor. "Don't ever forget," he said in a serious voice, touching my elbow and looking me in the eye, "that for some of the people who come through this court, you're the last chance they've got."

Stillman, Williams' partner on the heiress story, was a Harvard-educated man who had proven capable on suburban coverage and was ready for a more sensitive assignment. The two reporters spent many painstaking months unraveling the intrigue. One burly servant grabbed the medium-built Stillman by the shirtfront during an interview and almost lifted him off the ground. "If you f___ me," growled the servant, hoisting the reporter up to look him squarely in the face, "I'll kill you." Williams' greatest fear was that he might make a mistake that would allow those humiliated by the scandal (including some of the state's most powerful legal figures and a major bank) to seek retribution by a lawsuit or by otherwise pressuring his bosses. More than once, Williams woke up in the middle of the night frightened from such a nightmare.

No mistake occurred. News articles extending over several years showed that a powerful Hartford judge had abused his office to steer control of the fortune to an intimate friend and political ally. The revelations showed flagrant violations of professional ethics—violations protected by a huge conspiracy of silence.

The stories prompted the first impeachment effort against a public official in Connecticut's history. The judge cut it short by resigning, but not before a 160-page report by the General Assembly's investigator supported the newspaper's allegations in stunning detail. The judge and the other attorneys implicated in the scandal were allowed to practice law privately without any discipline. The newspaper then took the lead in exposing how Connecticut's system for investigating complaints about unethical attorneys was one of the most backward in the nation. It typified problems the American Bar Association had called a "scandalous situation" years before.

There's no point in identifying all the people involved or in describing further the heiress's ordeal. These things were brought out in a superb series in 1982 by a *Courant* magazine writer, and aren't vital to a book about newspapers. During my own research on the case later for a *Connecticut Magazine* article, I was struck by the extent of wrongdoing, the solid basis of the newspaper's reporting and the timidity of political institutions when the problems became known. "The biggest scandal," said a state legislator who led the fights for impeachment and disbarment proceedings when no one else would, "was that after the newspaper exposed the facts, no one did anything about it."

The newspaper, in other words, had virtues as well as shortcomings in 1981 when Times Mirror summarily replaced Executive Editor Dick Mooney with Mark Murphy, a longtime *Los Angeles Times* editor.

A brief corporate announcement said that Murphy had worked for the *Los Angeles Times* for seventeen years. As metro editor for ten years, he had supervised more than 300 journalists and all the paper's California news coverage. The *Courant* provided only a bit more information to readers in its news story the next day. It said that Murphy was forty-seven, married, with four children, and that his bosses were confident he "will very quickly gain the respect of both our staff and readers."

The news story ignored legitimate questions about the man who would take charge of all news and editorial operations at the *Courant*. What did independent analysts say of Murphy's performance in Los Angeles? What plans had he for the newspaper? Why was the change made? It might have interested readers to know that Murphy was the central model for the "Lou Grant" character in the then-popular television show based on the operations of a Los Angeles newspaper. Besides the job titles, though, the similarities between the Lou Grant character and Murphy proved far from clear. Murphy was a round-faced man with glasses who projected a self-satisfied air. Three respected veterans at the *Courant* recalled their introductions to him this way:

> —The magazine editor: "As soon as he met me, he said, 'It's not much of a magazine, is it?' "
>
> —The capitol bureau chief: "I told him I'd worked at the paper sixteen years, and he said, 'What the hell for?' "
>
> —A city hall writer, upon being described by his boss as one of the paper's finest reporters: "Murphy said, 'If he's so good what's he working here for?' "

These gratuitious insults foreshadowed the turbulence to follow. A note on the office bulletin board in February 1981 announced that the newsroom would be restructured. Virtually every job at the paper was going to be redefined and "posted." Those who wanted to keep their jobs would have to apply for them. No one was forced off the paper initially, however. Most job changes were promotions to more challenging assignments.

To implement the new order, Murphy brought in five men from the *Los Angeles Times*. The most important of these was Dick Barnes, aged thirty-six. He had been Murphy's assistant in charge of Orange County coverage in California. Barnes, a trim, sandy-haired bachelor, controlled all reassignments in the shakeup except for top newsroom management positions. He came to Hartford on a whirlwind tour. Barnes interviewed and assigned more than a score of *Courant* reporters and editors who wanted better jobs. Many of these interviews occurred on one day.

Three other new managers from the *Times* assumed control of national and foreign news; the photo and graphics departments; and the Washington bureau. The sports editor dubbed them "the Beach Boys" because of their laid-back, self-assured style fostered in the Tinseltown city almost unimaginably different from Connecticut. The nickname stuck. Murphy, who cared little for appearances and who had a carefree sense of humor, went further. Barnes, the all-powerful metro editor, was "Dickie-Pooh" to Murphy, even when talking to employees who barely knew either of them. "Fluffy" was Murphy's pet name for the long-haired, wisecracking editor from L.A. installed in charge of national and foreign news.

Murphy regarded the *Courant*'s allocation of personnel and space to local news as wildly disproportionate to its importance. He wanted every all-editions story to be lively and important—"a good read," as he was wont to say. Murphy had played a similar role in Los Angeles. His appointment as metropolitan editor there marked a major step in the *Los Angeles Times*' ascendancy in the 1960s, according to the history of the paper, *Thinking Big:*

> He constantly told his writers to think of their audience, to write in an interesting manner so that the mainstream reader could stick with the text. Good style replaced tightly edited copy as the criterion for a successful piece, and many of the staffers enjoyed the freedom to take days, or weeks, to file a feature.

The book also described criticism of Murphy in Los Angeles:

> But some of the copy editors grumbled about the length, and nonfeature-oriented *Times* staff criticized this overriding tendency toward 'soft' topics as a depoliticization of content. Any story that required complex and detailed analysis tended to be shunted aside in favor of one that lent itself to a looser prose form.

The same patterns became evident in Hartford, though the

paper rarely deigned to explain changes to readers. The old *Courant* had been aimed at the responsible citizen who wanted to know the workings of the community. Mooney developed a broader, regional perspective. But it was Murphy who fundamentally altered the paper. The new *Courant* provided more entertainment, more opinion—and far less local news.

My experience positioned me reasonably well to make the necessary changes that come when a local business is upended during a takeover. But I was troubled by all the frantic office politicking and seat-of-the-pants personnel judgments. It had once been an honorable thing (in Connecticut at least) to be a bureau chief or beat reporter at the *Courant*. During the 1970s, very few of the best reporters left for bigger papers (only about one a year) or tried to become editors. I went for long runs late at night at a high school track to ponder what I should do—and to try to get some sense of accomplishment that suddenly was missing from my government affairs writing. Murphy had scheduled the Sunday magazine for a major expansion. Because I had written many magazine articles and published scores of freelance photographs, I obtained an appointment as an interim editor there for six months before moving on to Boston for a newly created post covering the Boston Celtics full-time for the *Courant*.

Murphy saw shabbiness all around him at the paper. He brought in contractors immediately to tear up the old-fashioned newsroom. Out went the worn tile floors and the cheap wooden desks. Walls were painted or panelled with wood. Big potted plants were brought into the lobby. The central newsroom and editing offices were gutted within months of Murphy's arrival in order to install recessed lighting, carpets and other amenities.

Everyone but Joe Vetrano made the temporary adjustment to new quarters elsewhere in the building. The retiree continued to sleep each night in the managing editor's chair for weeks after the adjoining newsroom was closed off. Heavy sheets of plastic hung floor-to-ceiling outside it to contain demolition dust. Late that spring, shortly before his office was scheduled for its renovation, the Professor weakened and fell ill. With extreme reluctance ("The doctors and nurses are too damn young.") he consented to go to Hartford Hospital. Within days of his admission for pneumonia, he was found dead one morning near his hospital bed. He was in his favorite sleeping position: slouched in a chair.

The Professor, aged eighty-seven, had long been failing in health and the imminent disruption of his nest at the *Courant* cannot, in fairness, be regarded as the reason for his death. Nonetheless, it symbolized the end of an era.

Aggressive, practical-minded executives were intent on change. "We want to put our imprint on events," Murphy said. "In the past, the paper just shoveled in all the news it could. We want high quality here." Major expansions and improvements occurred in:

* The Washington bureau, which increased from one to three writers. It spent two-thirds of its time on national affairs under the new bureau chief from the *Los Angeles Times*.

* The business section, which tripled in size and provided hard-edged coverage.

* The sports department, which hired a new columnist ranging across the country and began covering professional teams in Boston and New York on a regular basis for the first time.

* Opinion-writing. Generally happy with the editorial page but bored with the paper's columnists, Murphy encouraged more provocative commentary within the news pages. He increased the number of columnists.

* The photography and graphics department, which obtained more equipment, better staff and more space within the news pages. When Times Mirror sought to applaud its journalistic changes in Hartford, it often pointed to the awards won by its revamped photo department.

* The magazine, which became the biggest showcase for Times Mirror's accomplishments in Hartford. Imported to run it was Lary Bloom, the brash and innovative editor of the *Miami Herald* magazine, *Tropic*. Bloom used evocative color photos and imaginative layouts and graphics. He provided enough space for

a story so it could spin out to a satisfying climax. Most of all, he stressed freedom in writing styles. He did not like "objective reporting."

The changes in Connecticut news coverage are worth describing at greater length:

The metro editor cut back on local news coverage by closing bureaus. Reporting became more regional, more in-depth. Barnes liked the kind of story that affected the emotions, which he called "a real gut-wrencher." As part of a nationwide hiring campaign, he went to Washington to hire staff from the *Star* when its closing was announced in 1981. He brought in six. Barnes' eloquence as a recruiter helped give the *Courant* a reputation among job candidates across the country as a place where high standards were becoming the norm.

He picked as investigations editor Tom Condon, a multi-talented University of Connecticut Law School graduate who handled *pro bono* legal cases in his spare time while working full-time at the newspaper. The New England Society of Newspaper Editors had selected Condon in 1980 as "Master Reporter" for his work during the decade. Murphy, for his part, was fearless (if not foolhardy) in pursuing lively fare, even if the stories might affront influential local figures or significant numbers of subscribers. Because of this emphasis on major projects, the paper achieved some notable successes. They included prize-winning features and consumer stories, as well as the continuing revelations about the fortune-hunters who had stalked Ethel Donaghue. Barnes said the feedback he received indicated that "a Golden Age" of journalism had arrived at the paper.

But Condon, among others, became disturbed over the staff's much-reduced attention to fact-gathering and careful development of news sources. He repeatedly told his superiors that too many reporters were sitting around the office trying to dream up major projects and polish their writing. "There's not enough information coming into the building," Condon insisted. As a gibe at the popularity of the feature-style, "soft-news" stories that flourished under the California management, Condon made up a poster he hung over his desk: "THANK YOU FOR NOT USING AN ANECDOTAL LEAD." It ridiculed a mood-creating writing style that was sweeping through many newsrooms in the 1980s and which was especially popular at the *Courant* under the Beach Boys. The poster showed a fanciful example of a trendy but fatuous treatment of a news event:

> Brendan Rodriguez sat disconsolately by the side of the road, his limpid brown eyes filling with moisture as he gazed wistfully at the fender of his beloved '71 Valiant.
>
> Rodriguez, a 43-year-old Irish-Hispanic deli clerk, was one of the lucky ones.
>
> Seventeen people were killed and 84 were injured in a nasty 47-vehicle collision on the Hartford street Rodriguez, a veteran of the Korean confllict, has called home for the past 11 years.

A decade previously, Condon had authored a jokebook published by Prentice-Hall entitled, *The Executive's Handbook of Humor.* But his California bosses were not laughing by early 1983. Supremely confident that techniques proven successful in Los Angeles would work elsewhere, they decided that Condon—one of the best journalists Connecticut could offer—had an attitude problem. He was demoted off the management team.

CHAPTER 6

The Fall

AT THE START of the Murphy era, the ringing, ringing, ringing of unanswered telephones around the building signaled trouble ahead. Sometimes the phone of an absent reporter would jangle for several minutes before the caller lost patience and hung up. Reporters inevitably leave their desks as they gather information. Yet the telephone is the lifeline of the news business. A breakdown in telephone communications was not simply a discourtesy to the public unprecedented at the *Courant*. It was foolishness.

Why did the phones begin to ring unanswered at this time? Massive personnel shifts caused many on the staff to obtain new telephone numbers. The structural renovations and the permanent shortage of computer screens forced many others to float around each day throughout the three-story building seeking an available work site.

More generally, the management upheavals removed restraints on selfish ambition. Employees jockeyed frantically to improve or simply to retain their positions. Reporters neglected the ordinary business of contacting newsmakers and writing up stories. Barnes, the metro editor, used to advise his staff, "Just do your jobs." But, rightly or wrongly, many reporters suspected that getting cozy with one of the editors and promoting a story idea was more important to their careers than the research itself. The paper's writers covering politics had a staff meeting in the spring of 1982 in which they tried to get some direction from one of their immediate supervisors, an assistant metro editor. The reporters told their editor they were confused. Were they supposed to be working on big stories that might take weeks to do? Or were they supposed to disregard a lot of the original Beach Boy rhetoric of the previous year and fill up the paper with breaking news, much as they had been doing before 1981? I was working nearby, and remember hearing the editor confess, "I don't know."

Like fearful employees traumatized by a merger in any other corporation, the *Courant*'s journalists wasted vast amounts of time trying to fathom omens. The telephones could wait. In an interview with the *Washington Journalism Review*, Murphy described the *Courant* as "worse than mediocre, an embarrassment to the profession." He told one reporter that he wanted to force out between a third and half of the newspaper's staff. The new editors largely avoided litigation by keeping outright firings to a minimum, especially after one copy editor committed suicide upon learning that his supervisor was recommending dismissal the next week. Instead, they forced resignations from targeted employees by making life at the paper intolerable for them. Some of these personnel decisions turned out to be wise. But some were so preposterous as to defeat the stated goal of improving the product.

Tough-minded personnel policies had their counterpart in relations with the public. One of many examples was Murphy's firm posture in dealing with Ned Coll, a flamboyant community activist in Hartford's black ghetto. Inspired by Robert Kennedy in the late 1960s, Coll founded a volunteer organization called the Revitalization Corps. To dramatize the scarcity of public beaches on Connecticut's shoreline, he repeatedly bused inner-city children to beachfront homes for impromptu parties on the tidelands of surprised cottage owners.

Murphy, unimpressed with Coll's media carnivals, reduced coverage of him and his activities almost to the vanishing point. Coll recognized that Murphy's decision was an extreme symptom of an across-the-board Times Mirror cutback of local news. So he organized a long-running protest: pickets, bumper-stickers ("The Un-Hartford Courant Hurts Hartford") and a hanging of Murphy in effigy. Coll, who would have the last laugh, also complained to Murphy's superiors in Los Angeles.

Murphy was so confident that he felt scant need to explain his changes to anyone. When the newspaper did deign to comment on its rapid transformation, the explanations amounted to little more than a bromide: Everything is getting better.

Editorial page cartoonist Bob Englehart repeatedly aroused controversy. One time was in 1981 just after Northeast Utilities asked state regulators for an increase in electricity rates it was charging the region. Englehart drew up a facsimile of the firm's "NU" corporate logo—but with a drawing of a huge screw substituted for the "N." Shortly afterwards, a subordinate editor raised a warning at the daily news conference that some subscribers were offended by the profanity implied in the cartoon. Murphy looked up at the critic and repeated the cartoon's joke, "Screw you." Other editors erupted into laughter.

Murphy and his boss, Publisher Keith McGlade, believed that some reader hostility was inevitable as they modernized the paper. Times Mirror had installed McGlade in 1980 to run the *Courant* after his career as business manager of two major Knight- Ridder newspapers in the Midwest, the *Akron Beacon Journal* and the *Detroit Free Press.* McGlade, a thoughtful man in his late forties, was aware of his lack of experience in editorial operations and of Chandler's trust in Murphy. McGlade largely left journalistic decisions in Hartford to the editor. "He was doing some things that were injurious," McGlade told me later. "Like shooting his mouth off. He'd say something wild just to get somebody's reaction. Murphy was probably his own worst enemy in some of the things he said, but he wasn't a bad editor." Others disputed that assessment. "It was Murdoch journalism," charged former *Courant* Director Millard Pryor, who complained to two Times Mirror vice presidents. "The theory was that 'bad news' sells newspapers."

During the 1982 Big East basketball tournament in Hartford, two Syracuse University basketball players were accused of raping a Villanova University coed in the aftermath of a hotel room party. A newly appointed sports editor pressured his staff, especially its female reporters, to track down the victim and interview her the day of the alleged crime even though the assignment was unnecessary, intrusive and tasteless. Reporters were unable to locate her that day. So they obtained the basic details through the normal procedure in such cases, her statement to police. But the newspaper's metro desk later pursued her for a story published in a Sunday paper. The slant offended some of us on the staff because it included quotations from Villanova students speculating that she might have invited the sexual attack. The story said, in part,

> Some talk of her friendships with men, many of them Villanova basketball players, who frequently make late-night visits to her dormitory room—to eat pizza and socialize, she says. She is too friendly, they say. She flirts and entices men and probably was 'asking for it' that night in Hartford.

Front-page publication of unattributed slurs by fellow students was a sensationalistic way to handle a rape story. Comments by the defendants, their attorneys and law enforcement officials would have been a better way to provide balance if, in fact, the newspaper had serious doubts about her credibility. Another acceptable method of dealing with dubious claims is by minimizing news coverage of them until they are resolved. Hartford's State's Attorney John Bailey blamed the front-page, Sunday story for ruining the prosecution. "She was so embarrassed [by it]," the prosecutor told me later, "that she dropped out of college and refused to testify." Bailey was forced to drop the charges. His finger-pointing at the paper was never reported.

"The paper became a major source of misinformation," recalled Theodore Driscoll, the *Courant*'s main investigative reporter for nearly a decade before Barnes demoted him to general assignment reporting. In interviews for this book, Driscoll described as "the ultimate in yellow journalism" the paper's exhaustive coverage of a drunk driving fatality.

The driver was Joseph Fazzano, an immigrant's son who went on to create a highly successful legal practice in Hartford. He had been the secret lobbyist for ITT in 1969 as it persuaded Connecticut's insurance commissioner to accept the Hartford Fire Insurance Co. merger. He was an eloquent advocate who numbered five dozen police unions in Connecticut among his clients. "I was earning more," he used to boast, "than the President of the United States."

Acquaintances who saw Fazzano early in the evening of April 27, 1983, said he seemed intoxicated and unhappy. Fazzano left a West Hartford restaurant about 8:30 p.m. About a half-hour later his Porsche fatally struck a ten-year-old Puerto Rican girl crossing a Hartford street. Some witnesses said the car sped away. A lawyer representing Fazzano contacted Hartford police ten hours after the accident and turned over the car. A probe led to Fazzano's arrest on two misdemeanor charges: negligent homicide and evading responsibility for an accident.

The *Courant* treated the story as a morality play: The rich, drunk, callous attorney had killed the poor, Puerto Rican girl standing at the curb in her own neighborhood. And then (according to the most important part of the newspaper's innuendos) the devious Hartford police tried to help the wicked lawyer escape full justice—all because he was well-connected and represented the Hartford police union. The *Courant* published many news stories and editorials suggesting this scenario. A front-page diagram purported to trace the path of Fazzano's car. It showed the vehicle hitting the girl virtually at the curb in a marked crosswalk section as the car swerved onto the sidewalk. The route and spot of fatal impact were published in red ink.

News stories harped on supposed police leniency to Fazzano:

1) failure to obtain a search warrant for his car; 2) failure to impound the car after it was examined; 3) failure to interrogate him; 4) delay of nearly a week after the accident before an arrest warrant was obtained; and 5) most of all, misdemeanor charges instead of a felony. Eleven front page *Courant* stories in the month after the accident largely focused on whether police were protecting Fazzano. While the stories inflamed the Hispanic community against police, they did little to enlighten anyone about normal police procedure in such a case.

"No search warrant was obtained in this case because the suspect's attorney of record gave the police consent to search the vehicle," said Hartford Police Chief Bernard Sullivan, whom I'd always found to be a forthright official. Sullivan's five-page press release continued. "This is standard, accepted police practice. The car was returned after the examination and not impounded. This is another normally standard police practice. We do not produce cars in courtrooms." Sullivan then explained that cars are sometimes confiscated when used in narcotics dealing, but never after auto accidents. "The most absurd question," the chief continued, "is whether or not it is normal for the police to interview suspects after an accident. It is, of course, normal for us to interview suspects after accidents. However, the Constitution of the United States guarantees all persons, whether they be prominent or not, the right to remain silent when being represented by counsel. Mr. Fazzano exercised the right of any citizen when his attorney advised us that his client would not speak to us."

The next day's paper virtually ignored Sullivan's explanations. A front-page story and its full-page runover on Fazzano and the week-old accident did not once quote the police chief on his rebuttal. An editorial headlined "MR. SULLIVAN'S UNACCEPTABLE DEFENSE" noted his explanation only enough to sneer, "If Mr. Sullivan believes that the investigation of Jeanette Ortiz's death was normal. . . . this city is in big trouble." An Englehart cartoon that day portrayed Sullivan as the bumbling movie detective Inspector Clouseau.

The *Courant* suspected a coverup because it did not learn of the accident until two days after it happened. Yet the paper's cutbacks of police coverage (it had no daytime police reporter, for instance, and its night reporter was otherwise occupied the night of the accident) made communications problems inevitable.

Nonetheless, the paper charged ahead. "From the start," the managing editor said, "we knew we had to have two investigations: one of the accident itself and one of the Hartford Police Department."

Driscoll was among those enlisted. "I was assigned to go to other police departments and check with lawyers and so forth, and find out what the Hartford police should have done and didn't do," the reporter recalled for me. "When I read the reports the thing that struck me most was: the most powerful evidence in there—the most powerful evidence anywhere that Fazzano was drunk, which would turn what he did into a felony—was an off-duty Hartford cop in West Hartford. He volunteered the information that Fazzano was stumbling around drunk and didn't know what he was doing shortly before the accident. And another Hartford cop, on duty on Trumbull Street, saw Fazzano having trouble getting into his car."

"If these guys were covering up," Driscoll continued, "they wouldn't have included that in the investigation. These guys were also setting themselves up for criticism later. Someone could say, 'Gee, you saw the guy having trouble and you know he's a big drinker. Why did you let him get into his car?' Yet these guys were dedicated enough to come forward." Driscoll next went to the court records to inspect the police department's original request for Fazzano's arrest. Underneath white-out marks and retyping, Driscoll could see that Hartford police had sought a felony charge. Curious about the discovery, he questioned State's Attorney John Bailey. "Bailey immediately acknowledged that the warrant application had a felony on it," the reporter continued. "He then gave me all the reasons why he didn't think they could prove a felony. The point is, when I went back to the paper with my story there was no one to deny it—because it was all on the record, from the key figures involved."

Driscoll's story undermined two weeks of earlier ones throwing suspicions on police. But it was kept out of the paper for days. Driscoll pressed his superiors for an explanation. He was told his story needed a news angle. "That's absurd," Driscoll told me. "It was its own 'news peg.' [Metro Editor Dick] Barnes just didn't want it to go."

Driscoll's story showed in a variety of ways how the police investigation of Fazzano met departmental norms. Also, it quoted the state's attorney as saying that when the girl was hit, she was ten feet into the road and eighteen feet from the crosswalk. In other words, the state's top-ranking investigator believed that the newspaper's diagram—published on the front page in red ink—was *entirely wrong*.

Driscoll's story finally ran May 24, nearly a month after the accident. His story was dumped on an inside page. Another story about criticism of the police department was displayed that day as the right-hand lead story on the front page—the most prominent position in the paper. "After that happened, I'm not even sure that I read any more on the issue," recalled Driscoll. "I was not given any more assignments on it. I was given the first bad evaluation at the *Hartford Courant* that I had gotten in seventeen years there. Barnes killed a project that I had worked six months on. That was all immediately afterward. In my evaluation, Barnes raised a question as to whether I had any of my 'news instincts' left. He denied me a pay raise."

The newspaper chose not to admit its misjudgments and factual errors in timely fashion. Instead, it published on July 17 (two and a half months after the accident) a Sunday magazine article that reflected a more balanced account than its news stories—but a history that was, nonetheless, far more charitable to the paper than it deserved.

Why reexamine the Fazzano coverage at such length here? Not because he should be excused for the crime he committed. But his culpability was not what kept the story on the front pages. The key element was the Hartford police department's role. The newspaper's coverage showed its willingness to smear an important institution (thus creating widespread public cynicism about the police) with an almost casual concern for the facts. In the end, it was the newspaper that disgraced itself.

The Californians' emphasis on bright writing overshadowed development of sources and careful documentation of the facts. Reporters on new beats often sat around the office trying to imagine what could be a career-boosting project while events in outside world passed them by. In the spring of 1983, allegations arose that the Hartford-based firm United Technologies Corp. was involved in Department of Defense cost overrun scandals. Several reporters worked on the articles, but they broke little new ground. At a national journalism conference during the summer of 1983, a producer for ABC-TV's *20/20* ridiculed the *Courant* for its haphazard coverage.

Other story ideas too numerous to mention were lost in the casual posture towards news-gathering that afflicted many editors and reporters. The office seemed permeated with the attitude that only small-timers would be caught writing a routine story or working late at the office. Barnes, the editor in charge of all Connecticut coverage, fragmented his energies into his law school studies and his long-distance running regimen. Others on the staff were putting much of their creative energy into applications for other jobs, fellowships and book projects. I myself was on leave from the paper during the 1982-83 academic year. "You went to Yale Law School," one reporter shouted across the city room on the day of my return, "and you didn't get a job someplace else?"

So much for the "Golden Era."

CHAPTER 7

The Kansas City Chief

RUMORS OF A MAJOR management shake-up raced through the newsroom during the afternoon of Aug. 29, 1983. As usual, they were true. An announcement during the mid-afternoon news conference confirmed that Mark Murphy was leaving the paper, spreading euphoria through much of the staff, especially my bailiwick, the investigations team. Three of my four colleagues there had been exiled from the daily news operation. They were too critical of it to be tolerated in positions of newsroom responsibility and too talented to be forced off the paper.

Shortly after the news conference ended all but the most urgent work ceased for the day. Reporters and editors clustered in small groups exchanging fragmentary information and speculating on its meaning. With a pang of sadness, I looked around the room for one of my close friends. Suddenly I felt like a stranger. So many people had left.

Shortly after 5:30 p.m., a jacketless Times Mirror executive named David Laventhol—white shirt opened at the neck and tie askew—came to the center of the newsroom to introduce the *Courant*'s new leader, Michael Davies. Laventhol himself was just a name to most of the sixty reporters and editors who surrounded him. A Yale College graduate in 1957, he had an affable, frank manner. After a stint at the *St. Petersberg Times* in Florida, he became assistant city editor, then city editor of the old *New York Herald Tribune*. Then at the *Washington Post*, he became a pioneer during the 1960s in fostering the flashy, contemporary "life/style" reporting that replaced traditional "women's sections" across the country. He went on to top news management jobs at *Newsday* in New York before becoming Times Mirror's vice president for eastern newspapers.

It had been a long day for Laventhol, but he beamed as he summarized Michael Davies' impressive credentials. President and editor of the Kansas City newspapers. Editor of papers that had won four Pulitzer Prizes. Just 39 years old. A great guy. It came time for Davies, also in shirtsleeves, to speak. He remained seated on the edge of a desk, demonstrating the casual air he managed to project along with a certain restraint and dignity. His white shirt, unlike Laventhol's, remained crisp and buttoned. A lanky six-footer born in England, Davies' appearance and Americanized accent recalled the young Peter Lawford, and created a similarly winning impression.

He started with a short speech that could have come right from my colleagues on the investigations team, so closely did it parallel our views of the paper's weaknesses under Murphy. Mike Davies wanted accuracy, community rapport, investigations and local news. "I don't ever want to see the *Courant* beaten on a Connecticut story," he said, "whether by the *Boston Globe* or the Manchester *Journal Inquirer*."

The questions began. Did he have any criticism of Murphy? "The *Courant* is a very fine newspaper with a fine tradition," Davies replied. "What's needed here really is fine-tuning and not a lot of wholesale changes." What did he think were the priorities for coverage? "I want to be able to pick up the *Hartford Courant* and find out what went on yesterday in the Greater Hartford area, in Connecticut and, in concentric circles, the nation and the world." What about the criticism that the *Courant* wasn't adequately covering local news? "At this point, I just don't know. Obviously a newspaper has to serve its community well. If there's some action that needs to be taken or some refocusing, then maybe we'll refocus." He handled every question in this amiable and urbane manner. No legitimate journalistic interest was threatened (who, after all, stands up for *in*accurate writing?), and nearly every valid gripe was mentioned with the implicit suggestion it would be addressed more fully later. It was an impressive performance.

The next day Davies began a series of staff meetings, first with top executives and then with middle-echelon editors and reporters who had been selected to carry back news to various departments. It defused rumors with facts, and contrasted with the palace intrigue atmosphere Murphy had created upon his 1981 arrival from Los Angeles.

Davies soon let it be known that Murphy had not been driven out. Murphy had been caught by surprise at noon on August 29th when Laventhol first told him at the Parkview Hilton Hotel that Davies was coming in as his boss. In the beginning, Murphy seemed inclined to go along with the plan. Within an hour, though, he had decided to walk out. He believed that his honor was at stake and he should make a stand: principle and pride are worth more than money and position. Davies, a fast-track achiever, tried to dissuade Murphy from leaving before he could find a new job. It's easier to get one from a position of strength, Davies advised the Californian, whose wife cared for their infant child at home. Looking back, however, Davies said of Murphy's walk-out, "In a bizarre way, I admire him for doing what he did."

Laventhol orchestrated the change, and it's to him one must go for the overview. Along with his vice presidency, he was publisher of Times Mirror's largest East Coast newspaper, *Newsday.* At his Long Island office, he described what he sought at the Hartford newspaper. The changes that took place in editorial content, the changes reflected in Davies' appointment, "had almost nothing to do with the economics of the *Hartford Courant.*" Revenues and profits were increasing in the first years of Murphy and Publisher Keith McGladc. "The issue that caused us to bring in Mike Davies was, first, the editorial direction that the *Courant* was taking was, in our judgment, a little off course. And two, the *Courant*'s ability to communicate to, and respond to its readership was not effective."

Laventhol believed that the best newspaper for Los Angeles or New York City was not likely to be the best for Connecticut. "Mark Murphy was an excellent editor. He enhanced the *Hartford Courant*. But I think the localness of the *Courant* suffered. I don't mean just the small chicken-dinner type of town news. This is a newspaper that exists in a community. People live there and they pick up the paper, and they want to know what's going on.

"When you assign your own reporters to do a story on a nursing shortage in the United States, and there's no nursing shortage in Hartford, and you have a limited number of resources to go outside of Hartford, it could be that you're a little off course. That was the journalistic issue."

"The second issue, communication, came somewhat late to newspapers," Laventhol continued. "People feel newspapers are arrogant, unaccountable, intrusive, do whatever we please. While we know our motive is unquestionably of the highest standards, they believe we're just trying to sell newspapers. I think the *Courant* in the pre-Davies time had those problems very, very seriously. It was a problem the management of the *Courant* was unable to deal with. It became my job. I went looking for someone who was an outstanding journalist on any level—and who secondly understood and endorsed the idea that a newspaper doesn't exist in a vacuum."

That man was Michael John Davies, born May 19, 1944 in Essex, an eastern part of England heavily bombed during the German blitz. His proper manner and cozy relationships with business and arts leaders would lead to a widespread assumption in Connecticut that he had been reared amongst the gentry. Not so. He was a hard-working, self-made man with a knack for impressing distinguished elders.

The Davies family was poor. "But," the publisher would later recall, "almost everyone was reasonably poor in England after the war." His family lived in public housing before emigrating to Savannah, Ga., in 1957 to join his oldest brother, who was working there as a plant manager for the Tetley Tea Co. The father ultimately found work as office manager for a construction company. Michael worked in the library of the *Savannah Morning News* during his senior year in high school. "I needed the money, needed the job," he remembered. "Part of the job was clipping stories for the files. And as I began reading them more closely, I thought, 'What an easy racket!' I went to the city editor and said, 'I bet I could do as well as some of these people.' I tried a couple of pieces, and I did and was hired."

He attended Armstrong State College and Georgia State University, graduating in 1966 with a bachelor's degree in journalism. Along the way, he continued to work for the *Morning News* and then the *Atlantia Times*. "English, writing, history, liberal arts," he said, "were always easier for me than anything involving chemistry or numbers." Midway through his senior year in college, he married Carol McCray, an attractive, blonde-haired homemaker interested in the arts. He received a copy editing job at the *Atlanta Constitution*, then moved to the Chicago area, where he obtained a master's degree from the Northwestern University School of Journalism while working part-time as a copy editor for a small chain of newspapers.

He impressed a visiting speaker to the campus, *Louisville Times* and *Courier-Journal* Executive Editor Norman Isaacs. "I'm English-born myself," Isaacs later recalled. "Mike had poise and presence, and after a short conversation, he was applying for a job." Davies began as a copy editor, then became editor of the Saturday afternoon edition of the *Louisville Times*, which had been lagging in sales before Managing Editor Robert Clark decided to put it into an innovative magazine-style format. Sales increased dramatically. Following Clark up the ladder in Louisville, Davies became managing editor of the *Times* and then, in 1976, managing editor of the larger and more prestigious sister paper, the *Courier-Journal*. "He's a very bright guy. He gets things done efficiently," commented Clark in 1985 when he was president of the American Society of Newspaper Editors, a major trade organization.

The 1976 Pulitzer Prize for feature photography went to Davies' photographers based on their report on busing in Louisville's schools. Davies himself was then picked to be a Pulitzer juror. The honor provided him with an exceptional education in how newspaper awards are bestowed. Shortly after Davies' Pulitzer duties ended in 1977, a devastating fire erupted at the Beverly Hills Supper Club in Southgate, Ky., a suburb of Cincinnati. The May 28 fire killed 164 in the overcrowded nightclub, which contained 1,300 patrons. Davies encouraged his staff at the *Courier-Journal* to pinpoint blame for the fire. A reporter showed that the club had had a number of fire code violations and had undergone lax enforcement. The paper's efforts prompted Kentucky's governor and legislature to strengthen fire safety enforcement. The reporter won a 1978 Pulitzer.

Davies seemed intent on creating a dignified bearing appropriate for an executive, recalled Richard Kirschten, one of his Louisville reporters who had moved on to become a writer for the *National Journal* in Washington, D.C. "Mike strikes me," the reporter said during an interview. "as one of these guys who at some point read a military manual that told second lieutenants, 'If you're liked by the troops you're probably not a very good second lieutenant. Your job isn't to be pals, but to establish authority and make sure they know who the boss is.' "

Davies' next job after Louisville came in 1978 as editor of the two jointly owned Kansas City papers. It was a rescue mission remarkably similar to that he would face at the *Courant* in 1983, although each of the Kansas City circulations was higher than the Hartford daily's.

The two Kansas City papers, like the *Courant*, were owned by employees, retirees and their families until sale in 1977. The same nationwide economic trends causing the *Courant* sale in

1978 allowed Capital Cities to offer $125 million in Kansas City. At that time, it was the largest purchase price on record for a single city newspaper operation.

Capital Cities was, of course, the firm that tried to buy the *Courant* in 1978. Just before Davies arrived Cap Cities had tried to streamline the Kansas City papers by bringing in two hard-nosed executives nicknamed "The Rodeo Boys" from its Fort Worth, Tex. newspaper, the *Star-Telegram*. Davies walked into a rather strained situation as a conciliator, and was accepted by the staff as an improvement over the Fort Worth executives.

Capital Cities Communications has long been known as one of the more efficient, profit-minded chains in the country. (Its net income as a percent of sales was the seventh highest of all Fortune 500 companies in 1985. Its New Haven television station, WTNH, reported $14 million in profits on revenues of $24 million). The Cap Cities newspapers in Kansas City during the Davies years published short news stories—sometimes ten or twelve on a page—and used graphics liberally.

Davies also saved some resources for the kind of in-depth journalism that wins awards. A *Times* national reporter won a Pulitzer in 1982 for a variety of stories. Davies also authorized a massive effort to determine why two sky walks collapsed during a Friday night tea dance at the Hyatt Regency Hotel in Kansas City July 17, 1981. The accident killed 113 people. Refining techniques he had learned from the supper club fire in Louisville, Davies provided what he called "the most concerted coverage of any single event" in Kansas City history. In the first week alone, the newspaper published more than fifty ad-free pages of news devoted to the Hyatt tragedy. By year's end, it had published more than 340 stories and hundreds of pictures.

The papers hired five engineers to analyze data provided by the newspapers. The probe found that a critical design change had been made in the sky walks that doubled the stress in key areas and probably triggered the collapse. Among other findings were that the hotel had thirty-five fire code violations and that city building inspectors were at the hotel site only eighteen hours during construction. The coverage won a 1982 Pulitzer.

To this coup, Davies added a deft follow-up. He decided to have his staff tail the Kansas City building inspectors for two months to see if the inspectors had learned anything from the tragedy. The findings led to the firing or resignation of twenty-one of the city's forty-odd building inspectors. Three others were suspended for two weeks. Davies' performance brought him a promotion to the presidency of the Kansas City papers. The job as second-in-command gave him oversight of their financial as well as news operations.

When Davies arrived in Hartford with an even better job, he quickly embarked on an exhaustive series of meetings with staff and community leaders. He asked everyone to tell him how the newspaper's news and opinion sections could be improved. Davies saw these meetings as an opportunity to learn—and to distance himself from the criticism. In the financial area, Publisher Keith McGlade's management had helped make the paper enormously profitable. Davies kept him for a transition period, and then assumed his duties and title.

CHAPTER 8

. . . and the Rest of the Tribe

MICHAEL DAVIES avoided any direct criticism of his predecessors for months after his arrival. Keith McGlade, of course, was still at the paper. Mark Murphy, reputed to have friends in high places at Times Mirror, continued to live in West Hartford while he searched for work. But finally, at one of the mass staff meetings Davies repeatedly organized, he said, "I've never seen a newspaper so out of touch with its readership."

Some of the theoretical differences between Murphy and Davies soon found concrete manifestation in the fate of one Joe Kirkup, magazine writer. Kirkup—his friends called him that, not 'Joe'—was a balding Vietnam combat veteran with a stubborn streak of independence, a love of animals and ill-concealed distrust for many of God's two-legged creatures.

When Lary Bloom was running the *Miami Herald* 's magazine shortly before he became editor of the *Courant's Northeast*, he saw Kirkup's angry letter to the *Herald* editor objecting to the hoopla over the release of American hostages in Iran. Where, Kirkup demanded, had been the parades for Vietnam vets upon their return to the U.S. from the jungles? Had they not been "captives?" Bloom was intrigued. He persuaded Kirkup to write a full-length magazine article about his wartime experiences. Kirkup had no formal training in journalism. He had worked as a car salesman, truck driver, jack-of-all trades. He called himself "a redneck." Nonetheless, the article was an extremely compelling memoir.

Bloom persuaded Kirkup to move north from Florida to be a regular contributor to the *Courant*'s magazine. Bloom turned him loose on subjects upon which Kirkup had strong opinions or, just for fun, upon those in which he knew next to nothing and therefore, presumably, had a fresh, provocative viewpoint. Among the latter was a piece on the writer's experiences (or more precisely, non-experiences) riding Amtrak. Bloom gave him enough money to ride the trains a few days. Based on that, Kirkup wrote a humor piece printed almost exactly as he wrote it.

Bloom embodied the flashy, irreverent aspect of Murphy-style journalism. And Kirkup's writing, in turn, struck Bloom as refreshingly brash, witty and (when Kirkup chose to be) sensitive. Just before Davies' arrival in late August 1983, Bloom devoted his Sunday column in *Northeast* to the tale of Kirkup's success and its lessons for others. "Invariably, whenever I'm out giving a speech, I'll be asked about Joe Kirkup. Joe always receives letters from readers—mostly from aspiring writers—after each piece appears. Not bad for a man who 'isn't a writer.'"

"And I admit," Bloom continued, "feeling great satisfaction when I sat in the audience a few weeks ago, as the Connecticut chapter of Sigma Delta Chi, the journalism fraternity, selected Joe's article about firemen, which he wrote last year for *Northeast*, as the best human interest story published in the state in 1982." Bloom went on to point to Kirkup as living proof of what it takes to be a published writer: "It isn't talent alone. It is instead a combination of talent and drive and life experience and guts. It is the willingness to put down on paper something of yourself; to risk an honest feeling, and to take the consequences for it. It is in the end writing—and not just talking about writing."

Two weeks later, the magazine published a Kirkup article poking fun at the Canon-Sammy Davis Jr.–Greater Hartford Open, a golf tournament run by the Junior Chamber of Commerce. The new editor lashed out at Bloom over the story, calling it sophomoric journalism. Bloom stood his ground, sneering at Davies' Sunday magazine in Kansas City. It was a blistering session, and was the talk of the newsroom for several days.

But Bloom and Davies needed one another too much not to patch up their quarrel. Bloom's magazine was losing hundreds of thousands of dollars a year. A snap of Davies' fingers could shut it down. And Davies needed Bloom, who had achieved a national reputation for *Northeast* and whose personality permeated a magazine that was an important status symbol for Times Mirror. The departure of Bloom, with all his magazine industry contacts, flair and technical expertise, might literally be ruinous for a magazine that was just achieving credibility with advertisers. The closing of the magazine would mean that losses Times Mirror had suffered on *Northeast* since its founding in 1982 would have been wasted.

It happened, though, that Kirkup was scheduled to have a cover story on animal trapping the same month as his golf piece. Unlike the tournament, which he cared nothing about and undertook strictly as an assignment, Kirkup was deeply moved by the suffering of animals held in steel-jawed, leg traps, sometimes for days, so their fur could be harvested for sale to make women's coats. *Northeast* had subsidized his research for two months on his $500-a-week retainer. The result was an article entitled, "The Not-So-Tender Trap." A color magazine cover had already been shot for the story when the *Courant*'s advertising department got wind of it.

An advertising executive believed the piece would offend fur-sellers, especially the large Connecticut department stores the *Courant* was trying to woo for magazine ads in a fall promotion on, yes, fashionable furs. The piece was postponed and subjected to extensive editing by the magazine's associate editor. Her position was that the article was being improved.

Kirkup became convinced that his carefully wrought phrases were being turned into clichés, and that his descriptions of animal suffering were being deliberately softened or eliminated for tawdry commercial motives. Kirkup and Bloom soon erupted into a long shouting match at the magazine's office suite. Kirkup said he could not stand working with that kind of editing. Bloom told him he was acting like a baby. After a considerable escalation beyond that, Kirkup said he was walking out of the office, forever. "Get back in there!" ordered Bloom, as he pursued Kirkup out to the elevator.

The magazine had already paid for the piece through Kirkup's freelance retainer and fees for artwork. It ran the edited version on inside pages. Kirkup refused to allow his byline on it, and vowed never to write for *Northeast* again. The official version of the dispute from Bloom was that Kirkup stopped writing for the magazine because he realized he was temperamentally unsuited to the editing process. Kirkup provided a different explanation. "I may be stubborn, but I'm not so crazy as to give up a $500-a-week job unless I thought there was a real matter of integrity at stake. That was a dream job for a freelance writer."

Bloom and the other editor with a national reputation, the editorial page's John Zakarian, were allowed to keep their jobs after they showed a willingness to adjust to the new regime. However, all the other top eleven Murphy editors soon left supervisory responsibility at the newspaper. In the new, more centralized *Courant*, Davies need have fewer worries that unseemly disagreements would arise with subordinates.

At first, many on the staff heartily endorsed Davies' public pronouncements. They searched his statements for clues about his intentions and how they could help him implement them. During this period, Davies was stressing in staff meetings and in his Sunday column that he intended no sharp break with the Murphy paper, but only "fine-tuning" that would emphasize local news and more accountability to the public.

Davies in reality was looking for those who had already proven to him their value and their understanding of his methods. That's common enough in business and politics. But Davies undertook such an extreme consolidation of power that he raised suspicions that he was seeking the loyalty Trilby bestowed on Svengali, the grateful, unflinching devotion that comes when people have been elevated to heights they might not otherwise achieve.

Marty Petty, just thirty years old and with three years as a professional journalist, was named to be the paper's top newsroom editor, in effect replacing both Murphy and his managing editor, who had worked at the paper more than two decades. A hard-working woman with a pleasant voice that seemed more Southern than midwestern, she was a native of St. Louis. In 1975, she received a bachelor's degree in journalism from the University of Missouri, where she met her husband, a photographer who also obtained his degree in journalism that year. She found work in public relations as an art director, an ad sales executive and as communications director of the National Dairy Association in Texas. Demonstrating idealism common to many journalists (especially early in their careers), she and her husband collaborated on an in-depth article about leprosy victims that was published by a New Orleans newspaper. She went to work for Davies in Kansas City as an assistant photo editor, and quickly rose to the position of assistant managing editor for photography and graphics. Her page designs and other suggestions there provided effective display for stories, including the prize-winners about the Hyatt Regency collapse.

Davies received blunt questions from the *Courant*'s staff about whether she was qualified for such an important job as managing editor. She had, the publisher responded, "the unusual ability to see and understand all parts of the news operation—from story generation, picture usage, to graphics. And she's extremely good in dealing with people and planning." He conceded, however, that she had never edited a news story in her career.

Another who had helped win the Pulitzer for the Hyatt Regency stories was Roger Moore. The forty-year-old blond bachelor was promoted from chief of the special projects desk in Kansas City to be *Courant* metro editor. A job as labor editor was created for Moore's close friend Mike McGraw, who had traveled with him from papers in Kansas City to Des Moines, back to Kansas City and on to Hartford. Joseph Stebbins, a reporter from Kansas City and University of Missouri graduate, was named senior deputy metro editor. He was, in other words, Moore's top editor in charge of Connecticut coverage.

Petty's undergraduate classmates from the University of Missouri soon arrived to receive editorships at the *Courant*. The names that follow are not really important to remember, only their interrelationships. The appointees included Michael Jenner, aged twenty-nine, who held a bachelor's degree in journalism (B.J.) from the Missouri Class of '75. He became the assistant managing editor in charge of the paper at night. Jenner's best man from his wedding, Randy Cox, (B.J., Missouri, '75) became assistant managing editor in charge of the photography and graphics departments. Jenner's wife, Jan Winburn (B.J., Missouri, '75), became the deputy editor at *Northeast*. Cox's wife, Joan Carlin, worked as a photographer in her husband's department and as a lay-out editor on the editorial page. John MacDonald, whom Davies knew from their work together in Louisville, became national editor of the *Courant*. His wife, Georgia MacDonald, became *Courant* bureau chief for the City of New Britain.

Marty Petty's close friend from college, Stephanie Summers (B.J., Missouri, '75), was installed as the editor of the life-style, arts, entertainment, real estate and travel sections. Former University of Missouri professor Ken Ross arrived as business editor. Appointed to be his boss was former *Kansas City Star* reporter Steven Woodward (M.S., Missouri, '79), who came in as executive business editor. Many other recent graduates of Missouri and employees of the Kansas City papers, including another husband-and-wife team, were installed in lesser editorships and reporting jobs.

"Missouri is a good school," explained Davies. "A lot of good people go through there." He also applauded his new editors' accomplishments beyond their college studies (which in some cases included editorships at papers outside of Kansas City), and attacked the in-bred atmosphere he found in Connecticut. "I think one of the real problems with journalists on the East Coast is their incredible myopia about what goes on in the rest of the country. There is a world beyond Connecticut. There is a world beyond the East Coast."

To put Davies' appointments in perspective, it is useful to know that in the 1980s three hundred colleges and universities offered four-year degree programs in journalism. The situation created an intense competition for whatever vacancies occurred in the estimated 51,000 news reporting jobs at all levels of experience existing nationwide in both newspapers and broadcasting. The oversupply of applicants was compounded by the preference of many leading news organizations for liberal arts graduates.

Traditionally, the *Courant* had hired from varied sources for its newsroom. Like nearly every other newspaper, it had always had a serious problem hiring enough racial minorities. Still, the commitment to newsroom diversity was strong enough so that only a few times in memory before the Davies era (mostly under Mark Murphy) had a spouse of a journalist been hired. Even these instances involved part-time or non-supervisory posts. An example provides the contrast. Linda Howell, a former *Courant* writer who had gone on to become a *Connecticut Magazine* editor, returned to the job market during 1980. But she believed ethics barred her from reapplying to the *Courant* for any kind of work because she was dating an assistant managing editor.

In announcing the appointment of Roger Moore to replace Dick Barnes as metro editor, Davies tried to dismiss fears that Connecticut's dominant news organization was going to be run by a tightly knit clique from Missouri. Davies told the staff in a mass meeting that Barnes had been urged to stay on, but had decided to leave for his own reasons.

It was a half-truth. Barnes had wanted to continue as metro editor, a position in which he had help dazzle scores of job applicants from all over the country who had left Hartford without an offer but hoping that some day, if they worked hard and greatly improved their journalistic standards, they could help Dick Barnes and Mark Murphy publish big stories in Connecticut. Davies offered Barnes an insulting demotion to a post out of the newsroom in the paper's public relations department. The Californian strode quickly out of a management meeting when he learned that his successor's appointment would be announced later in the day. In less than two minutes, Barnes cleaned out his possessions from his desk. Ignoring the office elevator, he rattled down the three flights of stairs, out of the building and into the chilly morning air, finally succumbing to tears. Within the month, Barnes would obtain a much better job—as city editor of the flagship *Los Angeles Times.*

Shortly afterward, the *Courant* boasted to its readers that it had been picked as the top newspaper in New England for 1983. The front page news story said that the New England Newspaper Association had bestowed two separate awards. One was for the best daily, the other for the best Sunday newspaper in the region from Connecticut north to Maine. The *Courant* did not mention in the lengthy story that Boston newspapers had not bothered to enter the contest.

The paper's new executives cleverly insinuated themselves into the publicity surrounding the award. "I think the thing that's terrific about it," Managing Editor Marty Petty was quoted as saying in the story, "is it was a team effort by the whole staff." Her comment was made on a Friday, a week after her deposed predecessor, a man named Reid MacCluggage, put in his last day at the newspaper where he had begun his career twenty-three years before.

That same week, a janitor holding two brass trophies commemorating earlier journalism awards came to the office of the newspaper's investigative team. "Do you think anybody wants these?" the janitor asked. A dozen of them had turned up while he was installing Petty's things in her new office. She had told him to get rid of them. But the janitor had had second thoughts before throwing them out. Each had been given to the newspaper or to an individual reporter for outstanding work during the late 1970s and early 1980s. To a conglomerate, the engraved keepsakes were as disposable as many of the people who earned them. On a staff of just over 240 reporters and editors, 106 left the *Courant* in 1983 and 1984, the bulk of them after Davies' arrival. Nearly all of the top editors leaving the paper under Davies had obtained their posts in 1981. That was during the first top-to-bottom transformation by Times Mirror.

David Laventhol, the chain's vice president for eastern newspapers, conceded during interviews with me that the dislocations in Hartford were like tidal waves. "They keep coming in a different way. And I think it's bound to take a toll on people." Laventhol believed the situation became stable after Publisher Michael Davies put his new management team in place. "Davies," Laventhol continued, "reasoned that it was best to move quickly in his transformations: 'Let's do them, get them done, settle down and not have any more tidal waves.' "

Not everyone was so hopeful. The Petty appointment, for example, raised eyebrows. Why would a newspaper seeking national stature appoint someone from another state with so little experience as its top newsroom editor? That she had worked longer in public relations than in the news business hardly inspired confidence. "Davies is basically an insecure guy, despite the image," commented former publisher Keith McGlade. "He needs to surround himself with loyal people." Why? And what did these in-house maneuvers mean for the public?

One thing was certain. At the top editorial levels of the paper, nobody knew much about Connecticut.

CHAPTER 9

PR and Pacification

LIKE CAMPAIGNING POLITICIANS, Davies and Petty courted community leaders all over town. Everywhere they went—breakfasts, brunches, lunches and dinners—they urged people to tell them what they thought of the newspaper. "The complaints were universal," Petty recalled. In seeking a Pulitzer Prize for Davies' columns on how to run a newspaper, she listed community criticisms of the Murphy era as follows:

* You don't care about what's important to us.
* Our newspaper is no longer 'ours.'
* Absentee owners don't care.
* You print only bad news and ignore the good.
* Your value system is different than ours.

Because of such comments Davies and Petty instituted new procedures in the newsroom. One improvement involved incoming telephone calls. Journalists were told to answer promptly any ringing telephones in their work areas. Davies hired clerks to answer calls, and installed a high-powered loudspeaker to summon reporters. The loudspeaker was abrasive but effective.

Davies himself began writing a weekly column "to demystify the *Courant*."

> We willingly and promptly correct errors on page 2 each day. . . . Reporters and editors diligently try to keep bias out of all stories. Whenever a story contains the opinions of the reporter, it is clearly labeled as something other than a normal news story.

After repeated suggestions from the staff that the paper needed an ombudsman, Davies created such a post and filled it with *Courant* veteran Henry McNulty. The appointment of a local man to such a high-profile post helped provide a vitally needed Connecticut image for the paper's management, even though McNulty had no supervisory power except over a secretary. The ombudsman's main job was to write a daily memo analyzing reader comments about the paper. He concentrated on pinpointing the blame for certifiable mistakes, which tend to be spelling, grammar and accuracy errors committed by writers and low-echelon copy editors. For example, McNulty rebuked the paper's highly prolific drama and film critic Malcolm Johnson for identifying a character in the movie *Hotel New Hampshire* as 'Suzie' when her name had been spelled 'Susie' in the novel by that name. Maintaining that his job did not involve second-guessing other editors on subjective decisions, McNulty rarely discussed any managers in his memos or in the op-ed columns he wrote four or five times a year. In other words, he focused on details. He thereby attracted the widespread scorn of newsroom colleagues, who dismissed him as a glorified proofreader even though his name and title, "associate editor," were emblazoned each day on the paper's editorial page masthead. Sadly, he presented the image but not the reality of a forceful, independent readers' advocate.

Such innovations assuaged readers who believed that the newspaper was aloof and uncaring. Yet many editors and writers worried that the publisher's efforts were excessive. His semantics obscured serious ethical issues. When Davies forbade *Courant* publication of edited staff-written stories, editorials and even "Doonesbury" comic strips—was that "editing" or "censorship?" It may have been a distinction without a difference to readers in a monopoly market. Similarly, was it "packaging" or "sensationalizing" when Davies, far more than Murphy, played up his investigations in exhaustive detail to win journalism prizes but ignored inconvenient evidence that went against the predetermined theme? Was it "community responsiveness" or "puffery" when the publisher asked for specific stories about civic leaders? Was it a normal boss-to-boss "warning" for *Courant* executives to seek out their peers at other newspapers and urge them not to hire journalists whose opinions differed from management's? Or was it an attempt to create a blacklist within an ever-more centralized industry? Such disturbing questions loomed constantly.

Davies' first troubles with his staff grew out of his custom of seeking stories about the businesses and prominent individuals he encountered during his rounds, which included directorships on the Greater Hartford Chamber of Commerce and the Greater Hartford Arts Council. Soon after his arrival, Davies met with Ned Coll, the community activist who had complained to Times Mirror's headquarters in Los Angeles. Returning from the meeting, Davies told the city desk to write about Coll's tutoring program, which had been in operation for years. As was usually the case, Coll was seeking volunteer tutors. "The story," recalled former City Editor Jack Kadden, "was obviously supposed to be rather favorable, and it didn't have a real news peg." The assignment was given to a black reporter who objected to the focus of the story. Kadden told her it was not her place to include any criticism or perspective on Coll. Eighteen inches of the required copy were duly published, though Kadden privately believed Coll's appeal for tutors would have been better summarized in a news brief.

More features, an editorial and a free-lancer's magazine cover story later treated Coll and his programs in flattering fashion. Staff writers familiar with Coll, his group and the overall dynamics of Hartford's ghetto approached their assignments with some reluctance. They regarded Coll as a well-intentioned white liberal with a highly uneven record of effectiveness. Beyond that, they believed it unfair that his programs should be singled out for special treatment when the city's blacks and Hispanics did not generally regard him as a spokesman—and when the paper virtually ignored similar programs run by minorities. Coll knew nothing of these maneuverings, only that the newspaper was publishing material about his Revitalization Corps and that Davies was promising better overall city coverage. Deftly neutralized, Coll suspended his bumper-sticker campaign and commended Davies in print.

I was among those who initially liked Davies' willingness to describe the newspaper's operations more publicly than had been done in the past. But his column began to be more of a self-serving public relations forum than anything else. "His column is a disgrace," commented James Napoli, the paper's chief editorial writer. "It's a collection of Journalism 101 clichés."

One of Davies' essays described the advantages to readers in having a Times Mirror monopoly in the city. "Not having daily competition has allowed us to support a much bigger, better-paid news staff with more news space with which to work," Davies wrote. "The Courant, in all probability, would be less fair and considerably less thoughtful than it is now. You can see this hit-quick-and-forget-it syndrome on television almost every night." The column had a recurring theme. Davies would identify a journalistic problem, then portray himself as the readers' defender against a swarm of arrogant, careless journalists poised to harm them. "THE MEDIA HAVE LOST PUBLIC TRUST" and "CLOSING THE CREDIBILITY GAP BETWEEN NEWSPAPERS AND THEIR READERS" were typical headlines. His columns, his speeches and his articulation of these themes in high-level private meetings helped make Davies a leading figure nationally in the industry's efforts to gain better loyalty from readers.

Public relations techniques permeated the newspaper's management. To enhance the image, executives dramatically increased the PR staff. One man was appointed "director of communications" with responsibility for handling other media. "One of the priorities we have set for the *Courant*," the top editors explained in their in-house newsletter to employees, "is the promotion of the newspaper within the industry." Consequently, distant journalism magazines blossomed with flattering references to the *Courant* and its staff.

Yet the paper's editors showed also that they knew how to minimize bad publicity by blocking access. "Any time the *Courant*'s been under fire for something, obviously we try to get a response," commented Richard Ahles, the news director of Connecticut's biggest television station, CBS-affiliate WFSB-TV. "We've never been able to get an interview on tape with the *Courant*, not with [Mark] Murphy, not with Davies."

A major turning point in Davies' relations with his staff occurred because of his 1984 column about Coleco Inc., a local manufacturer. Davies agreed with Coleco that the newspaper's business department had been unfair in reporting on the firm, which produced Adam, an unreliable, low-cost home computer. Coleco also manufactured the Cabbage Patch Kids dolls, a toy so successful in late 1983 that demand far outstripped supply. Davies cited "quality control problems" in his paper's coverage of Coleco. Among them was a news analysis by Robert Murphy, a financial columnist and former *Courant* business editor. The financial columnist (who is not related to Mark Murphy) began his piece with a quiz in which readers were asked to check boxes listing reasons for Coleco's problems. Beside one of the boxes was the name of Coleco's president, Arnold Greenberg. Greenberg had a reputation for being abrasive, and his performance had long been monitored with a skeptical eye by the out-of-state business press, including the *Wall Street Journal* and *New England Business*.

"In retrospect," Davies wrote in his column, "it does seem the [Murphy] story had a snide tone to it. The essence of the article, an analysis of the company's acknowledged problems, could have been presented in a different manner." John Tarpey, acting business editor, believed Davies' column was deeply harmful to the paper. Tarpey, a former reporter at the *Washington Star*, had come to the *Courant* in 1981. Before he left the paper in the late spring of 1984 to be an editor-writer at *Business Week* magazine, he helped obtain more than fifty staff signatures on a petition protesting Davies' apology. "The Davies column," Tarpey said, "sent signals all over town that if you have his ear and complain loudly enough, you'll have his sympathy. Bob Murphy was an expert on Coleco. His lead was thoroughly backed up by the story, and was mild in comparison with what many other news organizations were saying about Coleco." At the protest meeting at the Parkview Hilton Hotel, Davies further rebuked his staff. "Most responsible people would have some questions about whether we were being fair to those people [at Coleco]," he said, standing at the front of the ballroom.

He also spoke more generally about staff mistakes: "I want you to hurt from the gut, not just kiss it off and say, 'I screwed up.'" My view in listening to him was that the staff would (or at least should) accept legitimate criticism. After all, it had been the force pressuring Davies for months to appoint an ombudsmen. But the staff resented Davies' attacks because they distanced him from any responsibility and seemed mainly intended to enhance his own career.

The staff protests played right into his hands. In his column the next week under the headline "REPORTERS MISREAD STORIES, TOO," Davies wrote that he never intended for his employees to be soft on business coverage, only fair—and if they misunderstood him it was their own fault. He was so proud of his two columns that they were among those he submitted for a Pulitzer Prize.

Dissenting from Davies' position was *Wall Street Journal* reporter David Wessel, who had been a business writer for the *Courant* before Times Mirror's acquisition and a Bagehot Fellow in the business studies program at Columbia University. Wessel believed that Davies did indeed "send a signal" when he showed "he was going to take the side of a very controversial company that had frequently complained about *Courant* coverage in the days I was there, and publicly berate the reporter." Wessel, a New Haven native who continued to read the paper while working for the *Boston Globe* and *Journal*, thought Davies' original criticism may have been appropriate if given in private. "But," Wessel said, "editors and publishers have to be very careful not to send the wrong signals. Business desks at metro papers are often weak and full of fear. A lot of stories I see in the business section are embarrassingly puffy."

As the *Courant* sought to become a more attractive corporate citizen, it embarked on various projects requiring closer cooperation and fund-raising from the region's financial magnates. Chief among these was creation of the "Hartford Courant Center for the Performing Arts." Its largest benefactor was Aetna, with gifts valued at $800,000 (compared to $500,000 combined from Times Mirror and the *Courant*'s longstanding charitable foundation).

The newspaper's increasing institutional empathy for the insurance industry was suggested by its editorial relationship with retired Aetna Chairman John Filer. In late 1984, Davies helped encourage Filer to compile his memoirs on Hartford civic life for the main feature of the Sunday magazine's Anniversary Issue, its most highly touted of the year. But Filer was reluctant to undergo normal editing and he refused to describe why he had left his Aetna job. As an inducement, Bloom assured him that editors would not tamper with his manuscript except on minor points such as grammar.

This editorial posture was notable because the *Courant* had never adequately explored in its news pages the murky circumstances of Filer's departure from Connecticut's biggest corporation a few months previous. Filer, aged sixty, had announced what was headlined as a voluntary resignation. There was considerable private speculation around the city that Filer had actually been forced out because of Aetna's diversification into non-insurance fields and poor financial performance.

In his magazine story, Filer deftly side-stepped the issue of whether it had been his decision to leave the firm. The former chairman moved on quickly to other matters. One of them was an attack on the newspaper's performance before Davies. Filer said that other community leaders in the 1970s "were angry with me in the mistaken belief I could 'shape up' the newspaper. Believe me, the *Courant* was independent and unmoveable."

"All such efforts were frustrating, as nothing ever happened," Filer recalled of one of his 1970s attempts to complain about coverage. "Now, as with Hartford, progress has come to the *Courant* as well, I don't want Mike Davies to think he can relax, but the *Courant* is indeed a much better paper and with further effort it can live up to the standards that a city as fine as Hartford should expect."

The deference to Filer became a typical courtesy the paper extended to the powerful, especially in the business community. *New England Monthly* published an in-depth probe of United Technologies Corporation Chairman Harry Gray. It alleged that Gray had created a fictitious past to disguise his Jewish parentage and had systematically sabotaged other top executives with the help of wiretapping so he could remain in office longer. The *Courant*'s reaction? To publish an attack on the magazine by unnamed Gray subordinates at UTC. Judging by what the *Courant* published in 1985, it apparently did not even ask Gray's defenders to address the allegations in *New England Monthly*, whose story won a top prize in a national contest for investigative articles.

Some *Courant* staffers from throughout the paper confessed that they feared Davies and would not risk normal reporting techniques on powerful local institutions—whether they be businesses or "sacred cow" arts groups. "I have the subconscious feeling: 'The hell with it. Why pursue it?' " said Robert Murphy, the financial writer who had covered Coleco.

The *Courant*'s executives decided to protect reader sensibilities in other areas besides business coverage. Among newspaper editors nationally, Davies and Petty became leading opponents of cartoonist Garry Trudeau, whose strip "Doonesbury," was selected by *Courant* readers as their favorite.

Courant executives first attacked Trudeau for asking newspapers across the country to keep his strip at its traditional size. The cartoonist, who uses extensive dialogue, said he would rather not have the cartoons run at all than have them appear so small the words were hard to read. Davies, who wanted to reduce the size of all cartoons to save costs on newsprint, described Trudeau as dictatorial. "THE DOONESBURY GANG IS NOT SO FUNNY ANYMORE" was the headline of a Davies column that expressed the publisher's irritation with the cartoonist, including his anti-establishment humor. "First, it was unabated criticism of Ronald Reagan in the final stretch of last year's presidential campaign," Davies wrote. "Then it was a graphic account of an orgy in a motel room (which the *Courant* chose not to publish). And just recently it was a sequence of strips linking Frank Sinatra to the mob (the *Courant* declined to publish one of them.)"

> The irony, of course, is that for newspapers to explain why they didn't publish the comic, they are forced to write stories and relate the content just as I have done here. That, too, is getting tiresome.

Trudeau, with a home off Connecticut on one of the Thimble Islands, reacted mildly to the controversy after his Sinatra strip. "I consider it an enormous privilege," the cartoonist said, "to think about things, put them into my strip and then have those particular concerns show up in 800-some newspapers. So if it doesn't make it into each paper 365 days a year, it's nothing I worry about. I certainly don't characterize it as censorship."

Some subscribers felt differently. "Whom are you protecting when you censor something like this 'Doonesbury' strip?" wrote one *Courant* reader in a typical letter. "Please don't protect us anymore. Give your readers some respect."

CHAPTER 10

A Mirror of the Times?

THE NEW EDITORS IMPROVED suburban coverage for those readers most valued by the newspaper and its advertisers. The editors cut back elsewhere. The changes involved: 1) major reductions in reporting on the city of Hartford, where many of the region's poor lived; and 2) substantial improvements over Murphy-era coverage of affluent suburban regions, although the coverage was far less thorough than it had been before chain acquisition.

One of the first to recognize these patterns was City Editor Jack Kadden, a Hartford native in his early thirties whose ambition was to rise through the ranks of his hometown newspaper. Even during the Mark Murphy-era reduction of local news that prompted activist Ned Coll to call the paper "The Un-Hartford *Courant*," Kadden had a staff of a dozen reporters spending all their time covering the city. Soon after Roger Moore's installation as metropolitan editor in 1984, the paper creaked along with just three full-time city reporters. That number gradually rose to seven.

Moore's underlings questioned how the newspaper was going to make up for city desk reductions. He replied that it would get by as best it could—and that if necessary wire services could be ordered to cover certain city hall meetings traditionally handled by the *Courant*. Moore also said that city coverage would benefit from a new investigative squad, the "special projects desk," that had taken most of its general assignment reporters.

"I think this indicated the emphasis Davies is putting into winning awards," recalled Kadden, who argued at the time for a stronger commitment to ordinary city news. He was promptly removed as city editor and given a low-responsibility, late-night assignment he wryly described as "The Night Watchman." He soon resigned to take an editing job at the *New York Times*, sitting side-by-side with two other departees from Davies' *Courant*.

As recently as the late 1970s, the paper provided exhaustive coverage of zoning decisions, city council business and crime news. The newspaper ignored the vast bulk of it after Times Mirror's changes. The night police reporter, for example, covered the entire central Connecticut region by telephone under Davies and rarely visited a police station or crime scene. Criticism by the public was muted, however, in part because the paper stepped up its public relations campaign to convince readers that local coverage was better than ever. Indeed, a return to local news in the suburbs was a major step in the campaign to make the newspaper more popular. Davies told his staff, "I found very, very quickly when I came here that everyone, or virtually everyone, was mad at the *Courant*, from the governor to the waitress in the corner shop. The reason they all gave is the *Courant* had turned its back on what the *Courant* had been for two centuries: town news."

Fifteen reporters were assigned to a bureau in a 42,000-population suburb called Enfield. They collected and processed news from nine much smaller surrounding towns. Twenty-one reporters were based in the Manchester bureau, which covered news from fourteen white, suburban towns.

The paper boasted that its system of bureaus covered seventy-two of Connecticut's towns. (That contrasted with more than ninety communities before chain takeover.) But much of the

Times Mirror coverage was erratic, and the zones created artificial boundaries between communities. For example, the final edition of the pre-Times Mirror newspaper included local news from the city and all its immediate suburbs. Under the chain, that news was scattered through several separate editions. Residents of towns with historic ties had difficulty following one another's activities. Another problem was that many supervisors were from out of state and were thus unfamiliar with local conditions. In early 1986, the five *Courant* bureau chiefs directing coverage for the regional areas averaged just a year and a half at the paper.

David Laventhol, the firm's New York vice president in charge of the *Courant*, denied that its shifts of coverage were to appeal to prosperous readers to the detriment of others. "I don't think there's any exclusionary quality," he told me. "The *Courant*'s ideal goal would be to have one hundred percent of the Connecticut Valley region." Yet his boss, Times Mirror Chairman Otis Chandler, was on record as underlining the importance of demographics and advertising. "The economics of American newspaper publishing," Chandler told one interviewer, "is based on an advertising base, not a circulation base."

Back in Hartford, most low to mid-level journalists went about their duties with only a vague notion of why the newspaper might be changing. Even so, the results sometimes were all too apparent.

One manifestation was the ascendancy of incoming editors who fantasized the newsroom as a kind of Playboy Mansion, equipped with staffers who could provide double duty as employees and special friends. One married editor repeatedly made overtures to younger staffers, most of them direct subordinates. "When I'm around you," he said in the newsroom as he sidled up behind one writer, "I feel like John Dillinger"—a reference to the gangster's notoriously large sexual organ. To a different object of attention, he cooed, "You know what makes me happy? Fantasizing about *you*."

Another boss frequently gave the impression that homosexuality intruded upon his decision-making. Many in the newsroom had no concrete evidence about after-hours interests, of course. They had only their strong sense that sensitive assignments were often steered to a coterie of nattily dressed recruits who seemed to have a special bond. But certain things were clear. One was a series of highly unusual promotions for inexperienced members of the clique. Another thing was the company's remarkably prompt settlement of a workers' compensation action by Ron Winter, an earnest, hard-working ex-Marine who had labored for years as a *Courant* reporter. His written legal claim in 1987 said simply that he could not work any longer because of stress. But according to friends who worked with him before he filed the action, he endured a hellish two years after he rebuffed an editor's unwelcome homosexual advances. The torment, in Winter's view, was as bad as his combat experiences in Vietnam. Friends said that he obtained evidence to bolster his case by making secret tape-recordings. Just one week after he filed his claim, Times Mirror paid him $50,000. He refused to discuss his case after that. So friends surmised that the settlement required his silence. The payment was so prompt and so high for a stress claim that it must be construed as hush money.

Editors' sexual quirks obviously come more from individual temperment than from the type of management. Yet it's fair to speculate about what might encourage intrusive approaches to subordinates. One factor might be an environment where professional ideals are worn down by commercial realities. With lessened satisfaction from work, some might seek more private pleasure. Another cause for all kinds of abuses might be raw power. It increases when accountability is mostly to a distant home office that focuses on the big picture.

Whatever the case, the *Courant* and its top management were defendants in a remarkable number of employee complaints involving various civil rights. In mid-1987, the state of Connecticut's Commission on Human Rights and Opportunities was investigating nine cases alleging sex, race or age bias. Details were not public, although the newspaper knew about the filings because it was notified as defendant. It chose not to report the litigation except for one sex discrimination claim brought by fired sports writer Ginny Apple. By publicizing her action on television and in smaller papers, she forced the newspaper to write a news story.

Courant staffers with complaints about their bosses often obtained scant sympathy from Times Mirror's chief in Hartford despite his implementation of a host of modern management techniques such as employee breakfasts with the publisher. With considerable fanfare, Davies announced in his column a wide-ranging ethics code that forbade all employees, including editors, from abusing their power. Among other things, it banned nepotism and improper on-the-job romantic relationships. The latter was in keeping with the upright image of the publisher, a long-married father of two sons. Indeed, he helped preside over separate *Courant* inquiries into, for example, alleged adulteries by a judge and by a rival newspaper editor.

Yet his own appetite for women had created a legendary reputation and the nickname "Motel Mike" in both Louisville and Hartford. The name developed from a secretary's distaste for having to book his personal arrangements at a Louisville motel, according to numerous sources, including William Cox, former assistant to the executive editor at the *Courier-Journal*. Cox later became managing editor of the *Honolulu Star-Bulletin*.

Given Davies' repute, many on his staff awaited with curiosity his pronouncements upon the "womanizing" issue that ended the Presidential campaign of Democrat Gary Hart. In his Sunday column, Davies told readers that the *Miami Herald* had been wrong to rush into print with its story that Hart had spent the night with model Donna Rice. By that time, Davies was one of the country's most renowned practitioners of surveillance journalism—that involving editors' decisions to send a squad of reporters to spy on a specific target.

Davies pointed out that the *Herald* reporters staking out the candidate admitted that they had neglected to watch all entrances of his town house throughout the night. "A cardinal rule when doing an investigative story," Davies wrote, "is to nail down every fact so the published story is unassailable." But the *Courant*'s leader added that the mission would have been appropriate if conducted properly. "To invite Rice into his home while his wife was in Colorado was not only stupid, but fair game for the press."

Davies' 1986 lawsuit to divorce his college bride had left him free to date openly. He liked women active in the media, especially television news. One companion, for example, was WFSB-TV's Marlene Schneider, co-anchor of Connecticut's highest-rated news show. Davies moved in fashionable circles even by the standards of newspaper publishers. Demonstrating his social skills, he became so involved with family and friends of actress Katharine Hepburn that one of his subordinates referred to her as "Aune Kate." Hepburn, raised in a prominent West Hartford family and semi-retired in a home on Connecticut's shoreline, had long been known as an intensely private person, especially by Hollywood standards. But Davies not only established a friendship in his visits to Old Saybrook and Manhattan, but helped his magazine editors woo her help for a major *Courant* project. The plan required a vast amount of preparation, with public presentation scheduled for late 1987 or early 1988. It was for the newspaper to solicit funds from Connecticut's major corporations on behalf of noted artists. Each creator would be matched with a corporate donor who could thereupon claim sponsorship of a new, substantial work of art. Hepburn was either to provide a drama reading or, more ambitiously, to narrate a Connecticut Public Television documentary portraying the project.

Back at the office, all the long-festering turmoil made it difficult for many journalists to focus on the essentials of their business. One incident in early 1985 illustrated the extent of change. On that day, roving New England reporter William Cockerham heard shouts as he walked into the *Courant*'s main newsroom. Many things were different from the newspaper he had joined in 1968. There were no more manual typewriters. Stairwell walls were no longer encrusted with black ink airborne from the press room.

Instead, it looked like the model of an efficient and professional organization. Thanks to Times Mirror's expensive renovations, the corridor walls were tastefully wood-paneled. There were hanging plants. The reporters' work stations were computerized and separated by sound-absorbing acoustic panels.

Cockerham, whose stories were widely reprinted in other newspapers after transmission on the LA Times-Washington Post newswire, normally remained aloof from the Connecticut-based staff. By the mid-1980s, reporters and editors were coming and going so quickly at his paper that he did not even know many of their names by the time they left. But on this winter evening, the commotion on the far side of the huge room attracted his interest. He ambled over to a gathering of eight or nine reporters and editors near a big white-and-green wall map of Hartford. The police radio had just crackled out a report of an explosion at a place identified as East Service Road. The deputy metro editor, a 1983 arrival from Florida, wanted to rush a reporter and photographer to the scene. It was her voice that Cockerham had heard shouting.

"Where's East Service Road?" she demanded of her staff. "Where's East Service Road?" No one, including the police reporter, knew where it was.

"It's right here," said Cockerham. He pointed on the map to the service road running parallel to Interstate 91. The north-south interstate is a major thoroughfare that extends from the Canadian border to Long Island Sound. It runs the length of Hartford, a narrow city less than two miles wide.

In telling me the story later, Cockerham had a withering tone in his voice. "How in hell can you run a Hartford newspaper," he said, "with a staff that can't find East Service Road? That's how you get to the Hartford police station, to the post office, to the state jail and to the jai-alai fronton. For Christ's sake!"

The "explosion," it turned out, was simply a car backfiring near the police station. The larger question, it seems to me, was the staff's capability of assessing the inner-workings of the institutions in the area: the police department, for instance, or the gambling fronton that averaged more than 3,300 customers a night. No reporter who has ever covered police, jails or professional gamblers would underestimate the importance of developing good sources. Does it really need to be said that a newspaper should have a staff that knows its community?

Chain management recognized the image problems inherent in this style of newspapering. So Davies deftly created a strawman called "the advocacy reporter," referring to a type that lets private opinions affect news coverage. It is frequently associated with the ambitious, rootless, post-Watergate "scoop mentality." "I don't even want to smell advocacy reporting at the *Courant*," the publisher told his staff. "I have no use for it. I think that's one of the things we have to be most careful about in interviewing job candidates." In this, Davies was sounding a familiar journalism piety.

Yet it was far from clear whether his regime was part of the solution or part of the problem. About the same time that his Hartford police reporter was having trouble finding the only road leading to the Hartford police station, Davies himself was orchestrating a variety of power plays involving news coverage. These cemented his hidden alliances with powerful factions in the community, and dramatically affected Connecticut's public life.

CHAPTER 11

The Spike

SHORTLY BEFORE MICHAEL DAVIES' Hartford arrival in 1983, the head of the paper's investigations team walked into Mark Murphy's office for a decisive meeting. Feeling both exhilarated and apprehensive, squad leader Claude Albert was anxious to tell his boss about progress on a major probe.

The topic was insidious diseases in Connecticut workplaces. Albert and the rest of us on the story had learned that harmful exposures on the job—toxic chemicals, dusts and radiations—were sometimes vastly more dangerous than air and water pollution that receives much more publicity. In addition, the long incubation periods for the diseases frustrated prevention and detection. Victims often never realized what had disabled them.

Albert grew animated as he suggested that the newspaper identify Connecticut's major hazardous worksites and occupations. Detailed charts authenticated by scientific experts could explain the symptoms of the various ailments, helping workers in offices,

*To Spike: Originally, to make a cannon unusable by driving a spike into the fuse hole. In newspaper slang, to kill a story by impaling it on a spindle or vaporizing it from a computer screen instead of sending it to the composing room.

factories and construction sites trace the elusive connections. The cause-and-effect relationship has always been mysterious to the public because only a small proportion of those exposed actually sicken.

News media and government are often reluctant to address the problem except in response to the most obvious complaints. Partly this is because lingering disabilities and death are not "news," even though the causes might be unnecessary. Part of this lack of interest stems also from pressure by hazard creators, who have scant reason to want publicity and regulation.

Murphy, who usually referred to the investigations office as his "Snoop Coop," listened in his usual relaxed manner, leaning back in his chair. From time to time, he interrupted with questions.

Albert went on to describe two months of preliminary findings. These formed the basis for hard-edged news stories that would surround the charts. For example, Connecticut's largest employer, United Technologies Corp. (UTC), was extremely unhappy with the only environmental diagnostic center in the state, a clinic run by Yale Medical School and Yale-New Haven Hospital. UTC believed Yale was biased in favor of victims. Some Yale physicians, in turn, accused UTC of being arrogant and unusually reluctant to help workers identify and avoid the hazards around them. When asked to name the three firms with "the worst" attitudes in Connecticut, one Yale Medical School professor replied, "UTC, UTC and UTC!" Secret memos showed that UTC and the University of Connecticut were trying to set up a rival, business-funded clinic likely to be less sympathetic than Yale to employees and to those living near factories and complaining about pollution. The memos showed that the state university's leading negotiator was pushing ahead to get the money even though he expressed worries over UTC's "short-range motives" and "general anti-employee stance."

Also the team had learned that workers' compensation had traditionally been one of the most profitable lines for the private insurance companies that essentially run the system in most states.

More important, we had found that preventive measures were inadequate for long-latency diseases. "There's virtually no incentive for an employer to do something because of a fear of increased compensation costs," we had been told by economist Peter Barth, former executive director of a Presidential commission on the problem. The squad also unearthed some intriguing federal evaluations of Connecticut's state-run Occupational Safety and Health Administration (OSHA). Year after year, federal monitors criticized the state's health inspections as slipshod, timid and ineffective.

When Murphy encouraged Albert to continue digging for more facts, the investigations editor quickly promised he would push the innovative series into publication by mid-December, four months away. "I don't work that way," Murphy responded. "Take as much time as you need to do it right." Managing Editor Reid MacCluggage finally spoke up. Second-in-command to Murphy, the longtime editor had been leaning against a wall next to Albert's chair. "This could be the most important project the *Hartford Courant* has ever published."

Conservative by nature and a supporter of Ronald Reagan for President, Albert did not want the stories to be accusatory in tone. He believed that workplace ailments were caused by ignorance and bad luck more than anything else. The correct remedy, he felt, was not scandal-mongering, but an explanatory style that would, nonetheless, reveal dangerous conditions and disturbing public policies.

The workplace project had had its beginnings in the spring of 1983 when Albert and two others on his staff conducted preliminary interviews with experts. I began working with them after my June graduation from Yale Law School, where I had earned a master's degree with honors during a leave from the *Courant* on a grant from the Ford Foundation. Legal issues relating to health hazards were among my chief interests there. One seminar focused entirely on workplace disease. Two others were taught by nationally prominent scholars in toxic hazards and insurance law, Peter Schuck and Guido Calabresi.

Albert envisioned a team approach. He and I would do the preliminary research. Reporter Larry Williams would concentrate on the insurance industry. He was a veteran of the news business who was studying accounting to improve his skills. His wife worked for Aetna.

Albert and I proposed a separate insurance story. Hartford was nicknamed "the Insurance City" because its environs were home office to fourteen major insurance firms. Williams disparaged the idea because he did not think insurance claims practices would make interesting reading. He changed his mind after he began studying profits statements and visiting the homes of diseased workers in Connecticut's Naugatuck Valley. He soon focused on an old-fashioned, red brick foundry called the Farrel Corp., located forty miles southwest of Hartford. Since the mid-19th Century, it had made cast-iron machines, ranging up in size to those weighing seventy tons and used to refine sugar.

The casting process involved heating molten iron to 2,800 degrees Fahrenheit, then pouring it into frame molds packed with sand. When the molds were removed, chunks of sand adhered to the metal. In a special cleaning room, workers used jackhammers to remove sand fragments. Hammers rattled. Air hoses blasted. Sometimes the swirling red and black dust blocked visibility after five feet.

The sand used in the casting contained silica, a mineral valued for its hardness and resistance to heat and chemical change. Silica also causes a sometimes fatal scarring of the lungs called silicosis. A national study of foundry employees in the 1930s found that they were dying of lung disease at 2.3 times the rate of other workers. The Liberty Mutual Insurance Company raised Farrel's workers' compensation premium based on a 1960 analysis that Farrel's foundry was causing a high risk of silicosis.

Despite the extra premium, insurers used reprehensible tactics to stall or avoid payment. Walter Sadlik, an employee of Farrel for forty-two years, filed a claim for compensation in March 1983 after his physician said he had silicosis. He had worked without a dust mask nearly his whole time at Farrel. Aetna, Hartford's biggest insurance company and authors of the famous, "Aetna, I'm glad I met ya" television advertisement, had replaced Liberty Mutual as the foundry's carrier. After an eight-day investigation that included an interview with Sadlik, Aetna's claims adjuster denied the claim with an obvious stalling tactic—a statement that the sick man had "no proof of employment" at Farrel. In commencing the litigation process with him, Aetna also raised six other legal defenses, including, "No exposure to toxic chemicals or fumes with this employer-respondent."

In Connecticut and most other states, private insurance companies make the initial decision on which claims should be paid. When insurers deny claims they go before state-run compensation commissions that operate without the time-consuming procedural rules of courtrooms. The system was set up around the country during the World War I era to provide modest payments promptly to workers. In return for a system of subsistence benefits without extensive litigation, workers lost their right to sue their employers in regular courts.

We found that the insurer's delaying tactics in the Sadlik case were commonplace, and were just one of many disparities between the system's purported goals and its performance. "The system ain't working," Professor Barth said, distorting his language to emphasize his point. He was speaking of payments for diseases. Claims for accidents tend to be much more routine.

Insurers have an obligation, of course, to fight dubious claims to protect their shareholders and keep rates reasonable for the public. But insurers are almost never assessed back-interest for delaying payments even if their defenses have no merit whatsoever and the claims remain unsettled for years. Meanwhile, the companies continue collecting interest on the money received from the employers as insurance premiums. (Workers, conversely, are generally docked for the insurers' lost interest when a lump-sum settlement is reached.) "Starved out" workplace victims—sick, out of work, without benefits—often settle their cases for a tiny fraction of what a similar ailment would bring in a lawsuit. Cancer cases averaged just $12,010 for the victim, according to the major federal study on the point.

An insider's opinion came from Dr. Edward Bernacki, vice president of Tenneco Inc. of Houston, and former medical director of UTC. Liberty Mutual was the world's largest provider of workers' compensation coverage, and UTC was its largest single customer. Dr. Bernacki said Liberty Mutual fought valid claims—in violation of the principle that payments were supposed to be speedy, with a minimum of litigation. "The insurer would contest cases that were obviously occupational. Their mechanism for reducing claims is to delay them. It's probably not a bad strategy, but it hurts people." Adding support to this view was Dr. Arnold Rilance, a New Haven lung disease specialist in private practice. He said that between 100 and 150 of his patients through the years (and he was just one physician in the area) had been Farrel employees or retirees suffering from various stages of silicosis. He said that Liberty Mutual routinely accepted his diagnostic opinion when it favored the insurer—but ignored it when he said the worker deserved compensation.

John Antonakes, Liberty Mutual's vice president for claims, became visibly angered in his Boston office during our interview seeking his response. "I resent accusations that insurers contribute to delay," he said. "Maybe they do, but Liberty Mutual doesn't." He declined to discuss specific cases, saying only that, in general, if a worker's condition was diagnosed by a "physician whom we know to be impartial, we will generally abide by the findings of that examiner."

Connecticut records revealed that just thirty-one claims had been filed by Farrel's workers since the early 1940s, apparently because the occupational cause of many lung ailments was going unrecognized. Insurers disputed twenty-seven of these claims. Despite this aggressive posture, the only case the insurance companies won outright was on a claim barred by the five-year statute of limitations that began ticking when the man left employment.

I found my visits to the homes of disabled workers the most

moving experience of my career. The difficulty of our task inspired me to work six and seven days a week during the project, and many times far into the night. My efforts were inconsequential compared to the unpaid contributions of those helping us. Charles Bergin of Waterbury got up from his deathbed to talk with me, show me his medical documents and pose for photographs. He was a former school principal, age fifty-six, with the fatal lung disease mesothelioma, which has been caused by asbestos in well over ninety-nine percent of reported cases. "I want people to know how dangerous the damn stuff is," he choked out, a teacher to the end. "I didn't know it, and none of my staff did. I never heard the words 'mesothelioma' or 'asbestosis' until I got sick myself." He died four weeks later.

I was struck by ordinary people's faith in the power of our newspaper to shed light on the problems. It recalled my predecessor Dennie Williams' exhortation when I began courthouse work as a young reporter. By the early 1980s, journalism periodicals were publishing many commentaries on growing mistrust of the media. Only once, however, did we encounter a significant problem of resistance during the dozens of interviews we held with disabled employees around the state. That was when a former Farrel jackhammer operator balked at allowing his name to be published. The silicosis victim spoke of a fear of retribution from the company and its insurer. "When you don't have anything, you can't take chances," he wheezed. We ultimately persuaded that man, Albert Henderson, to share his story on the record.

We asked more than three dozen victims to provide intimate medical records that we needed for authoritative stories. Every single person did so. These records included some of the most sensitive information imaginable. A half dozen men were diagnosed as sexually impotent from their work around lead fumes in a steel mill. Some workers were brain-damaged. One was incontinent. Another suicidal.

December was a hellish month of writing to weave the massive research into a series. Davies, who had replaced Murphy as *Courant* editor, wrote Albert a terse and ominous note. "Beware the Ides of January," it said, invoking the soothsayer's warning to Julius Caesar before his demise. Marty Petty, who had taken over from MacCluggage as managing editor in December, studied our three-page, single-spaced outline explaining the theme of each story, its documentation and its photo and graphics possibilities. Her only two suggestions were: 1) that we finish the project quickly and 2) that we enhance it with photographs of secret documents and widows crying at gravesites.

The production pressure made Albert eager to bring his longtime subordinate Tom Condon onto the project. Carrying the title "chief investigative reporter," Condon had won more journalism awards than any other writer at the paper. He began massive revisions and cuts in the stories that the rest of us on the team had prepared. No sooner were these revisions made than the new metro editor, Roger Moore, arrived from Kansas City. He ordered that the series be further cut in half.

Moore scheduled the much-reduced version for publication in a special section Sunday, April 22.

Michael Davies read the stories, and on the afternoon of April 17th his word came down in brief, simple terms: The project was spiked. None of it would appear.

There were no outbursts from the investigative team after the project was killed. Some setbacks are so overwhelming that they paralyze the emotions. Besides, Davies and his new editors kept us apart by ordering the paper's investigative squad abolished and the office vacated. Confronted by such a resolute use of power, no complaints on our part would have helped get the stories published.

We tried a low-key approach: a request to hear his reasons. Albert, Condon and I met him Friday, April 20. In shirtsleeves and with a gentlemanly manner, he came out from behind his desk to sit with us around a coffee table in a corner of his office. "The series just didn't work for me," he said. Davies went on to say it was poorly organized and would bore readers. "I don't want to spend any more staff time on another revision." Condon and I made a last effort to save part of it. Suspecting that Davies was especially concerned about how the business community viewed his stewardship of the paper, I pointed out the increasing interest of business executives in workplace health issues. Some of our earliest research had found an authoritative insurers' prediction, "Occupational disease will be one of the most important and difficult issues for the insurance industry in the eighties." Condon asked for a chance to work all weekend on his own time to make a last revision for delivery Monday morning. It would consist of four things, along with photos: 1) a relatively short main story on the disability insurance program for workers; 2) short human interest vignettes on the sufferings of such victims as the deceased school principal, Charles Bergin; 3) an informational chart listing disease symptoms and possible causes; 4) and a brief item on where readers could seek help if they suspected a problem.

"Give it a try," Davies said.

From our many hours of interviews with top insurance company executives, Condon selected more of their viewpoints to appear high in the main story. With a lawyer's eye for nuance, he eliminated any implication that the newspaper believed any private businesses might be doing anything wrong. The provocative quotations from Tenneco's Dr. Bernacki and from the New Haven physician, Dr. Rilance, were relegated to the bottom half of the story, naked of their supporting evidence.

Davies approved the new version. Larry Williams was so disturbed by its softening of our findings, however, that he withheld his byline. I supported Condon's revisions because if he had not made them exactly that way, no information at all would have appeared. The soft version bounced around the office for another couple of weeks under the scrutiny of various editors.

Late Sunday, May 6, the newly appointed editor in charge of the paper nights, Assistant Managing Editor Michael Jenner, allowed the main story to run in the Monday edition. Jenner spiked the rest of it. These were the human interest stories; the explanation of how to obtain help; and the detailed informational chart on disease symptoms. The chart, of course, had been one of the primary reasons for the project in the first place.

Even within the newsroom, knowledge of what had happened to our series was not widespread. In the tradition of investigative reporters, we had generally kept quiet about our research for competitive reasons while we were doing it. We did the same afterward for reasons of our own. It seemed unprofessional and pointless for us to voice our disappointment. Journalism is not a science. And in any dispute about this series, Davies had vastly more rhetorical power. His past accolades were impressive, and he controlled the only respected public affairs forum that would have had any deep interest in exploring this in-house dispute—the news and editorial columns of the *Courant* itself.

Nonetheless, I was troubled that our many hours of interviews with disabled people and their families had left them with the false hope that something significant would come out of it. And what about the many scores of experts who had contributed their time—wasted time—to help the newspaper? Subsequent reporters attempting to interview them would surely suffer. I wrote thank-you notes to thirty or so of those who had been most helpful.

The material deserved a chance to be tested on the open market. I quickly wove parts of it into a sample chapter and outline for a book on environmental hazards. Then I tried to learn about the world of book publishing. The next month I obtained representation by one of New York's top literary agents, Peter Shepherd of Harold Ober Associates.

Coincidentally, one of my best tipsters in Hartford told me that a Hartford federal judge had been the target of a four-year criminal investigation because of a long-standing, never-reported sex scandal involving abuse of his office staff and dereliction of duty. I kept silent about the information. Partly it was because my new assignment at the paper was simply to write headlines in the sports department on the late-night shift. That wasn't the main reason for my reticence. I had always been a team player, ready to share information with my colleagues. But who was "the team" in 1984? Virtually every news editor I'd ever worked with was gone or stripped of power. Under those circumstances—and after the incoming editors' callous treatment of our sources on the health project—what right did I have to ask my tipster and the judge's victims to entrust their jobs and reputations to the *Courant?*

I resigned in July 1984 so I could pursue my research and writing independently as a freelancer. I had loved being a newspaper reporter—so much so that I had missed just three days of work for illness or personal reasons during my fourteen years at the *Courant*. On my last night, I wore a Hawaiian shirt and a bright purple tie in a forced attempt at midnight light- heartedness on the sports desk. Actually, I felt solemn to the point of being numb. I could hardly wait to leave.

Ultimately, other writers' efforts (especially an excellent 199-page, four-part series in the 1985 *New Yorker*) preempted the information I had wanted to disclose in a book. Nonetheless, all of the five magazine stories I sent out were published in versions close to the ones originally submitted to the *Courant*'s editors. Three of my articles appeared regionally with minimal editing and were republished nationally virtually word-for-word. But, this kind of dissemination did not serve the purpose of the research. Many of the people who most needed the information were never going to see it. They weren't subscribers to upscale magazines or glossy professional journals. They were ordinary working people who relied on their daily newspaper.

In the wake of the *Courant*'s gutting of the project, Davies, Petty and their "readers' representative" became well-known in the newspaper business nationally for the sense of community interest they ostensibly displayed at the newspaper. But never once to my knowledge did any of them express a moment's concern for the more than 200 interview subjects who had spent countless hours helping the *Hartford Courant*.

One of them was Trudi Townsend. In October 1983, she had aided us in understanding what had happened to her husband,

Oscar, a grinder at Farrel who left the job at age fifty in 1974 because of the lung disease silicosis. He died two years later. She frankly described their life, even the heavy drinking that helped kill him after his shortness of breath cost him his role as provider.

"I'm going to die," she remembered Oscar saying. "I'm just suffering." Later, six years of litigation with insurers wore down her resistance so that she accepted a $14,500 settlement (from which medical payments and fees for five attorneys were subtracted) for her husband's injuries and death.

She telephoned the newspaper in October 1985, some two years after she had been interviewed. "You probably don't remember me," she told Larry Williams.

"Of course I remember you," the reporter thought grimly to himself, remembering his shame over his paper's behavior.

"I wondered," she continued in a quiet voice, "did the story ever come out?"

The fate of the *Courant*'s workplace disease project was one of many indications of the new publication standards in force after Davies replaced the top echelon of editors. The final slant revealed extreme deference to corporate interests. "Thirty or forty years ago, editors would boast of interfering with the news," Ben Bagdikian of the University of California would tell me later. "No longer." The journalism school dean described the subtle methods used by modern news executives (perhaps subconsciously) to achieve corporate purposes and protect their careers. "They simply decide that certain things really aren't news, or that maybe, 'It's not that interesting.' It's rationalized away, because if you isolate it [the decision to spike], it looks like a violation of one of the most important ethical values of journalism."

Michael Davies was installed in Hartford to placate the community antagonized in a variety of ways by Mark Murphy. Was the new editor too deferential to business? During a taped 1985 interview in his office for my book, Davies explained how he proved his independence from pressures in Kansas City, a place he described as more controlled by Hallmark Cards Inc. than

Hartford was by insurers. "There you had one company, Hallmark, which was like all of the home office [insurance] companies here put together," he said. "That was its dominance in Kansas City." Davies recalled the many hard-edged stories he had published in the *Kansas City Star* and *Times* after the 1981 collapse of the Hyatt Regency sky walks killed 114 people. Davies said the stories angered Hallmark. "They owned the hotel. It was their land. They financed the building of it."

It's human nature to look back on our shining moments with hazy appreciation. Yet the fatalities from the collapse of a downtown hotel clearly required in-depth analysis. Moreover, standard business reference books show a marked contrast between the power of Hallmark and that of the insurance companies. Hallmark had 19,000 employees nationwide in 1985, the bulk of them in Kansas City. Connecticut-based insurance companies employed 48,000 people in Connecticut, all but a thousand or so in the Hartford region. Aetna alone had 41,000 employees nationwide, some 15,100 in the *Courant*'s circulation area.

In addition, the financial influence of insurers would be vastly greater than that of a greeting card manufacturer even if their workforces were equivalent. Insurance companies acquire tremendous leverage because of their billions upon billions of dollars of stockpiled premiums, which become investments. Aetna, for example, was a major force in Hartford redevelopment—including the civic center and an adjoining thirty-nine-story skyscraper.

A decline of insurers' overall profits made them especially sensitive to criticism in 1984. With top executives being forced out right and left, the industry was gearing up then for its massive public relations campaign from 1985 to 1987 to pressure Congress and legislatures in all fifty states to enact restrictions on personal injury lawsuits. These lawsuits had only a tangential relationship to the questions raised by our series, of course. But its fate seemed controlled by unarticulated, gut sentiments, not by specific, constructive criticisms that we could discuss and incorporate.

Davies liked to say that the *Courant* could not print the health series because it was boring and poorly written. An outside newspaperman who ultimately caught wind of the publisher's power play asked Tom Condon if Davies' assessment were true. "Much of it's been published in other places," Condon pointed out. "Read it for yourself and decide."

CHAPTER 12

Business "Realities"

AT THE 1985 ANNUAL CONVENTION of the American Society of Newspaper Editors, a major trade association, Michael Davies took the podium to speak on "Business Realities: Their Impact in the Newsroom."

"If there's one thing an editor-turned-publisher discovers very, very quickly, it is that 'profit' is not a four-letter word," Davies announced to those gathered at the Washington Sheraton Hotel in the nation's capital. "Going from running a newsroom of about three hundred to worrying about the present and future welfare of about fifteen hundred employees [throughout the newspaper] is very, very sobering and gives one a very quick and deep appreciation for those who bring in the revenue—and bring it in reliably."

"The newsroom has to be included in strategic planning and overall company goals," he continued in the speech, which was televised nationwide on the C-Span cable network, available in twenty-one million homes. "I don't believe that equates with selling out or lowering standards at all." He was politely received by his fellow editors, many of whom doubtless hoped to emulate him one day in ascending to a publisher's chair. Davies spoke in his usual mild, understated tone and couched in his theme in acceptable ambiguities. Yet back home in Hartford, Davies had come under serious attack by his staff, which knew better than outsiders how the newspaper really functioned:

* While the publisher publicly described his profit-seeking in terms of his concern *for* his employees, company-sponsored morale studies showed that employees felt that a harsh regime was extracting profits *from* them.

* The studies also reported a widespread view on the staff that the newspaper was selling out its ideals to the business community.

The newspaper initiated the morale studies in late 1984. The company picked two groups of ten journalists, with no obvious malcontents. These were twenty reporters and editors who had done well under Times Mirror. They were asked to describe their feelings about the newspaper, especially any suggestions they might have. The journalists trouped to a hotel for two separate sessions, and their comments were recorded. The tone of the discussions was similar, with a summary of one saying:

> Many people report seeing friends and respected colleagues who are valuable employees treated unfairly or unjustly, forced out of jobs, harassed, fired without notice.
>
> It is believed there is a total disregard for humane treatment on the part of management, something that was referred to as seeing people "drawn and quartered" for what many suspiciously view as non-professional reasons.

The summary, compiled by a copy editor, included attacks on management's minority hiring record, "nepotism and cronyism" and middle-management ignorance about Connecticut that caused news stories to be "missed or mishandled."

> The view that departments are understaffed, that employees are treated on the basis of favoritism rather than

> professional ability and that they are expected to regularly put in 12 to 14-hour days without claiming overtime are among the major complaints.
>
> There is a view that there is too much bureaucracy—too many bosses, too many editing desks to go through—and that in working for an "absent landlord" many at the management or supervisory levels are content to pick the bones of employees as clean as they can for self-advancement within the chain.
>
> There is also a perception that the newspaper management is too closely linked to the business community and that management has shown itself to be a tool of the Chamber of Commerce and business by ordering stories written to satisfy or mollify advertisers, by discouraging 'tough' business coverage and by ensuring that reporting does not go against the grain of business.

The copy editor ended on a conciliatory note, saying the tone of the criticisms was constructive and that there was no attempt to denigrate the talents of specific newcomers, many of whom were praised as "valuable additions." A separate inquiry solicited the opinions of 181 supervisors in the advertising, circulation and production operations of the newspaper. The results showed that they expressed many of the same frustrations as journalists, including concerns about job security and ability to perform their public responsibilities.

The results shocked management, according to one high-placed insider who said the newspaper's executives never would have allowed the damaging (albeit confidential) comments to have been put in writing if they had known what was coming.

Davies and his new senior vice president for administration, an attorney and former banker named Alberto Ibarguen, minimized the reports during an interview with me. Ibarguen was silent for much of our discussion. But he commented at one point that the morale studies showed "a fundamental loyalty" to the newspaper. "That's one of the things that comes through on the employee survey," he said. "You don't speak with that kind of vehemence about a place you don't care about."

Davies corrected his aide. "Number one, it's not a survey. There's nothing scientific about it." The publisher stressed his belief that the studies—whatever they're called—were a unique effort at the *Courant* to solicit opinion on what was wrong. "Whenever you do that, whether at *Newsday*, the *New York Times* or at Kodak, the result is going to be predictable. You open the dam, and over that dam flows an enormous amount of vituperative commentary, a lot of it, frankly, flotsam and jetsam, some of it substantive."

The studies brought temporary improvements in conditions, but the central problems persisted. One such sign was the abrupt firing of Ginny Apple, who had been a schoolgirl tennis and basketball star and the sports editor of the University of Oklahoma's student newspaper. Her hiring by the *Courant* in 1975 made her the first full-time female sports writer in Connecticut's history and one of just a handful in the nation. Mainly covering tennis and Yale football, the personable Texan averaged more volunteer speeches to school and civic groups than anyone else from the paper during most of her career. But her new bosses did not appreciate her writing style. And they were unimpressed with her knowledge about running, skiing and women's sports. They emphasized mass-spectator, professional events.

"She's been a problem since she got here," Davies told the sports staff in series of bitter meetings. "That's not true," responded a former sports editor who had supervised her virtually her entire career. Her colleagues alleged management attempts to build an unfair case against her by giving her unusually difficult assignments, secretly clocking her movements and, in one instance, sabotaging a story when she succeeded. Davies remarked that if he worked at a place where things were as bad as the staff claimed he would leave for another paper. One infuriated writer had to be restrained by a colleague's armhold around his neck. "I was born here," spat out the writer, shaking his finger in Davies' face. "I was raised here. AND I'M NOT LEAVING!"

That the new executives had trouble taking such complaints really seriously was apparent in the newsletter they write, *Under-Currents*. It quoted Metro Editor Roger Moore as saying,

> While I would stop at nothing to hire all my friends in Kansas City, I would never hire a relative. Also, the next busload of Kansas City chums will be arriving this week to fill positions in Enfield, Manchester, Middletown, West Hartford, New Britain, City Hall, Specialties, Government/Politics and Projects.
>
> There's not a Moore among them. Please make them feel at home.

Moore's comments, taken from a note he posted on an office bulletin board, apparently were his idea of a joke. With this kind of humor, he was emulating his leader. In Davies' televised Washington, D.C. speech to fellow newspaper executives on "Business Realities," he blamed his reporters for not knowing enough about their communities. "News-people, at least on the newspapers I've been associated with," he said, "are reluctant to get out in the community. They eat lunch with each other, they socialize with each other, they marry each other—or at least live with each other."

He paused on that laugh line, which received lightly scattered snickers from the audience.

Davies proceeded to answer questions. The *Boston Globe*'s managing editor asked the *Courant*'s chief whether there were not a danger in his belonging to a variety of civic groups, including the board of directors of the Greater Hartford Chamber of Commerce, while seeking out stories as editor and publisher. "How do you explain to your readers," the *Globe*'s editor asked, "that it's not going to affect the way you cover some of those issues?"

"I think there is *some* danger in the publisher being involved in *some* community activities," Davies responded. "I think there is a greater danger in not being—and withdrawing and being aloof." There seemed scant danger of such isolation. In one of a number of swank affairs for the powerful, Davies led a Times

Viorel Floresco, *Bridgeport Post-Telegram*

ıterstate 95 lies in ruins after a hundred-foot-wide section collapsed in Greenwich, Conn. ıring the early morning of June 28, 1983. It killed three motorists and seriously injured ree others. The follow-up investigative series by the *Hartford Courant* duped journalism perts nationwide.

Thomas Giroir

Courant Editor and Publisher Michael Davies, left, clowns around with Aetna Life and Casualty Chairman James Lynn, center, and Connecticut Lt. Gov. Joseph Fauliso at the ground-breaking of the Hartford Courant Center for the Arts. Aetna made $800,000 in gifts to the center, far exceeding the newspaper's contribution.

Andrew Kreig

Joseph "The Professor" Vetrano nods off during the wee hours one morning after the departu of the workforce. The retiree, a symbol of the paper's informal ways during the 197 preferred sleeping in an editor's chair to his bachelor hotel room.

Alan Decker

Mark Murphy relaxes after his 1981 installation as editor. The former metro editor of th *Los Angeles Times* was the real-life model for TV's "Lou Grant" character. Irreverent an self-confident, he implemented a top-to-bottom transformation of the newspaper he calle "an embarrassment to the profession."

Bob Englehart/*Hartford Courant*

ıitorial page cartoonist Bob Englehart portrays Hartford's police chief as a bumbling detective ing to solve a fatal hit-and-run by a prominent attorney who was intoxicated. The cartoon ıects the themes of the paper's front page news stories in 1983. News editors minimized suasive evidence that the police chief and his department did little if anything wrong.

n a neighbor's balcony in downtown Hartford, *rant* reporter Theodore Driscoll overlooks the re- he covered for two decades. He struggled with ıewspaper bosses to present a realistic appraisal of lrunk driving case.

Hartford Police Chief Bernard Sullivan commented privately, "Ted Driscoll restored my faith in journalism."

Charles Bickford

Barry Zitser, the state-employed attorney representing consumers before utilities regulators, alleged deceptions by Times Mirror right at the start of the chain's entry into the Connecticut market.

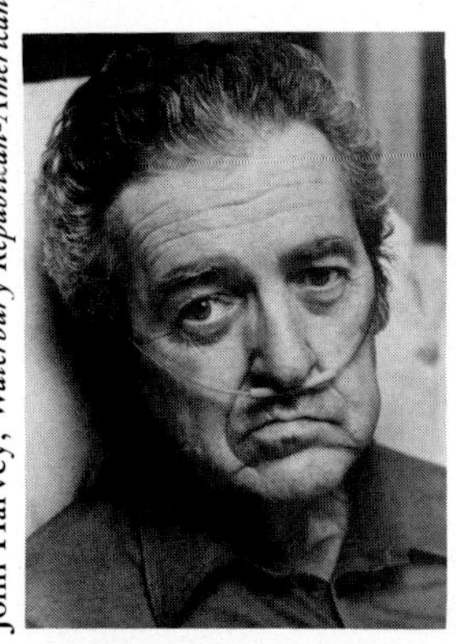

John Harvey, *Waterbury Republican-American*

Just four weeks before his death from an asbestos-caused cancer, former high school principal Charles Bergin describes the dangers of asbestos in school buildings. He was a teacher to the end. *Courant* executives spiked the story.

Mark Murphy is hung in effigy by community activist Ned
Times Mirror ultimately felt it had to silence Coll. And it did

Times Mirror

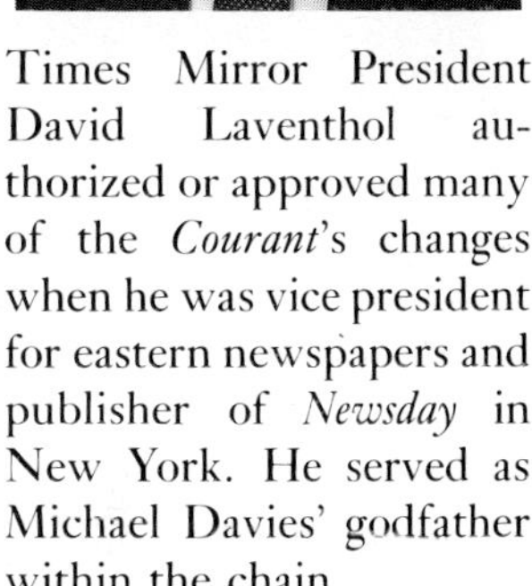

Times Mirror President David Laventhol authorized or approved many of the *Courant*'s changes when he was vice president for eastern newspapers and publisher of *Newsday* in New York. He served as Michael Davies' godfather within the chain.

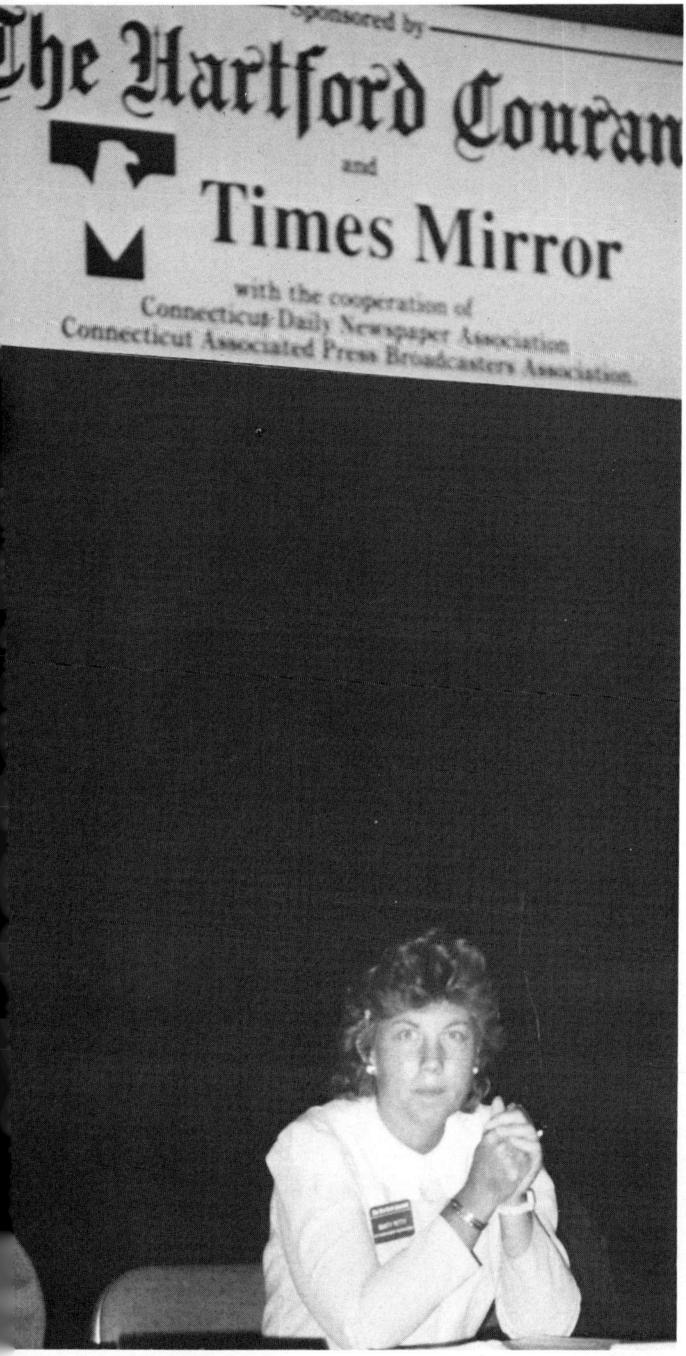

Charles Bickford

ng one of many public relations efforts by the *Courant* and
arent chain, Vice President Marty Petty helps lead a panel
ssion on journalism problems. Davies installed her as the
r's second-ranking editor in 1983 although she had never
d a news story during her three-year career as a professional
alist.

The author, second from left, covers a 1982 Boston Celtics playoff game after appointm as the *Courant*'s first full-time pro basketball writer. Times Mirror dramatically increa spending for national sports coverage. Also at courtside in Boston Garden are, from left, *Quincy Patriot Ledger*'s Mike Fine, and the *Boston Globe*'s Larry Whitesides and Mike Madd

Russ Adams

Ginny Apple tape records an interview with tennis star Ivan Lendl in 1982 as he tells that his aloof image stemmed from shyness and a fear of being misquoted by the press. A became the first female sports writer in Connecticut and one of the first in the nation w she joined the *Courant* in 1975. Her brutal treatment and abrupt dismissal in 1986 prov her sports colleagues into a confrontation with the publisher over her "unjust firing."

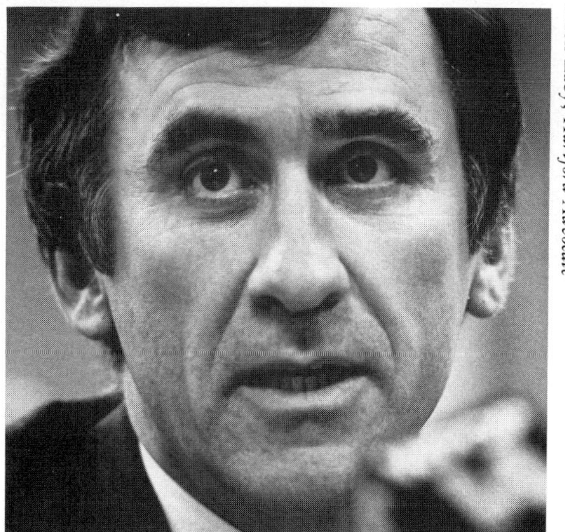
Nick Lacy, *Hartford Advocate*

Austin McGuigan, Connecticut's chief prosecutor from 1978 to 1985, says the state's grand jury investigation convinced him that the newspaper was wrong about a vital allegation in Davies' award-winning probe of bridge inspectors.

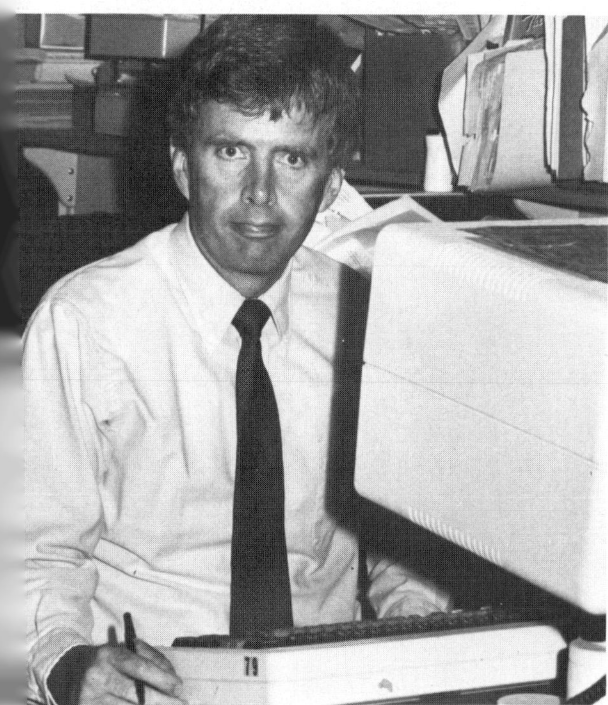

's columnist Tom Condon is a lawyer, author and ected reporter—and an outspoken critic of misman- ent of his newspaper. He began work at the *Courant* 71 after returning to his home state from Vietnam at.

Kansas City Star

Roger Moore ran the special projects squad at the *Kansas City Star* before his appointment in 1984 as editor of the *Courant*'s Connecticut coverage.

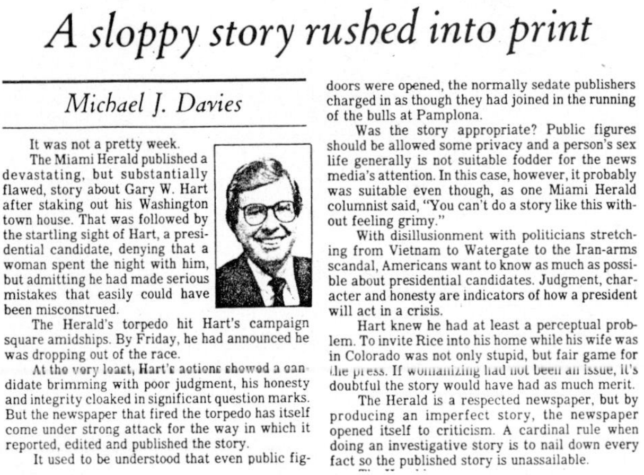

A sloppy story rushed into print

Michael J. Davies

It was not a pretty week.

The Miami Herald published a devastating, but substantially flawed, story about Gary W. Hart after staking out his Washington town house. That was followed by the startling sight of Hart, a presidential candidate, denying that a woman spent the night with him, but admitting he had made serious mistakes that easily could have been misconstrued.

The Herald's torpedo hit Hart's campaign square amidships. By Friday, he had announced he was dropping out of the race.

At the very least, Hart's actions showed a candidate brimming with poor judgment, his honesty and integrity cloaked in significant question marks. But the newspaper that fired the torpedo has itself come under strong attack for the way in which it reported, edited and published the story.

It used to be understood that even public figures' doors were opened, the normally sedate publishers charged in as though they had joined in the running of the bulls at Pamplona.

Was the story appropriate? Public figures should be allowed some privacy and a person's sex life generally is not suitable fodder for the news media's attention. In this case, however, it probably was suitable even though, as one Miami Herald columnist said, "You can't do a story like this without feeling grimy."

With disillusionment with politicians stretching from Vietnam to Watergate to the Iran-arms scandal, Americans want to know as much as possible about presidential candidates. Judgment, character and honesty are indicators of how a president will act in a crisis.

Hart knew he had at least a perceptual problem. To invite Rice into his home while his wife was in Colorado was not only stupid, but fair game for the press. If womanizing had not been an issue, it's doubtful the story would have had as much merit.

The Herald is a respected newspaper, but by producing an imperfect story, the newspaper opened itself to criticism. A cardinal rule when doing an investigative story is to nail down every fact so the published story is unassailable.

In his Sunday column and frequent speeches, Michael Davies projects the image of a progressive-minded executive vitally concerned with journalistic ethics.

Businessman Millard Pryor says, "I like everything about paper now." He found the Times Mirror *Courant* boring, Mark Murphy's style too sationalistic.

Davies, center, discusses ethics with then-FBI Director William Webster, right, and Sen. John Kerry (D-Mass.) on a series televised nationwide by the Public Broadcasting Se in 1987. Davies, who initiated the series produced by Columbia University, later pun Connecticut's public television network with fierce, behind-the-scenes pressure after it dec to broadcast each of the four, hour-long segments during prime time.

Mirror-paid junket of prominent *Courant* advertisers (such as Bank of New England Chairman Walter Connolly) to the 1984 Olympic Games in Los Angeles.

Executives today are fond of saying that the time is past when a single advertiser, no matter how prominent, would have the influence to cause a major newspaper to downplay or drop a legitimate news story. Instead, the debate at metro-sized newspapers focuses on innumerable subtle concessions largely unnoticed by the general public. One area of controversy involves special supplements that are primarily intended as a means of obtaining more revenue. Special sections on sports, products, travel and education are especially frequent. The text sometimes is straightforwardly labelled "advertising" (usually in small type) and comes directly from press releases. Other times it is presented as staff-written news. Either way, it is almost always supportive of the advertisers' interests.

A don't-make-waves attitude within the main news sections is more serious. Most readers are sophisticated enough, one hopes, to sense that a story in a food section is not prepared with the same standards as front page news. Why would newspapers, especially profitable "monopolies," ever compromise standards? Three-quarters of newspaper revenue comes from advertising, the rest from subscriptions and daily sales. Although a large advertiser might not be able to switch its business to a rival newspaper in the age of monopolies, alternative media are not only available, but increasingly attractive. Television and direct mail are the major threats to the traditional leadership position of newspapers.

In 1987, a full-page black-and-white advertisement cost $12,606 to run in the *Courant* on a Sunday. That was nearly triple the rate five years earlier. The price was eleven times the rate when I arrived in 1970. Such increases helped Times Mirror achieve an annual profit level reliably reported to have soared from $8 million to $24 million in the first five full years of chain management.

CHAPTER 13

The Pundits

SOON AFTER HIS ARRIVAL in 1983, Michael Davies decided that the newspaper's editorial page and its op-ed columns did not adequately reflect the interests of readers. In contrast to Murphy, the new editor took great interest in the *Courant*'s editorial positions and at times enjoyed baiting board members by saying their ideas lacked common sense and were out of step with the community's. These differences came to a head during the 1984 presidential election. The board had attacked President Ronald Reagan for most of his major policies during his first term. Massive deficit spending. MX missiles. "Star Wars." Contra adventures in Central America. The members of the board regarded them as practically unsound and, in some cases, as morally offensive. Before the 1984 Presidential election, there was little doubt about the board's viewpoint. Each of the ten members except Davies (who was on the board ex officio) was solidly for Democrat Walter Mondale.

Davies wrote a Sunday column explaining how the board would reach its decision. It was headlined, "WHOM WILL WE ENDORSE IN NOVEMBER? IT'S A MATTER OF CONSENSUS." Two weeks later, the *Courant*'s editorial endorsement appeared, coincident with a major salute to the paper's place in history. Memoirs and accolades about the paper's past came in from some of the nation's leading experts in journalism, including author David Halberstam and Fred Friendly, former president of CBS News. These essays were displayed along with *Courant* memorabilia over nine full, ad-free pages. Davies' column was enhanced by a new photo that showed him with an ear-to-ear smile under the headline, "A HISTORY INTERTWINED IN AMERICA'S."

The section also included a Reagan endorsement that was to provoke an in-house stir over whether it deceived readers about the paper's decision process. The editorial's rationale for Reagan support was that the President's image made him "the symbol of hope" for Americans. The editorial (written by Editorial Page Editor John Zakarian with Davies figuratively looming over his shoulder) conceded that Reagan's record was "anemic" on the ideals of preserving the environment, compassion for the disadvantaged, insistence on civil rights for all citizens, respect for freedom of information, restoration of a semblance of balance in the budget and separation of church and state. "But," the editorial said, "Mr. Reagan wasn't just a bystander while America reinvigorated itself—after sixteen years of listlessness caused by the Vietnam War, by Watergate, by the Arab oil embargo and by the hostage crisis in Iran. He was the principal cheerleader, the preacher who used the bully pulpit to best advantage, the politician who projected his amiable personality and the actor whose command of the medium of television was the envy of his rivals." The *Courant*, then, was saying Reagan would be the better president because he had become "the symbol of hope."

Protests from confused readers soon poured in. "To pick a president on his charisma is pretty sad for a newspaper," one angry caller told the paper's reader representative. "An editor is supposed to have a few brains." The readers' confusion was understandable. The Reagan endorsement did not disclose how much it broke with the newspaper's previous editorial positions.

In the flurry of public comment on the endorsement, the newspaper's management continued to suggest the board was a unified body. Davies used the ombudsman's internal memo to float this view. The publisher said the board was forced to choose between two candidates, and "neither we thought was particularly strong." His use of "we" and "us" in the memo maintained the illusion that the board acted together. Actually, several members privately agonized over whether they should resign in protest.

The weekly *Hartford Advocate*, acting on fragmentary information, revealed the publisher's power play. Some Democratic politicians wanted to issue a strong statement attacking the *Courant* for public deception in its selection process. But the Mondale staff's fear of antagonizing the state's most powerful newspaper prevailed.

Davies deflected attention from his maneuver by denying that the board had ever "voted" for Mondale, as an erroneous initial report had said. His point was a red herring. The issue was not whether there had been a formal "vote" with the expectation it would be decisive—but whether everyone on the board except him had favored one of the candidates. Even the political party of the candidate, in fact, was not as important as whether the paper had been honest and reasonably open about its decision-making. Disclosure of the editorial process, claimed a *Courant* editorial, "would stifle unfettered discussion—brainstorming if you will." It continued, "More importantly, newspapers are private institutions. Their editors, publishers and editorial writers are not elected by the people." These same arguments, of course, are commonly used by all manner of groups to resist inquiries from outsiders, especially from the news media. In dismissing his paper's public explanation, Chief Editorial Writer James Napoli later remarked, "The last refuge of a scoundrel is 'privacy of the individual.'"

Davies exercised far greater control over the pages than had Murphy. "Davies reads all the proofs [printed drafts] and sends back comments and occasionally kills editorials," Napoli said. "It's unlikely that an editorial writer is going to risk his editorials being killed. You know the areas that are verboten."

Napoli described the difficulties in maintaining a consistent editorial policy at chain newspapers. "In the old days, there was a publisher-owner who was there forever and the editorial page really reflected what he thought. Those papers would have a group of professionals writing editorials who were comfortable with what the publisher wanted." At group-owned newspapers such as the *Courant*, on the other hand, there are rotating executives. "So a publisher walks in and says, 'This newspaper is really irresponsible and liberal. I think I'll change it.' Two years later the LA *Times* revolves him out of there, and someone else comes in and says, 'What a bunch of right-wing bozos, let's get some intelligence on this page.' I don't think that's a problem the chains have really grappled with."

For his part, Davies repeatedly derided Dick Polman, the paper's main public affairs columnist, in private conversations with the editorial board. Yet two of Polman's closest friends were on the board, and most of its members generally sympathized with the columnist's views. A developer helping the *Courant* expand to new offices complained after Polman revealed in early 1984 that city officials were angry over part of the plan. Davies apologized in print for his columnist, who promptly began job hunting.

The *Courant*'s CEO heard that Polman had been spotted seeking work in the newsroom of the Knight-Ridder chain's *Philadelphia Inquirer.* So he telephoned *Inquirer* Managing Editor Eugene Foreman to warn him about Polman, who was hired anyway. "I have friends at every newspaper in the country," Davies blandly told me in explanation of his call to Foreman. "We talk about things."

Polman fired a parting shot at Davies and Times Mirror on a television talk show. "It's not a good situation at all," the columnist said of the *Courant* newsroom. "Davies is ready, willing and able to jump on the people on the staff, including myself, for reporting he perceives as too aggressive" towards the business community. "At least I will be going to a good, stable paper with a sense of mission instead of one that changes its mission every six to eight months like the *Hartford Courant*."

Davies' call to Philadelphia was not an isolated instance. Other incidents showed management attempts to sabotage careers. Davies, for example, pressured the *Los Angeles Times* to fire an editor on its wire service desk who had been a witness in an unsuccessful bias suit against the Kansas City papers under Davies' presidency. Davies threatened to cancel his wire service subscription unless the young editor were fired. A *Times* internal investigation produced a six thousand word, in-house report that cleared the target of Davies' accusation of perjury.

But he was still frightened at Davies' influence in the industry when I talked with him. At the end of the interview, after I had first ascertained the facts from other sources and then confirmed them with the target, he asked that his ordeal not be revealed for fear of angering the *Courant* publisher further. "I've got a family," he explained. "I've finally put that behind me."

A thirst for vengeance apparently was passed to Davies' top newsroom subordinate at the *Courant*, Marty Petty. When a reporter resigned to take a job at the *Los Angeles Herald Examiner*, Metro Editor Roger Moore urged him to explain his action immediately to the managing editor or face her efforts to prevent him from ever again working at a Times Mirror newspaper. The reporter was appalled when the metro editor confided that he had needed two hours of persuasion with Petty to soothe her ruffled feelings about the resignation. The offense? The *Courant* management, after promoting the reporter from town duty, regarded him as an ingrate because he did not remain at the newspaper. It was yet another indication of narrow-minded thinking at an organization ostensibly devoted to openness. Mark Murphy had brought in five high-ranking aides from Los Angeles during the Beach Boy regime. The Kansas City Chiefs tried to extend this kind of patronage and diehard loyalty down to the level of ordinary reporters.

After Polman's departure his columnist's job was left vacant for seven months. During that time, the company's in-house poll confronted management with the extremely low level of staff morale. Petty sought out longtime reporter Tom Condon to be columnist, although she warned him from the start that his predecessor, Polman, would never again work for Times Mirror. Condon had been assigned to reporting on the Hartford Board of Education after Davies scuttled the investigative project on workplace diseases. A few of his stories were so local that they appeared solely in the weekly regional news tabloid, the *Town Courant*, along with such fare as the details of real estate closings. It was the first time since his early days as a reporter that his articles appeared in just certain editions. Condon made the best of the demotion by unearthing some excellent stories. But much of his talent went into other projects, including a screenplay and a short story on Vietnam combat. Drawing on his knowledge as an attorney, he wrote a well-received book on labor law, *Fire Me . . . . . And I'll Sue! A Manager's Survival Guide to Employee Rights.* Condon's guidance to employers on better staff relations was excerpted in a full-length *Harvard Business Review* article.

Condon accepted the new assignment at the paper, and within a few months became the paper's best-read columnist, according to the *Courant*'s poll of readers. His repertoire included humor, personal experience and mini-investigations. Yet some of his most pithy observations could never be published in his paper. "Times Mirror," he would say privately, "is making the same mistake the federal government did across the country during the 1950s and 1960s. They keep sending in visiting experts who try to reinvent the wheel." He believed that the *Courant* was at its peak in 1980—before Times Mirror started making changes. His reasoning? Not that it was a great paper then. But he believed its staff was, on the whole, considerably more talented and more public-spirited than afterward.

He compared the successive management teams to World War II invaders. "The *Courant* under Times Mirror is a lot like Poland. First, it was overrun by the Germans. Then by the Russians."

CHAPTER 14

Prize Hunting

"TIMES MIRROR made journalism history," the firm's 1984 annual report announced, "when it became the first media company ever to win four Pulitzer Prizes in a single year." It continued, "More than 100 other major awards were won by Times Mirror newspapers and journalists in 1984."

The report described the acclaim given to individual publications in such detail that it would be a foolish editor indeed who ignored the implicit directive. Beyond advancement within the chain, a prize is valuable for editors and reporters seeking better jobs at other news organizations. "It's like money in the bank," Pulitzer Prize Board Secretary Robert Christopher told me during an interview, "particularly if you win it when you're reasonably young." Unlike a journalist's reputation within a community, a prize is tangible—and therefore more portable across state lines.

News organizations, as well, have powerful incentives to accumulate prizes. Much as Saks Fifth Avenue carves out a different niche in the retail marketplace from Macy's or a discount store, newspapers use editorial quality to distinguish themselves from rivals. Straightforward profiteers, usually operating in small cities removed from competitive pressure, expend little effort to build up an image of public service. A chain such as Gannett, however, wants both its twenty-two percent annual pre-tax profits and a good reputation. So the country's largest newspaper owner (more than ninety dailies, including the nationwide *USA Today*) circulated a list called "Gannett's Pulitzer Prizes." It turned out that at least twenty-seven were won before the group bought the papers. Times Mirror aims at an even higher spectrum of the market. Therefore it is willing to spend more money on the kind of high-profile stories that attract favorable attention, especially from prize committees and from other media seeking a quick index of quality.

The Pulitzer Prizes, the most respected in the profession, have been bestowed by Columbia University in New York City since 1917 in honor of the late publisher Joseph Pulitzer. Winners receive just $1,000 apiece. Yet the awards (twelve in journalism, and seven in letters and music) are so highly regarded that the competition has become aggressive. There were 1,560 applications for newspaper awards in 1985 compared to just 985 in 1979.

Reporter William Cockerham witnessed the changes over a fifteen-year period at the paper he has long nicknamed, "America's Oldest Newspaper Without a Pulitzer." He told me, "When [former *Courant* Editor Bob Eddy] decided to enter some of the stories I'd done in 1969 and 1970, he sent in a Pulitzer application that looked like a kid's report in school. He reproduced the clippings on that old cheap kind of coated copying paper. He pasted them into a scrapbook—crooked and with hand-lettered titles. You couldn't even read some of the words because there were date stamps all over them. I was embarrassed at the application." The practice in the mid-1980s was far different. "I'm not kidding," Cockerham said, "when I tell you that there were five people working virtually full-time on prize applications for the first six weeks of this year."

Pulitzers are granted in a two-stage process. Jurors, a group of some sixty-five distinguished volunteers, read applications and recommend winners. Another panel of even more eminent volunteers, the seventeen-member Pulitzer Board, makes the final decision. Christopher, the board's top-ranking employee and a distinguished author and editor in his own right, said, "Prize committees probably do pay more attention to impact than the general reader does. But, at least in the case of the Pulitzer Board, I would hasten to add that doesn't mean they don't highly value fairness."

Contest judges try to exclude overblown or otherwise inept entries. Yet they are busy people and do not have time for an independent review of the facts. "There's no way you can check out the reliability of twelve hundred entries," Christopher said. "I'm innocent enough to think that daily papers are edited by responsible people and they're not going to print things they know are not true." The system is built on such trust. And, except in the rare libel lawsuit, no one with clout or credibility—not contest judges, not rival media, not academics—subjects investigative methodology to real scrutiny.

"Someone should take a hard look at this process," a federal prosecutor warned me years ago when I was a court reporter. He worried that, in a few instances, his office's routine follow-ups to news stories were being cited in prize applications to glorify the articles— even when the official inquiries later failed to substantiate the themes. The prosecutor could not discuss his specific concerns because they stemmed from grand jury evidence that was secret by law. But he believed that someone within the journalism community—perhaps an ombudsman or nationally syndicated columnist—should systematically explore the problem of inflated prize applications.

The potential for abuse in prize contests, I suspect, comes from misguided zeal by the media more than from deliberate falsification. "All of us march to some sort of inner drum," My Lai investigator Seymour Hersh once said. "In twenty years in the newspaper business, I've never met a reporter who published something he knew to be wrong."

Those of us in the media like to describe ourselves as "professionals," much like lawyers or physicians. Yet only the most backward states still rely exclusively on unpaid volunteers to maintain professional standards in law or medicine. Why? An answer comes from Yale Law School professor Geoffrey Hazard, who was once described by the *National Law Journal* as the country's leading expert on legal ethics. He told me that volunteer peer review is undermined by lack of incentives for hard digging and by what he called the Good Ol' Joe Syndrome. "Panel members instinctively believe 'good ol' Joe' couldn't really be a bad lawyer because he never acted that way around them."

The journalism awards bestowed by volunteer committees are simply a carrot for good behavior, of course, not a stick. Still, they have great influence on professional conduct because no other official sanctioning process has been widely used. The First Amendment generally precludes discipline of unethical or incompetent journalists except by their own bosses or by courts. "Free press" principles also severely undercut the influence of the National News Council, which was founded in 1973. It foundered a decade later from lack of support. The *New York Times* was among the news organizations that from the beginning flatly opposed outside investigation of complaints against the media.

This situation survived even the debacle caused by *Washington Post* reporter Janet Cooke. She won a Pulitzer in 1981 for describing "Jimmy," a narcotics-addicted child said to live in Washington, D.C.'s ghetto. Some of her own co-workers as well as the city's mayor insisted, to no avail, that there was no "Jimmy." Gross lies in her autobiographical sketch were eventually exposed only because of the publicity surrounding her Pulitzer triumph. *Post* editors, shamed by the fraud in her resume, then interrogated her about the story until she broke down and admitted that she had created the boy. Cooke returned the Pulitzer and left the paper in disgrace.

The *Post*'s embarrassment caused many newspaper editors throughout the country to reduce reliance on anonymous sources for investigative projects. Another trend was to publish stories in which much of the evidence came from the direct observations of the reporters. This kind of documentation was said to enhance newspaper credibility with readers. The *Courant*, for example, commonly adopted the techniques of surveillance by reporters. Editors in Hartford touted this method repeatedly to readers and to prize committees as ensuring credibility and fairness. Yet any technique can be abused. And a nationwide study of newspaper credibility by a trade association revealed a disturbing state of affairs. Sixty-three percent of the public believed newspapers take advantage of ordinary people. The same belief was shared by fifty-two percent of the journalists polled.

Following up the concerns voiced by my former editor, Charles Towne, I visited the Pulitzer offices—a couple of rooms furnished in plain, academic style on the seventh floor of Columbia's Journalism Building. Although prize applications are reputed to be self-serving and extravagent, they are not open for public inspection until after the awards are announced each April. After that, only a few people a year (most of them graphics designers seeking tips on better presentation of their papers' submissions) ever bother to look at them, according to longtime staffers. Robert Christopher told me he knew of just two writers (one published in a Welsh journal and another in German magazines) who had ever looked up applications and independently checked their claims. "I keep waiting for a student to propose it," commented Christopher, who held a journalism professorship at Columbia, "but no one has."

I set out to examine the *Courant*'s award-winning bridge project, published the previous year and unsuccessfully submitted for a Pulitzer. My next two chapters show: 1) the facts as the *Courant* presented them to readers and various prize committees; 2) the facts known at the time to those in the newsroom; 3) the facts as confirmed later in sworn testimony and in other evidence available to anyone who wanted to check the record.

"Could 'Janet Cooke' happen again?" I asked the Pulitzer Board's administrator.

"We do everything that we reasonably can to try to prevent

it," Christopher replied. Yet he added, "In Vietnam, I asked General [Creighton] Abrams if he thought Tet could happen again. He looked at me and said, 'Mr. Christopher, that's the last question I ask myself before I go to bed every night.' I sort of feel that way about Janet Cooke."

CHAPTER 15

Inspecting the Inspectors

SHORTLY AFTER HE RESIGNED his *Courant* job as chief editorial writer in 1985, James Napoli reflected upon his five years at the paper. He was relaxing in blue jeans at a friend's apartment before leaving for Egypt, where he was joining the faculty of American University for two years while his wife wrote for a wire service in Cairo. They left the newspaper voluntarily, eager to begin the adventure of work overseas.

Napoli was displeased at Michael Davies' close editing of the editorial pages. "He's a Babbitt publisher. He's going to go any way the wind blows. He's going to do whatever is good for Big Business. He's a booster. There's no inspiration in his writing, and that's kind of reflective of the guy." Neither did Napoli think much of daily news coverage. "Still fairly lousy" was his terse description. "We don't know what's going on in state government most of the time. That bothers me a lot." Yet when Napoli was asked to pick the best year overall for the newspaper he picked a Davies year, 1984. Why?

"The projects now are really effective, really comprehensive." Napoli singled out for praise Davies' 1984 probe of government bridge inspectors. It went on to win more prizes than any other investigation in the *Courant*'s history. "I didn't think it was Pulitzer Prize material. But it was exhaustive, innovative and exactly the kind of thing that Roger [Moore] is good at organizing. And we've seen repeats of it—emissions [a probe of government automobile exhaust inspections] and a few other things. I liked it."

Davies' plan was to show that state bridge inspectors were failing to perform their duties in the wake of the fatal, I-95 bridge collapse described in the first chapter of this book. He began enlisting newsroom support for the project within months after his 1983 arrival in Hartford. The probe would follow his formula for investigations in a number of ways. First, his targets were usually involved in government work. Therefore almost all background documentation for stories was available to the newspaper (usually at government expense) under the liberal provisions of state and national Freedom of Information laws. Davies typically went after low-echelon functionaries assigned to perform specific tasks, usually connected with safety. The newspaper spent enormous sums to show that some of those people were not performing their jobs adequately. This incompetence, malingering or petty theft was then portrayed as scandal.

High officials had an option after the *Courant*'s revelations. They could defend their subordinates. Or they could join the newspaper's accusations. Most learned the advantages of allying themselves with the state's most powerful news organization. Gov. William O'Neill was especially adept at gaining headlines by announcing immediate investigations to punish wrongdoers identified by the newspaper. The newspaper then cited the governor's actions in its prize applications and editorials to show the impact of its stories on public affairs. The stories seemed to antagonize relatively few readers. Organized labor was weak in the state. And how many people, after all, sympathize with state workers accused of being lazy and greedy?

Even when Davies ranged beyond his standard formula, he tended to go after comparable targets: taxi drivers who overcharged, rock concert ticket scalpers, acid rain polluters from distant states and child molesters. When the *Wall Street Journal* reported bizarre wiretap allegations surrounding the resignation of United Technologies Corp. President Robert Carlson in 1984, the *Courant* simply parroted the Hartford-based corporation's brief denials of wrongdoing. The *Courant* stories were so vague that it was difficult to determine the thrust of the allegations—that the firm itself might have been responsible for bugging Carlson's house--much less their likely veracity.

Yet it's more reasonable to explore what Davies did than what he omitted. There are, after all, many important things to investigate, and a newspaper's resources are limited. The bridge inspection series, Davies' first major *Courant* investigation, began Sunday, June 24, 1984, with an eight-column, front page headline about the state Department of Transportation (DOT): "FRAUD, LAXITY MAR DOT BRIDGE INSPECTIONS." The stories took up the top half of the front page for five straight days. The front page treatment and inside runover on those five days totalled eleven full pages, none of which included any advertisements.

Davies summarized his view of the series in a 1985 letter nominating it for a Pulitzer Prize. "Connecticut and the nation," he explained to the contest judges, "awoke on the morning of June 28, 1983, to the shock of a bridge collapse that had killed three people and injured three others." He continued:

> A 100-foot span of the bridge carrying Interstate 95 over the Mianus River in Greenwich, CT. had fallen; blessedly, the bridge collapsed in the early morning hours, thus sparing society from the far greater loss had the heavily travelled span gone down under heavier traffic.

He then described how the newspaper assigned six reporters, a photographer and an editor to a systematic surveillance of the state's bridge inspectors in the field. Spying on the eighteen surface inspectors and two divers began in mid-March 1984 and lasted sixty-five days until shortly before the first anniversary of the accident.

Reporters also copied many thousands of pages of government reports and payroll accounts. These records included logs of inspectors' daily activities, their mileage vouchers and their actual inspection reports. The *Courant* hired a private consultant, Dr. Carl Kurt, an associate professor of engineering at the University of Kansas, to re-inspect some bridges.

"The extensive three-month investigation," Davies continued in his Pulitzer application, "found that the bridge inspection was seriously flawed despite the tragedy at Mianus."

> The *Courant* discovered some bridge inspectors spent little time inspecting bridges. Rather, they killed time by driving roundabout routes, taking extended coffee breaks or lunches or sitting in their trucks. The two men [divers] assigned to inspecting the underwater portions of bridges were the worst offenders. During seventy-seven hours of surveillance, they only dove once, but collected bonus pay as if they had routinely entered the water to inspect the bridges. Interviews with the inspectors' supervisors showed a wide gap between their guidelines and how the inspectors actually did their inspections. The supervisors also did not have any idea how much time the inspectors wasted.
>
> The *Courant* presented its findings in a major package of five stories, graphics and photographs. The response was immediate. On the Sunday of publication, Connecticut Transportation Commissioner J. William Burns launched a full investigation which resulted eighteen days later in the firing of the two underwater divers for fraudulently collecting bonus pay. Burns also disciplined ten other inspectors for goofing off on the job. Four of them were docked pay for non-productive use of their time. Still pending is a criminal investigation into the underwater inspectors' conduct that was begun the day after the package was published.
>
> Also on that Monday, Connecticut Gov. William A. O'Neill called all his commissioners to an early morning meeting and ordered them to improve the management

of their agencies. He told them to meet with their middle managers and tell them that he expects every state worker to put in a full day's work.

The stories also led DOT to issue new orders to bridge inspectors and their supervisors to improve accountability. Inspectors now must record in writing the times they start and stop inspecting a bridge. They will be provided trucks equipped with two-way radios and required to report when they arrive and leave a bridge they are inspecting. Supervisors will start making unannounced spot checks. The public response also was dramatic. Gov. O'Neill said the *Courant* performed a distinct public service and the newspaper received dozens of congratulatory letters from readers.

We believe this effort represents journalistic accomplishment and public service at the highest level. A significant problem affecting the lives and welfare of hundreds of thousands of citizens was identified, vast resources and time and money were dedicated to investigate the situations in the face of considerable obstacles; the most professional standards were maintained throughout the effort; and, with a high degree of responsibility, the results were displayed in a manner appropriate to the conclusions. The impact of the report was immediate and widespread—resulting in firings, disciplinary actions, legislative hearings and a major overhaul of the program.

Sincerely,
Michael J. Davies.

The letter summarized the aggressive tone of the stories. It also conveyed the thrust of the paper's massive follow-up effort that continued well into the following year, 1985. "I wish I'd had that story," News Director Richard Ahles of the CBS-affiliate WFSB-TV told me shortly after the series appeared. His reaction was typical. Other media echoed the *Courant*'s findings, reported government reactions and helped keep the story alive.

However, a careful analysis of the stories shows that the total quantifiable "fraud" alleged by the newspaper was $881. That sum was paid in apparently unwarranted bonus pay to two longtime inspectors with base salaries of under $20,000 a year. The newspaper's consultant, Professor Kurt, did not find anything wrong with the state's inspections reports. A Hartford reader was in a small minority when he wrote a letter to the editor, slightly condensed here:

> As I piece it together, a corps of reporters under the inspired leadership of their editor . . . uncovered a shocking story worthy of the coverage of the attack on Pearl Harbor or the assassination of a president.
>
> Thank God you unearthed the woeful tale of wanton sunbathing on an extended lunch hour by one of the 4,000 employees of the DOT, and the equally scandalous episode of the procuring of laundry from the dry cleaners on company time.
>
> You played to a receptive audience eager to believe another story of government failure. You have made your headlines with the well-orchestrated 'creation' of news.

The hidden history of the bridge series revealed carelessness and management-inspired zealotry far different from the image of thoughtful public service the newspaper sought to purvey.

The bridge fell down while Mark Murphy was still in charge of the newspaper. All through the summer before Davies' arrival, the *Courant* provided extensive coverage of the tragedy, including the causes. The bridge, built in 1957. collapsed when a rusted pin-and-hanger assembly broke, increasing stress on another assembly that also sheared off. Authorities and the news media quickly identified maintenance problems and a questionable design as likely causes of the collapse, although the precise allocation of blame awaited the outcome of lengthy litigation. The pin assembly had rusted because a defective drainage system permitted rainwater mixed with road salt to cascade upon it from the highway. Penny-wise and pound-foolish, the state had scrimped on maintenance. It saved $160,000 in 1982, for example, by not replacing a "snooper" truck that had a boom-type apparatus to lower inspectors over the side of bridges to look at the underside. Instead, inspectors made their checks from the riverbank by binoculars, as best they could.

Davies, taking charge of the newspaper, wanted more lively fare. He was convinced the same "inspect the inspectors" story used in Kansas City might work again. As described earlier, Davies' editors in Kansas City assigned two reporters in late 1982 to follow eighteen Kansas City inspectors for two months in the wake of the Hyatt Regency Hotel collapse. The *Star* published the story Jan. 30, 1983 under the banner headline, "TAX-PAYERS LOSE AS INSPECTORS CHEAT." In six ad-free pages over the next three days, the paper charged, "Many city inspectors responsible for ensuring the safety of buildings in Kansas City regularly lie about their working hours, loaf at home or in bars and restaurants when they are supposed to be on the job and steal tax money by falsifying work and mileage records." The day of publication, the city suspended all the inspectors. Fifteen of them either quit or were fired. The city fired six more inspectors upon its subsequent investigation. The total, then, was twenty-one firings—nearly half the city's total of forty-six inspectors.

The Kansas City papers published similar stories about inspectors in other communities in the region. In the fall of 1983, the efforts won the first-place public service award in nationwide competition sponsored by the Associated Press Managing Editors Association. On Dec. 10, 1983, after Davies had already come to Hartford, the *Kansas City Times* uncorked the story again under the headline "ONE-THIRD OF K.C. INSPECTORS STILL LOAF." A new, forty-one day surveillance showed that nine of the twenty-five inspectors followed "are still loafing on the job and falsifying their daily work reports." The city later suspended four of the nine, and fired four others. In reviewing the stories, it appeared to me that the papers had identified a serious problem in Kansas City and that the stories were a legitimate journalistic effort.

During the early winter of 1983, Davies had trouble persuading mid-echelon staff in Hartford to make a full and enthusiastic commitment to his idea for a similar probe of Connecticut bridge inspectors. Claude Albert, head of the newspaper's investigations team, and one of his subordinates, Clifford Teutsch, privately expressed reservations. Former DOT Commissioner Arthur Powers, accused of bribery, had been convicted the previous year on reduced charges. Teutsch, the paper's main reporter covering Powers and nine other DOT corruption cases, said that the state's continuing grand jury probe made DOT one of the last places in state government that the paper was likely to succeed on a fishing expedition. Metro Editor Dick Barnes also dragged his feet in implementing Davies' idea.

There was no more delay after Marty Petty and Roger Moore arrived from Kansas City and got their bearings as *Courant* managing editor and metro editor, respectively. They told reporter Christopher Bowman to copy every bridge document possessed by the state transportation department. Bowman, a hard-working young man who had joined the reporting staff eleven months previously, was flabbergasted when he went to DOT headquarters in mid-February 1984 and discovered the enormity of the task. But his new bosses told him to finish the copying within a month so the newspaper could begin its reporting. At that point, the *Courant* had scant idea whether Connecticut's bridge inspectors were loafing on the job. Usually investigative reporters take a preliminary "sniff" on a story before committing massive resources. Petty and Moore already knew what they wanted.

Bowman, somewhat nervous from the pressure, obtained use of a special room from the DOT to conduct the copying operation. The newspaper hired at least five men from a temporary personnel agency and rented two copying machines to help Bowman and the newspaper's legal researcher copy the documents. They began putting in nine, ten and eleven-hour days copying reports and blueprints, some of them huge. DOT officials cooperated with the newspaper under threat of Freedom of Information Act (FOI) litigation. The officials did not know the focus of the newspaper's probe.

When Bowman stopped by the newsroom one morning in late February, reporter Larry Williams calculated on a computer that even if he could keep up his exhausting pace it would take three more months to finish the assigned copying. The mission was aborted after one week. By then, the newspaper had copied some 25,800 pages from about 650 files. Bowman later said hardly any of documents were ever used, or even read.

Moore, a high-strung, enthusiastic man, took control of the *Courant*'s bridge inspectors investigation in March upon his arrival in Hartford. In Kansas City, Moore had directed the *Star* special projects team that showed inspectors were goofing off in the wake of the Hyatt collapse. Moore's Hartford reporters used motor-driven cameras with long-distance lenses and a special clock that printed the date and hour on each photo negative. A car rental company agreed to swap reporters' cars daily so that bridge inspectors would not detect them. "Hand radios were rented with hidden antennas," recalled Craig Baggott, a senior reporter on the surveillance along with Bowman. "[Synchronized] watches were critical: with two reporters taking minute-to-minute notes, timing had to be on the money."

Baggott's story was published in the *IRE Journal*, a quarterly tabloid going to some 2,300 members of the group Investigative Reporters and Editors. In the article, Baggott promoted the theme that his newspaper carried off its investigation with flawless precision. Also, he obscured the management initiative behind the project and the theme of worker fraud and laxity. Instead, Baggott implied that the probe arose in the more normal fashion: because reporters convinced editors to risk the costs of documenting the reporters' suspicions. "By late January we had decided on surveillance," Baggott told IRE members, "Michael J. Davies, the new editor and publisher, and Marty Petty, the new managing editor, sat down with Moore, checked the costs and gave us the nod. They knew it was a gamble; they knew we had to do it."

Baggott went on to describe the daring nature of the probe, and to portray its highlights. "Ron Winter, an ex-Marine, often called on his camouflage experience to blend in with the surroundings, sometimes creeping on his stomach to within 25 or 30 feet of the inspectors, radio and recorder in hand. Back at the office one night, he claimed he had lain still for nearly an hour in the woods, so still, he said, that a bird landed on his back. We couldn't believe that. So he played his tape, and the bird was on it." Baggott, in his early thirties, was a tall, curly-haired reporter who had worked for years in the newspaper's local bureaus before being promoted to the central office during the Mark Murphy transformations of 1981. During the middle of the bridge project, he reacted angrily one day when Larry Williams (laboring on the soon-to-be-spiked health hazards probe) joshed him about his less-than-cerebral duties spying on inspectors for Davies. "If people'd spend more time doing their jobs around here instead of criticizing the new management," Baggott snapped at Williams, "we'd get a lot more done."

The series was intended to run in late June to coincide with the first anniversary of the Mianus River Bridge collapse. But the surveillance wound down in June without discovery of the kind of flagrant dereliction of duty that Davies, Petty and Moore had found during their project in Kansas City. Then the Hartford reporters learned two things (or thought they did) that provided the appropriate whiff of scandal. First, pay records obtained under Freedom of Information law showed that two underwater inspectors received bonus pay for diving almost every day. The reporters, going through their old notes, believed that only one of the divers had dived during seventy-seven hours of observation—and even that diver had gone down only once. The so-called "divers who didn't dive" would be by far the most serious abuse the newspaper found in its sixty-five days of surveillance. Yet the divers had had nothing to do with the fall of the Mianus River Bridge, which was caused by problems on the superstructure.

The second supposed breakthrough came from John

Cavanaugh, head of the DOT bridge inspection unit. He remarked to reporters grilling him in June that a bridge inspection should take at least thirty minutes. Nineteen of the fifty-four supposed "inspections" observed by the newspaper apparently occurred in less than thirty minutes. Cavanaugh's statement was the principal basis for the newspaper's claim that its exposé revealed a continuing safety hazard—although the newspaper's own engineer, Professor Kurt, said that a safe inspection did not necessarily have to take thirty minutes.

The day of publication, Davies devoted his Sunday column to the story. The Hartford exposé "should make every resident of Connecticut see red," he wrote. "It's a classic account of how public servants waste taxpayers' dollars by loafing in ways big and little and, more seriously, of how some inspectors fake their reports and put in for premium pay without doing the work." In Kansas City, his column had similarly charged, "PUBLIC'S TRUST BETRAYED." The newspaper's management team never disclosed to Hartford readers that it had done essentially the same investigation in Kansas City. Yet Davies' role in the project was so important that he personally insisted that the word "FRAUD" be in the Hartford headline, recalled Mark Stillman, one of the two reporters who followed the divers.

After publication, the *Courant* pounced on the governor to demand his reaction. The newspaper's crusade presented him with a sudden choice before he had the full facts. He could try to defend the low-ranking targets of the probe, or he could join the hue-and-cry and reap favorable headlines himself. It was not a difficult choice for any politician worthy of the name. "DOT VOWS PROBE OF ABUSES" was the headline of a story bannered across the top of the *Courant*'s front page on the second day of the series, June 25. The story by reporters Bowman and Baggott implied that state officials should file criminal charges against the divers:

> Stanley C. Jones, the leader of the diving crew, and his partner, Charles A. Banky, each collected more than

$420 in bonus pay after reporting on their time sheets that they had dived April 24, April 25, May 1, May 10, May 18 and June 4. The *Courant* watched them on those days and they made no dives.

Under state law, someone collecting unearned pay could be charged with larceny.

Austin J. McGuigan, chief state's attorney, could not be reached for comment Sunday.

"O'NEILL CALLS CRIMINAL PROBE OF INSPECTIONS" was the eight-column, top-of-the-front-page headline the next day. "ASSEMBLY DEMANDS REPORT ON DOT INQUIRY IN 30 DAYS," was another front page headline that same day. The governor and the newspaper served one another's purposes through the rest of the week: "O'NEILL PUTS PRESSURE ON TOP OFFICIALS" and "GOVERNOR WARNS: NO GOOFING OFF" were other front page *Courant* headlines. This treatment continued, to a lesser extent, for many weeks. The newspaper even paid for a public opinion poll to test statewide reaction to gold-bricking by government workers. Results were published on the front page.

State transportation officials convened a disciplinary hearing for the divers June 28. It proceeded despite protests by a union representative, who called it "a kangaroo court." The divers' attorneys pleaded in vain for a delay, saying they had had less than an hour to learn about the case. The divers, on the advice of their attorneys, declined to testify because of the pending criminal investigation.

The hearings provoked a constitutional skirmish between the DOT and the newspaper. The DOT investigators asked reporters about unpublished information. "The *Courant* refused such an outrageous demand," Davies wrote in his column. "If we allowed an arm of government to rummage through our files and find out the names of confidential sources, those sources would dry up immediately. They would know the newspaper couldn't be trusted."

> Similarly, we have to maintain our independence from all government agencies. If we furnished them with everything in our files, it's doubtful we could claim to be properly performing our constitutionally mandated role as a watchdog.
>
> In this particular case, there are no confidential sources. The unpublished information merely echoes what has been published. There are no bombshells. There is nothing in our notes that would convict or exonerate any state worker beyond what has already been published.
>
> What we are fighting for is a principle. If we turn over notes and other unpublished material today, we will have to do it in the future when confidential sources and sensitive material are involved.

Davies' position provoked vehement protests from the divers' attorneys. The DOT deputy commissioner in charge of the inquiry board agreed with them. "I really don't believe the *Courant* can write an article such as this and walk away from it," he said. "Basically, everything was negative in the newspaper. Now we want to know the rest."

"We're not running away from our story," responded Ralph Elliot, the newspaper's regular attorney on retainer and the incoming president of the Connecticut Bar Association. "But we are trying to cooperate within certain parameters that preserve our rights." The reporters answered some questions but not others during the hearings. Bowman, for example, said, "I'm a trained professional observer.... I'm willing to stand behind what is written in this article."

"'Fraud?'" asked a diver's attorney, referring to the most explosive word in the headline of the main story.

"That's an accurate headline. That's an accurate word," Bowman replied. The reporter then refused to describe the basis of the newspaper's claim that the divers submitted false records for bonus pay. The newspaper's attorney quickly interjected, "The *Courant*'s article is not on trial here." Afterward, the newspaper's editors used their news and editorial pages to castigate the DOT for seeking more information from the newspaper than it was willing to provide. "We have even offered to show DOT officials how to do their own detective work," Davies sneered. "So far, they seem to be inclined to do nothing but probe the veracity of the *Courant*'s reporting and to waste time by issuing outrageous demands."

The stories continued through the summer. "STATE FIRES 2 DIVERS, REPRIMANDS 10 INSPECTORS," said the newspaper's banner front page headline July 19. A closer look showed that only four inspectors besides the divers received a tangible penalty beyond a letter of reprimand. They were docked two hours pay for overlong breaks.

While the newspaper played up the penalties (weak as they were) on its front page, it relegated to an inside page a related finding by Burns, the DOT commissioner—even though it undercut the entire rationale of the project: the theme that the inspectors' work habits endangered state safety. Burns said the state had hired independent engineers to re-inspect every bridge cited by the *Courant* as an example of a too-brief inspection. The new inspections, conducted at substantial expense to taxpayers in response to the newspaper's claims, found no significant discrepancies between the conditions originally reported by the state inspectors and those found by the independent consultants.

"There is not one shred of evidence," Burns concluded, "that the bridge safety inspectors did not competently, thoroughly and adequately inspect the bridges assigned to them."

CHAPTER 16

Sworn Evidence

WHILE THE NEWSPAPER'S FOLLOW UPS to its bridge exposé thundered across its front pages in 1984, Ombudsman Henry McNulty assisted the cheerleading. "As we anticipated," he wrote, "the public reaction to our DOT bridge inspection story has been quick, intense and positive." McNulty himself found nothing to criticize about the series, and virtually nothing wrong with its many follow-ups, which extended into the next calendar year.

He provided a comment for a press release the project's supervisory editor wrote about the series. The account ran virtually intact as a full-length article in the national trade magazine *Editor & Publisher*, according to one reporter who saw both the press release and the published article. The trade journal included the statement, "Readers [sic] reactions to the report have been very positive, according to Henry McNulty, The *Courant*'s reader's representative." By publishing the flattering material as if it were a news story, *Editor & Publisher* helped the Hartford paper's campaign for wider recognition and prizes.

One person not swept up in the general hoopla was Austin McGuigan, Connecticut's chief state's attorney. A slender man with piercing dark eyes, the prosecutor seemed an unlikely person to scrutinize the press. McGuigan had often been accused of being a publicity-seeker himself.

But the tenement-raised prosecutor also had a stubborn streak and a self-image as a defender of the common man. Named Connecticut's chief prosecutor in 1978, he had undertaken a number of courageous investigations. One attacked the links between organized crime, legalized gambling and politicians. Another probed illegal campaign contributions provided by architects, engineers and highway builders who received lucrative state work at the DOT. In the early 1980s, McGuigan obtained the resignations and convictions of two of Gov. O'Neill's commissioners. One was Arthur Powers at DOT, who pleaded guilty to charges involving a $1,000 gift from an architect. The other was Agriculture Commissioner Earl Waterman, convicted of a $38,500 theft when he was a town official. Veteran political observers in Connecticut said that McGuigan was the first prosecutor in state history to convict a governor's commissioner of a crime.

In complying with the governor's order to investigate inspectors identified by the *Courant*, the prosecutor learned that the divers' attorneys advised them not to talk to authorities during the probe. McGuigan decided to force the divers' cooperation. He gave them immunity in return for their testimony before a grand jury that was trying to learn if higher-ups were involved in a fraud against the state. McGuigan reasoned that the divers had been punished enough by the shame of their exposure in the media; their firing after lengthy careers; and the DOT's administrative action against them requiring return of unmerited pay.

He also believed that DOT accounting procedures were so loose and bonus payments for divers so common that the state could not prove the divers had "criminal intent" in collecting it. For many, many decades in Anglo-American law, proof of a criminal state of mind has been necessary for conviction in serious cases (but not such things as parking violations). The requirement, known by its latin name *mens rea*, might appear to be a mere technicality. Yet it reinforces the strong social stigma attached to conviction by ensuring that only the morally culpable are found guilty. "If the state doesn't have a procedure for how people get paid," the prosecutor told me during an interview at his home, "you're going to blame the diver? Blame the state!"

The *Courant* accused McGuigan editorially of coddling the divers. McGuigan remained firm. "We go after people who can fight back," he told a young prosecutor assigned to the state's elite squad of attorneys operating out of the central office. Only McGuigan provided the divers a fair chance to tell their side of the story. The *Courant* had ambushed them the week before the story ran and cleverly selected their quotations to put them in the worst possible light.

Prosecutors learned many things during the four months of secret, sworn grand jury testimony from DOT officials, the divers and *Courant* reporters. The testimony indicated that the DOT had indeed been lax in accounting procedures and that the divers obtained unmerited bonuses totaling $9,200 over a number of years. The DOT reached the figure by showing that only one man had dived but both had put in for diving pay—a payment plan once used but discontinued. The two doubtless deserved to be fired for accepting such pay, especially when they admitted that neither had dived on two of the days of surveillance. But this finding was short of the newspaper's insistence that only one man had dived—for just eleven minutes—during the seventy-seven hours in question.

The grand jury report also said the DOT's lack of supervision "could result in abuses which might detrimentally affect the safety of the public." Once again, that fell far short of the newspaper's innuendos that public safety had already been endangered by a "significant problem affecting the lives and welfare of hundreds of thousands of citizens." In its Pulitzer application, the newspaper claimed that it displayed its findings "with a high degree of responsibility" and "in a manner appropriate to the conclusions."

In fact, it made an astonishing number of subjective decisions and factual mistakes in its effort to reap acclaim. The *Courant:*

1) created public fears about the quality of bridge inspections far out of proportion to reality; 2) goofed up on its central allegation—that its surveillance was flawless, proving that the divers did not dive; and 3) was not willing to admit even the possibility of error to the public or to contest judges. Ron Winter, the Vietnam veteran who had taken his assignment so seriously, was proud of his own careful tracking of the inspectors assigned to him. But he told me about foul-ups, such as finding a colleague sleeping on duty and seeing an editor jeopardize the project by bringing visitors to a surveillance site. Winter was especially disillusioned by what he perceived as intense politicking over what facts would be presented to readers and who would get the glory. "These people showed me," he said, "that the only thing that mattered was what they got in their hand at the end of the story. Whether it was accurate, whether it could have gone further, or whether it was a disservice doesn't matter. It's whether they got an award for it."

The newspaper misled readers by its main, front page photos for the series June 24. These photos (copyrighted by the newspaper, as if they were priceless evidence of negligence by the inspectors) showed supports for a bridge in the western Connecticut city of Torrington. The concrete looked badly eroded to the layman's eye. In the context of the story, it seemed as if the state were ignorant of this danger because of the "fraud, laxity" of its inspectors. The text of the story said that the reporters observed inspectors spending only twelve minutes at the site of that bridge. The photos, therefore, were presented as chilling evidence that motorists' lives were endangered by the practices the newspaper was exposing.

The newspaper never mentioned that in March of 1984—the same month the newspaper began spying on inspectors—independent engineers from Massachusetts hired by the DOT completed a report of twenty-nine pages on that bridge's structure. The engineers noted the concrete deterioration as a problem. They recommended that the bridge be replaced. They provided a detailed cost-benefit analysis of three different ways to do it.

The engineering report contained many photographs of the deteriorated bridge supports. When the newspaper began its probe, in other words, the state was already monitoring the Torrington situation closely. Yet the paper went ahead and used the photos unfairly for their shock value, without explanation.

The first insider I approached with my findings was Mark Stillman, one of the two reporters who had tailed the divers. I trusted him to be candid. As recounted in an earlier chapter, "The Beach Boys," Stillman had done much to improve discipline of unethical attorneys in Connecticut by exposing the various schemes by fortune-hunters stalking the disabled heiress Ethel Donaghue. Stillman was covering town news in 1984 when his bosses drafted him to help tail bridge inspectors. When I met with him two years later, he had left the newspaper business and become a student at Columbia Law School. He retained his characteristic good humor, and welcomed me into his studio apartment in New York City.

I first showed him the engineers' report on the Torrington bridge, then the newspaper's treatment of that bridge in the exposé. "It's misleading," Stillman conceded, with his voice sounding troubled over the discovery. "If this is the worst bridge in the state and the state has already done this [he pointed to the engineers' report] what's lax about it?" Stillman also spoke of Professor Kurt, brought in by the paper from Kansas "with the thought he might be able to establish these were poor inspections. But apparently his conclusion was that the quality of the inspections was pretty good. That got very little play."

To put the divers' bonuses into perspective, the newspaper should have pointed out that they only performed work that surface inspectors refused to do. Some diving assignments—wading into the water and the like—were easy. Yet the divers also worked year-round. Icy water, rats and snakes were part of their environment, as was polluted water that posed threats of hepatitis and cancer. Even normal diving with air tanks could be dangerous, and the state's divers had to do such things as swim up culverts to perform some inspections.

Grand jury testimony indicated that the DOT's practice was to grant diving bonuses liberally in recognition that the divers' base pay of under $20,000 annually was lower than that of surface inspectors who had much easier jobs. "My own interpretation," testified John Cavanaugh, supervisor of all inspectors, "is if the diver walks into the water he would be performing his duty as a diver [and thus be eligible for per diem bonus pay]."

Stillman's recollections showed that the newspaper had imposed its own definition of "dive" without warning readers that it was different from Cavanaugh's. "I think we assumed," Stillman recalled, "a dive was when they completedly submerged themselves and put on diving equipment. . . . I didn't think that merely entering the water constituted a dive. But the question was never really asked in my presence."

"Why was that?"

"Nobody thought of it," Stillman replied. "If 'dive' means 'wade,' maybe they dove."

While the state's definition might seem too generous, the final result was hardly a scandal of the magnitude the newspaper suggested. Even with all bonuses, deserved and undeserved, Diver Stanley Jones's annual income extrapolated over his last year before his dismissal was $32,152. That was after thirteen years with the state. Banky's was $29,933 after eighteen years of state work. The independent divers hired by the DOT to check the work of Jones and Banky cost between $600 and $650 a day. They found essentially the same things the state's divers had already recorded.

The grand jury testimony also seriously undermined the results of the newspaper's visual surveillance. The *Courant* continued to maintain essentially what it printed during the first day's story: that "during seventy-seven hours of surveillance, Jones, the team leader, dived eleven minutes and his partner, Charles A. Banky, did not dive at all." The immunity deal with the divers stipulated that they could be charged with perjury (which carried a prison term of up to five years) if they lied on the witness stand. Both Banky and Jones admitted they had received undeserved diving pay on some of the six occasions cited by the newspaper. But the divers each insisted that the newspaper had slipped up on other occasions in its surveillance.

Prosecutors were especially interested in the April 25 inspection of a bridge over the Fenton River in an eastern Connecticut town named Willington. Russell Lucy, a divers' aide who was not accused of wrongdoing, swore that Jones submerged to look at an underwater piling of the bridge. "I remember giving him the mask," Lucy testified. The bridge was new, and had never been inspected before. Jones' report on that day noted undercutting of the bridge piling five feet below the surface. That condition was soon confirmed by the two private divers hired by the state. Prosecutor McGuigan's assessment of Jones? "His report conclusively proves that he looked at it, 'cause there was no previous inspection and he found all kinds of problems under the goddamned water—five feet of cloudy water."

Stillman, in testifying at the June DOT hearing, had matter-of-factly conceded the possibility of an error. There was nothing misleading about his testimony. His description and that of his partner, Bowman, showed that the reporters were so worried during their surveillance about being spotted by the divers that they hid deep in the woods and constantly moved about. The intermittent surveillance was quite different from the image the newspaper had fostered publicly. The testimony:

> Stillman: I had them in view for approximately fifteen minutes [out of a thirty-seven-minute inspection April 25].
>
> DOT: So for some twenty minutes or so, then, you did not have them in view—them personally in view?
>
> Stillman: That is correct . . . .
>
> DOT: Did your period of not having them in view coincide wth Mr. Bowman's?
>
> Stillman: It may have.
>
> DOT: You don't know?
>
> Stillman: I don't know, no.

DOT: Okay. Is it possible that they were out of view of both of you for a certain period of time?

Stillman: Yes. I think it's possible.

Bowman testified that he personally watched the divers "at most, ten, fifteen minutes" at that bridge—much of it from a hundred yards away while he was hiding in a swamp. Bowman insisted, however, that the newspaper stood by its story: that the divers did not "dive." Yet the basis of his view was that they would not have had time to don a wet suit and diving tanks without being spotted.

The testimony before the grand jury undercut another major theme of the series—that many inspections were so brief that they could not possibly have assured safety under Cavanaugh's remark that inspections required thirty minutes. The divers Jones and Banky testified that sometimes when they were observed they had been performing partial inspections, or else simply orienting themselves on what equipment they would need when they performed an inspection. The newspaper assumed the inspectors' brief visits to bridges were full-fledged inspections that fell short of Cavanaugh's thirty-minute guideline. That issue was not explored in the published stories.

One thing that disturbed me as I discovered documents and witnesses in 1985 discrediting the bridge series was how little interest anyone in the media had shown about doublechecking on the story. A judicial order made the grand jury transcripts public in March 1985. They sat on top of a gray filing cabinet in the clerk's office of Hartford Superior Court. A courthouse clerk told me that virtually no one had ever looked at them except for the first day after they became public—and then only to bat out brief daily news stories for the next day's editions.

The *Courant*'s overall credibility was still high, despite such lapses as Hartford Police Department-Joseph Fazzano stories (which at least stemmed from a breaking news event). The Hartford daily's reputation for conservative standards for investigative stories had been built up by many generations of journalists. Other media did not suspect that the *Courant* would be grossly mistaken about the premises of a long-term, carefully planned probe such as the bridge series. Journalists tend to trust large daily newspapers more than other media such as television or magazines. Wire service reporters, for example, routinely rewrite newspaper reports and send them out nationwide.

When the grand jury transcripts became public the newspaper's reporters and editorial writers refused to point out its own mistakes. Instead, the editorial board called on McGuigan to arrest the divers on perjury charges because they had contradicted the newspaper. But the chief state's attorney was offended that Connecticut's most powerful news organization had used so much muscle on such lowly targets. He refused to put his finger on the scales of justice.

"Mike resented me over that," McGuigan told me one afternoon. He sat in his living room chair and nervously pulled a tennis shoe on and off his left foot. "Mike's English and fancies himself a Southern gentleman. A 'club player,' don't you know. Me? I was driving a truck when I was sixteen years old."

McGuigan's tone grew fierce and a vein started to bulge in his neck. "Read the editorials they wrote: Prosecute the bridge inspectors! Well, you've got to understand something. If you goddamn think I'm going to prosecute somebody to make *them* happy, you got to be s_______ me!"

As described earlier, the bridge series was the biggest award-winner in the newspaper's long history. It took all the top regional prizes: public service from Connecticut's Sigma Delta Chi, the professional journalism society; and the Associated Press and United Press International prizes for public service in New England.

In June 1985, after the award season had ended, I visited the Pulitzer offices in New York to examine how the *Courant* had touted its bridge series and how the method compared with that of other newspapers. Spencer Klaw, the Harvard Class of '41 grad who worked as editor of the *Columbia Journalism Review* (the profession's major watchdog), wheeled his red bicycle into the conference room where I was studying applications. The *Review* is across the hall from the Pulitzer suite. After Klaw locked his bicycle to a radiator, we embarked on a wide-ranging conversation about the news business. He was surprised that anyone might have any criticism of the bridge inspection series. "We gave it a 'laurel,'" he said. "What was the matter with it?"

The following week I went to Chicago for the national convention of Investigative Reporters and Editors. I was inspired by the energy and idealism that pervaded the IRE discussions. It came not simply from the cub reporters. That's expected. It was apparent also in the veterans with highly responsible jobs. For years, many of them had licked envelopes and performed all the other chores necessary to create a group that would encourage better investigative stories for the public.

On the last day of the sessions, I breakfasted with *Courant* reporter Chris Bowman. David Hayes, who had been his counterpart on the *Kansas City Star* and *Times* inspector surveillance in 1983, then sat down beside us on one of the sofas in the lobby of the convention hotel. Hayes told Bowman the *Courant* had been silly to pattern its story so precisely on the Kansas City model—right down to using a Kansas consultant, Professor Kurt. Hayes said he knew an engineer in Washington with excellent credentials who might have been more supportive of the newspaper's theme. Bowman agreed. He had worked hard on the bridge series, and genuinely seemed to believe it was a great success. He was not alone. A chorus of the sages of journalism had sung its praises.

To obtain further honors, Marty Petty nominated her boss for a Pulitzer in the "explanatory journalism" category. "Davies' column has explained the *Courant*'s policy of striving to be fair, accurate and balanced," she wrote the judges. "Today, 58 columns later, *Courant* readers are still saying thanks." Davies fell short of a Pulitzer his first year in Hartford. But he could take satisfaction in the many other accolades from the trusting journalism experts who praised his efforts. He himself was elevated to the position of juror for Pulitzer Prize entries in 1986. "It was my lot," he modestly explained in his column before the year's prizes were announced, "to be chairman of the general news category, which is defined by the Pulitzer board as reporting that meets the daily challenges of journalism, such as spot news or consistent beat reporting."

Davies also gave a pep talk to his top editors, with a transcript of his remarks prepared for lesser *Courant* employees. "Nationally," he said, "when people are totaling up their list of which papers should be in the top ten, or top twenty, or top twenty-five, the *Hartford Courant* damn sure will be up there." He continued:

> We don't have the particular resources or peculiar audiences of the *New York Times* or the *Los Angeles Times*, but there is absolutely no reason why we can't be thought of at least as much of a regional powerhouse in terms of standards and quality as, say, the *St. Petersburg Times* or *Chicago Tribune*.

No substantial criticism of the bridge series ever surfaced. A book published by IRE took the series at face value, and twice described it as "a model surveillance effort." Among the project's many honors, it was selected as the best public service story nationwide in the 1985 competition sponsored by the Scripps Howard Foundation. The newspaper was co-winner of another nationwide first-place award from Scripps Howard—one for enhancing First Amendment values. That award cited a *Courant* series on government reluctance to comply with Freedom of Information law, and various columns by Davies and his ombudsman, Henry McNulty, that helped "ensure public trust." It was the first time that one newspaper had ever won as many as two of the five Scripps Howard prizes in the same year.

The publisher, Petty and Moore led a contingent of eight *Courant* staffers to Cincinnati for the black-tie awards ceremony in which Davies' acceptance speech recalled the *Courant*'s courageous efforts to continue publishing during the Revolutionary War. In return, the recipients heard lavish praise from the

Scripps-Howard judges for the paper's award-winning efforts. "It checked every second, used surveillance," the judges commented in describing the bridge inspection series. "In a very systematic way, it followed every checkpoint of a good investigation. In a textbook case of public service journalism, the *Courant* made an extraordinary pursuit of the truth."

And of prizes.

CHAPTER 17

What's News?

"While it is not possible for the media to tell the population what to think, they do tell the public what to think about."
—Ben Bagdikian in *The Media Monopoly*

THE BRIDGE INSPECTOR SERIES was the trial run. It incorporated techniques that later permeated *Courant* investigations. The newspaper published more high-profile special projects than ever before. They were displayed more spectacularly. Impact was heightened by charts, photos, editorials and editors' columns. Judging by published letters-to-the-editor, reactions of other media and the garnering of awards, these techniques also seemed to be more successful than those of any comparable period.

Senior reporters grumbled that their assignments too often were to find facts to support the theories of editors from out of state. Davies, for his part, blamed reporters for not coming up with good ideas. So he and his editors provided strong direction.

Most of the *Courant*'s reporting was routine news coverage, of course, and some of it was legitimate enterprise work that deserved laurels. "But its stories are sometimes so unfair," said Daniel Schaefer, a thoughtful career attorney in the state attorney general's office, "that even when it does do a good job people are constantly wondering whether there's a hidden agenda or some other kind of deception."

Courant insiders privately spoke of heavy pressure to attain outside recognition. "Stories are being written for prizes," said Charles F.J. Morse, the paper's most senior political commentator. "You've got to bring that out in your book." Nationally, however, there seemed scant perception that such efforts could ever be a problem at a newspaper. The group Investigative Reporters and Editors invited Roger Moore to speak at its 1987 annual convention. And the administrator of a major awards program glossed over prize-hunting in the annual ethics report of the Society of Professional Journalists. "I've never seen any evidence that newspapers that consistently win in major contests devote much energy to tailoring their coverage to a set of contest rules," wrote George Pica, director of the Penney-Missouri Awards Program at the University of Missouri. "If a shoddy newspaper does tailor its coverage to suit the rules of reputable contests, there's a good chance that the contest organizers have identified viable needs and are, in effect, helping communities throughout the nation by setting agendas for otherwise directionless newspapers."

After the bridge inspection extravaganza, the *Courant* repeatedly went overboard in crusades. Five of these deserve brief examination:

* An attempt to win a Pulitzer by discrediting the reliability of Connecticut's auto emissions testing—even if it meant suppressing the newspaper's own tests that exonerated the program;
* An all-out effort to duplicate the bridge safety successes with a similar campaign for fire safety;
* A long-running smear of the chief state's attorney that helped drive him from office;
* A campaign for "tort reform" that helped insurance companies win major legislative victories and record profits;
* A corruption investigation that demonstrated gross zealotry by the newspaper.

Connecticut's auto emissions tests, like those in other states, began in 1983 out of public fears that faulty car exhaust systems posed a danger for fetuses, infants, the elderly and other adults with chronic lung disease or allergies. Yet the program attracted criticism because many drivers begrudged the time for thorough annual check-ups.

The *Courant* in 1985 appointed a newly hired reporter from a small paper in New Jersey to be lead investigator for a squad auditing the reliability of Connecticut's program. A mechanic assisted the team at times. "Reporters took a car through all 16 safety inspection stations and all 18 emissions testing stations," Davies wrote in his Pulitzer application. "The car had been adjusted so that it should have failed the emissions tests, and sidelights from the car were removed, a failure the safety inspectors should have caught."

"[The reporter] found that safety inspections were perfunctory at best," Davies continued, "and no more guaranteed the safety of a vehicle than did a carwash." As for the emissions? "Even though it had been adjusted to fail the emissions tests, the car passed at 13 of the 18 testing stations with readings all over the scale." The newspaper's massive, copyrighted exposé in August 1985 dominated the top of a Sunday front page with the headline, "SAFETY, CLEAN AIR TAKE A BACK SEAT IN STATE AUTO TESTS." Next, the newspaper pursued the familiar practice of pressuring top politicians for reaction. Five months later, Davies would boast in his letter to the Pulitzer judges, "The ramifications of the story are still being felt. The governor and legislature both have called for reorganization of the DMV [Department of Motor Vehicles]. Legislative leaders are forming a committee to study whether a private corporation could do a better job of running the department. We are proud to submit this effort for your consideration."

Let's look at the real story. As soon as they learned of the *Courant*'s methodology, experts from private industry joined state and federal experts in denouncing the newspaper's testing procedures. The experts essentially said that the newspaper's tinkering with the emissions device did not necessarily mean that it should have failed the state tests. As a reaction to the exposé, the U.S. Environmental Protection Agency examined Connecticut's testing centers and found that they were operating reliably.

A month after the original story, the *Courant* secretly decided to undertake a new testing procedure incorporating the criticisms it had received. Four more reporters, posing as ordinary motorists, sent their cars through tests twenty-nine times. The results exonerated the state's program from the original claims of unreliable emissions tests. Nonetheless, the newspaper's top management decided that the second round of testing was not news. The material was spiked. Neither readers nor contest judges ever heard about it.

It festered on some consciences in the newsroom for more than a year, however. In 1986, an insider anonymously mailed various Connecticut news organizations a detailed statement alleging fraud and cover-up by *Courant* editors on the emissions project. No one published a story, partly because of the tradition that the internal affairs of other news organizations are not "news." Upon learning of the matter in 1987, I obtained copies of the test results. The state Motor Vehicles Department checked its records and confirmed as genuine the testing results cited in the letter. By then, the newspaper's recklessness had seriously undermined an important toxic control program. The motivation? To win prizes and, later, to avoid embarrassment.

"If no one in the media will act on this information," I asked a ranking Motor Vehicles official, "why don't you just call a press conference yourself and present the evidence?"

"We thought about that. But we decided it would just look like sour grapes."

Even more than the emissions testing project, the *Courant*'s 1985 examination of Connecticut fire safety enforcement recalled the bridge inspection series, as well as Davies' Pulitzer-winner on fire safety in Louisville. It was the familiar formula of 20-20 hindsight blaming inspectors after an accident. The "news peg" this time was a boarding house fire that killed eight people in

1984. Thirteen reporters fanned out across the state to seek out potential fire code violations at more than 100 buildings used by the public. Some of the reporters privately described intense management pressure to find fire code violations—even minor, technical ones—to support the predetermined theme that government officials were overlooking a serious problem. Yet buried some 260 inches into the *Courant*'s main story was the curious statement, "Statistics from the U.S. Fire Administration show that since at least 1977 Connecticut has had one of the lowest fire-death rates in the country." For all the hoopla in dozens of stories and editorials, the newspaper could point to just three fire fatalities statewide during the previous year in locations open to the public. There was no indication that code violations were a factor. Once again, the paper demonstrated a serious lack of proportion.

Nonetheless, the institutions of government responded to the newspaper's campaign. "The governor demanded immediate and sweeping action," wrote Davies in his application for the Pulitzer in the prestigious "public service" category. "Manpower and money for fire safety was [sic] increased, and inspection procedures overhauled. Three separate statewide task forces also were formed to develop long-term improvements."

The governor did not hurt his stature with the newspaper's management by such cooperative responses. Indeed, the *Courant* endorsed his 1986 re-election bid even though Davies and the editorial page editor were the only ones on the ten-member board to favor him over his Republican challenger, Julie Belaga.

Chief State's Attorney Austin McGuigan, on the other hand, became a favorite punching bag in both the news and editorial sections. His vulnerability arose when he tried to exert more prosecutorial control over criminal investigations traditionally run by state police. The police counterattacked to protect their turf. In their traditional heavy-handed fashion, they spread innuendoes about McGuigan and prominent judges who supported him. Although judges backed McGuigan in written decisions on key legal issues, he and his aides were left essentially alone to face a gathering force of all the enemies he had collected during his career as a corruption-fighter. His manner (abrasive at times) and his cavalier approach to administrative chores had also created opponents in the media and government.

Early on, the *Courant*'s new executives and the reporters they assigned to the story largely cast their lot with the state police. Editors blocked many suggestions by reporters who admired McGuigan, and kept the story mainly in the hands of two who disliked him. They relentlessly pursued inconsistencies in his statements with front-page stories. Meanwhile, serious allegations against the state police faded away. "I thought the stories were very heavily weighted to make McGuigan look bad," editorial writer James Napoli would concede later. "I thought the news coverage was very bad and the editorial coverage, in retrospect, was more vehement than it needed to be and didn't take the state police to task for many of the same things we branded McGuigan with—namely, manipulation for their own advancement." The two news reporters maintained that their stories simply reported the facts along with the opinions of responsible public figures. But some views never seemed to surface in print. One came from attorney Stephen Traub, who was president of the Connecticut Trial Lawyers Association and vice president of the Connecticut Bar Association. "The *Courant*'s coverage was vicious," Traub maintained, "positively vicious."

The investigation of McGuigan fascinated Davies. McGuigan had been a friend of Davies' predecessor, Mark Murphy. And while Davies also sought out the prosecutor early on in quasi-social encounters, McGuigan's cocky, self-assurance (demonstrated in his refusal to prosecute the bridge inspectors) did not find nearly such a receptive audience with the polished Davies as with the irreverent Murphy.

As chief state's attorney, McGuigan was in charge of criminal prosecutions. A separate official, the attorney general, controlled civil litigation. For months, it appeared from the *Courant* stories that McGuigan might have been covering up serious corruption, including that by the just-retired chief justice of Connecticut's

Supreme Court. (State police leaked information that they had initiated a gambling investigation of the retired chief justice, a longtime McGuigan supporter.) Davies, eager to nail McGuigan, distributed to his staff confidential state police documents undermining the prosecutor. Rick Hornung, editor of the weekly *Hartford Advocate*, recalled that Davies telelphoned during this crusade with a most unusual request: that Hornung let the rival *Courant* break his story that a judge critical of state police had had a romantic affair ten years previously with a secretary. The *Courant* editors were so keen on the allegation that one ordered a female reporter friendly with Hornung to worm the facts out of him so that the *Courant* could get the scoop. She protested the assignment vigorously, to no avail.

My own review of McGuigan's career for *Connecticut Magazine* convinced me that the newspaper had blown up the main issues vastly out of proportion. The gambling accusation against the retired chief justice is a good example. Despite all the police and a media fascination with it, not a single witness ever testified that the justice knew about (much less participated in) gambling at a country club where he co-owned the land. Missing from the paper's analysis was a vital historical perpective. McGuigan had long irritated Connecticut's entrenched Democratic machine by publicizing political corruption and other white-collar crime involving influential figures. State police, until their turf was threatened, had rarely ventured into that explosive realm.

Although other newspapers besides the *Courant* were attacking McGuigan editorially, the prosecutor regarded the *Courant*'s opposition as decisive. "It made it easy," he said, "for political people to come out of the woodwork and say, 'Let's do it. [Oust him from office.] We can actually pull it off.'" Gov. William O'Neill, who had seen two of his aides convicted by McGuigan, was only too happy to topple the loose cannon overboard. The governor's commission picked a new chief prosecutor who promised to let state police set the investigative agenda.

A great deal of the *Courant*'s enterprise activity in early 1985 was devoted to keeping the controversies alive. Shortly after publication, the major stories were reproduced in an expensive process that created clear-cut copies suitable for contest entries. Yet by the end of the campaign, it was obvious that there had been no scandal involving McGuigan to justify a prize for the paper's news coverage. "Austin McGuigan was the best prosecutor I encountered in Connecticut in my ten years in the state," commented *Boston Globe* Business Editor Lincoln Millstein, who had held the same title at the *Courant* before his 1983 resignation. "The politicians in Connecticut finally have what they want in the justice system. And what saddens me most is that my old newspaper helped them."

In another major editorial campaign, the paper sought to focus public attention on the need to "reform" civil liability laws in Connecticut and the nation. The purpose was, ostensibly, to help the public by assisting insurance companies and manufacturers in holding down costs. More than a hundred locally produced news stories in the *Courant* helped the insurance industry keep the topic at the forefront of the public agenda. In several of his Sunday columns, Davies argued for severe cutbacks in the American jury system on the grounds that it was awarding too much money to victims of accidents. In one column headlined "CONNECTICUT CAN BECOME A NATIONAL LEADER IN CIVIL JUSTICE REFORM," he suggested such radical changes as: 1) abolition of the contingency fee system; 2) disbarment of lawyers if they file as many as two "frivolous" lawsuits; and 3) forcing the losing party in a case to pay the victor's legal costs. He even floated the idea that losing plaintiffs routinely sue their lawyers for negligence.

To be sure, there were aspects of liability laws that unfairly penalized insurers and other corporate defendants. But Davies' recommendations went far beyond redressing them. His suggestions would sharply tip the justice scales in favor of hazard-creators and against victims. Take the proposed change in lawyer payment plans. In the contingency fee system, plaintiffs' attorneys get their payment only by sharing in a victory, not by charging on a pay-as-you-go basis. After the Mianus River Bridge collapse truck driver David Pace and his wife were suffering from broken backs. His parents, who were essentially supporting them during recovery, each had cancer. Suppose the family had to pay, up front, the $60 or even $100 an hour an attorney might charge to litigate for years against the state of Connecticut and Aetna, its insurer, for compensation on the I-95 bridge collapse? The Pace couple would begin knowing it had a powerful moral claim to damages—but that its lawsuit was risky because technicalities and precedents were against it. Would it undertake the effort knowing that if it lost it would have to pay not only its own legal costs, but whatever bills the insurers' attorneys (certainly in excess of $100 an hour) were running up? What incentive would defendants have not to engage in stalling tactics to starve out plaintiffs ill-prepared for long court battles?

As it happened, the victims of the bridge collapse ultimately won substantial out-of-court settlements. Connecticut Attorney Gen. Joseph Lieberman, who had been troubled all along by the implications of the state's court fight against the victims, commented that the belated publicity about the Paces' plight assisted the family greatly in obtaining a proper amount of money from the state and its insurer.

Encouraged by the *Courant* and bulldozed by Connecticut's powerful insurance lobby, the state legislature created a "tort reform" package that was among the most favorable in the country towards insurance companies. Their profits jumped to record highs, aided by dramatic price increases camouflaged by the public relations campaign castigating greedy lawyers and victims.

The price a community can pay for headstrong news crusades became apparent in another way. Managing Editor Marty Petty deployed ten reporters in a month-long attack on what she believed to be thievery by Hartford housing officials and consultants. Only one feature story resulted, however, and it simply warmed over larceny charges against one unscrupulous developer that the paper had routinely reported the previous spring. But the high-pressure tactics prompted one observer to speak out.

"The technique was The Big Lie and make it come true,"

charged Arthur Anderson, who had a contract from the city to administer its low-income housing program. Though not a target of the paper's investigation, he witnessed its massive scope at first with mystification, then anger. "People in the quasi-public sector tend to believe reporters are usually objective and pretty accurate in their facts," Anderson told me. "When they're fishing, you know. But when they come up and say, 'Let me tell you, this guy and this guy are going to get arrested with four other guys'—you say that to seven or eight people around a town this size and it ruins a lot of reputations. By the second or third week it was very clear it was nothing more than Petty getting bad information and pushing reporters to go out and get more information about some big conspiracy. It's very simple: it hasn't gone on. I called up Agent Double-O-Seven [Anderson's nickname for Metro Editor Roger Moore] and said, 'Listen, buddy. I'm sick of your reporters. I'm sick of your innuendo.' "

Newspaper targets and their friends often complain, of course. One thing made Anderson's objections noteworthy, in my mind. When I talked with five of the experienced reporters assigned to the investigation all said that they, too, believed that the paper's editors had recklessly initiated and pursued it. The reporters were just following orders. McGuigan, after doublechecking with a subordinate prosecutor, also told me privately that nothing substantial turned up in the probe.

"I don't think I'm unusual," said Anderson, describing the newspaper's diminishing stature in his eyes. "The *Hartford Courant* used to be a topic of discussion. I haven't felt that way for two or three years. It used to be fun to poke fun at it, or worry about it. I think everyone used to feel ownership of the *Courant*.

"I think the issue is whether a reporter has grown up in town," he said, mentioning a number of those whom he had watched progress through the years. "Tons of them. They don't come in trying to prove anything, but come in doing obituaries and town news, and learning and learning, as opposed to coming in and having a significant post and asking questions of people—just banal, stupid questions.

"An awful lot of people, and I am too, are afraid of the power that paper has," Anderson continued. "They can kill you, whether they print anything or not. I always felt I could talk with a reporter and ask, 'What the hell is going on?' When you talk to reporters now, they say, 'I don't know. These f ______ people are doing this.' And so it's time to say, 'Goodnight,' close up shop and say, 'To hell with 'em.' "

CHAPTER 18

Conclusion

"The very purpose of most journalistic organizations: Not presenting the truth, but presenting the appearance of the truth. Now, often the best way to create the appearance of the truth is to report the facts accurately. But where there is any conflict, [truthfulness] has to give because it's not the primary purpose."
—speech by author Edward Jay Epstein

MICHAEL DAVIES AND TIMES MIRROR went on to create impressive reputations as proponents of honesty in journalism. The *Courant* chief was installed on the Credibility Committee of the American Society of Newspaper Editors. Much more prominent was his work as president of the national association for AP members, the Associated Press Managing Editors Association. "Readers and Journalists: Bridging the Credibility Gap" was a major report released at its annual convention in San Francisco. In a press conference, Davies called also for a Times Mirror-sponsored forum by news organizations to improve coverage of terrorism. Davies played a key liaison role between his chain and Columbia University in providing $300,000 to the Graduate School of Journalism for four, hour-long panel discussions on ethics that were broadcast nationwide on public television in 1987. He himself was one of the panelists along with such figures as CIA Director William Casey and FBI Director William Webster. But when Connecticut Public Television aired the last three segments at 11 p.m. instead of the 10 p.m., prime time slot he favored, Davies mounted a secret campaign of retaliation. He forbade staff appearances on the statewide educational network. And he wanted to end the Hartford Courant Foundation's charitable sponsorship of the McNeil-Lehrer NewsHour's Connecticut broadcasts.

During this period, *Courant*'s parent firm undertook a massive advertising campaign in its newspapers and in national magazines entitled "The People & the Press." The promotional series disclosed the findings of the firm's specially commissioned Gallup Poll on popular attitudes. "There is no credibility crisis for the nation's media," the chain's experts said. "If credibility is defined as believability, then credibility is, in fact, one of the media's strongest suits."

At this same time, Times Mirror's Hartford executives were living with a guilty secret. Their private poll revealed a marked increase in the number of readers who found the paper unfair. Nine out of ten readers polled in 1981 believed the *Courant* reported the news fairly. That figure had declined to two out of three by the fall of 1985. In response, the paper's executives beefed up the public relations staff and reinvigorated the campaign to create an image of openness.

With Davies' appointees controlling the region's dominant news organization as tightly as they did, few readers were in a position to learn its secrets, much less make a meaningful objection. A former Kansas City reporter, speaking privately, described Petty's value to Davies primarily in terms of her loyalty: "Why did Petty rise at the *Kansas City Star?* Simply because she never stabbed him in the back and always told him, 'You're right.' He wants 'Yes' people around him. And someone who's totally honest with Davies will never get anywhere. He has fifty people jumping to get something done. They're all afraid their careers will be ended if it isn't. And if his instincts are basically correct, he comes out with either a good piece or a good design change or some good moves in personnel."

That's fine if all these initiatives are wise. But what if they're not? "I could fill up the Civic Center with people who hate Mike Davies," claimed Hartford attorney Steven Seligman, speaking off-the-cuff and doubtless with exaggeration. Nonetheless, the lawyer's statement is noteworthy because his only involvement with the *Courant*'s publisher was reading Davies' Sunday column.

After these op-ed columns failed to win a Pulitzer in 1985, Petty submitted a new batch with another fulsome letter of nomination. "This past year," she wrote the judges after she studied the paper's poll of 1,400 readers, "his column has delved more deeply into the process of deciding what is news and how to handle it. His frank and honest treatment of a number of issues provoked readers and reporters and made the column one of the best-read features in the paper."

In fact, the poll showed that Davies scored close to the lowest readership of any of the *Courant*'s staff columnists.

What of the former executives who preceded him?

Former Executive Editor and Vice President Dick Mooney (1976-81), who had been summarily replaced after overseeing the paper's news and editorial operations, returned to the *New York Times* as a member of its editorial board. He wrote me several encouraging notes. One said that even the classic insider's account of the news business, *The Kingdom and the Power* by former *Times* reporter Gay Talese, "was incomplete, woefully, because the bosses wouldn't talk with him." By that time, Mooney was the only news executive of his rank or higher who had not given me his views. He never provided his thoughts, doubtless out of reluctance to be mired in the past or to second guess his successors. But he did mention that the *Courant*'s transformation was significant enough so that he had once thought of writing a book about it.

Former Editor Mark Murphy (1981-83) endured a job hunt for many months after he walked out of the *Courant* upon Davies' arrival. Then the former *Los Angeles Times* metro editor became managing editor of KCBS-TV in Los Angeles. (The move, by coincidence, paralleled "Lou Grant's" shift on TV from a newspaper to a television newsroom.) He left the CBS-network station to become editor of the 48,000-circulation *Spartanburg Herald-Journal*, a newspaper located in the Piedmont region of South Carolina. Then Murphy abruptly resigned, reportedly after a dispute with the publisher on the best ways to change the paper. The downward-spiraling editor left no forwarding address.

Keith McGlade, Times Mirror's first *Courant* publisher (1980-84), helped create a Connecticut-based network of small newspapers providing business and other specialized news and advertising. Over breakfast, he reflected on his top management experiences in the two chains widely regarded as the best in the country, Times Mirror and Knight-Ridder. "If you look at their P and L's [profit and loss statements] they certainly look well run," he began. But he said newspapers at both chains had begun to suffer from excessive interference from corporate headquarters. "I had a headhunter talk to me, a search guy, and he said, 'You know, about the time you went to Times Mirror I thought it was the best managed media company. Now I think it's the most political.' That's sort of a universal feeling." McGlade spoke of the difficulties the Times Mirror was having in the "real world," places such as Dallas and Denver where the chain competed against locally owned papers. Times Mirror, acknowledging that it could not win its Dallas newspaper war, sold the *Times Herald* to a Texan.

"Obviously, I don't have a great, high regard for those folks," McGlade continued. "Frankly, I think Davies does much of his stuff, almost all of it, with [Vice President David] Laventhol's guidance. He talks to him a lot." McGlade's view of close cooperation between the two Times Mirror executives undercut a fond hope retained by many low-level *Courant* staffers: that things would get better if only Laventhol, with his *New York Herald Tribune* and *Washington Post* background, knew what the executives from Cap Cities' Kansas City papers were doing in Hartford.

Laventhol, in effect Davies' godfather within Times Mirror, received a promotion to the presidency of the chain. With this, he received the power to oversee all operations nationwide under Otis Chandler's cancer-stricken successor as chairman, Robert Erburu.

Davies installed a longtime crony, Michael Waller, in a newly created job: executive editor and vice president in charge of all *Courant* news and editorial operations. Waller had worked with

Davies fifteen years, first in Louisville and then in Kansas City. "This is really a terrific thing for the *Courant*," the paper quoted Petty as saying about Waller. Perhaps as consolation for not getting the job herself, she received a promotion, to vice president and deputy executive editor. Her college classmate Michael Jenner succeeded her as managing editor. That meant that six of the paper's top seven on-line editors for Connecticut news coverage were part of the University of Missouri and *Kansas City Star* management clique.

In keeping with Times Mirror's efforts to make it seem that everything was getting better for its Connecticut readers, the story announcing Jenner's appointment included an outright falsehood—that he would direct "a staff of more than 300 reporters and editors in Hartford and 10 in bureaus across Connecticut, in Boston and in Washington, D.C." That figure (never challenged by the ombudsman) inflated the size of the staff by at least forty-five, even using the newspaper's own official in-house tabulating system.

Of all our media, newspapers have the most important role in maintaining democratic and community values. Magazines reach an audience that is too fragmented. Television sweeps with too broad a brush and must be supplemented by the print medium. In addition, the corporatization process described in this book is even more advanced in television than in newspapers. The trend was aptly summarized in *TV Guide*, "Network News Today: Which Counts More—Journalism or Profits?" and in 1987 Congressional hearings.

The *Courant*'s handling of the workplace health series more than anything else demonstrated the real-life consequences of news judgments deferential to so-called sacred cows. Who, actually, was directly harmed when Davies led the businessmen's junket to the Olympics? The health series, on the other hand, would have broadly disseminated information not readily available in any other forum. It had the potential to prevent needless suffering and to tell unwitting victims about issues that could directly improve their lives. In fairness to Times Mirror, I should say that the frugal *Hartford Courant* of the 1970s never would have paid for research of that magnitude. However, I am absolutely confident the information would have been published if it had been in hand, even when local insurance companies owned part of the newspaper's stock.

There were voices in the community who believed the paper under Davies was better than ever before. After receiving special, flattering coverage under Davies, community activist Ned Coll repeatedly praised the new publisher. Businessman Millard Pryor, a *Courant* critic for years, concurred. "I really like the paper," said Pryor, "I like everything they do now. The publisher is a very smart guy. I run into him all over town selling that paper and what it stands for." Circulation continued to grow, rising from 215,000 to 223,000 daily copies in the eight years after 1979, with Sunday circulation gains even higher.

The newspaper undoubtedly became easier to read under Times Mirror. The layout, photography, graphics, the magazine, color reproduction, national sports coverage—all these were far superior to anything in the past. Overall, however, I could not help but feel that much of the newspaper's success was from image-building that verged on deceit. Take Pryor's assessment of the readers' representative. The ombudsman rarely criticized his superiors. Henry McNulty earned a reputation among many colleagues as a management toady. Yet Pryor had the impression, from afar, that the ombudsman courageously risked his career by watching over top management. "I'm not sure how I'd like a guy in my shop telling me and everybody what a lousy job I did." Pryor chuckled. "It must be a little hard on him. I don't know where Henry's going to go after this job."

A high batting average is not good enough for a newspaper, especially when the failures tend to be in the areas that make it most distinctive: its investigations, its editorials, its ethical judgments and what it publishes about itself. The hidden imperatives and taboo subjects that I discovered squeezed all pleasure out of work for me. And as I uncovered new scandals during this research, I began to feel, at age thirty-eight, like an Ancient Mariner burdened with a tale that had to be shared.

"The bottom line of it is that they have turned this into a dishonest newspaper," reporter Theodore Driscoll told me in his deep, resonant voice. In his mid-forties and earning some $40,000 a year, Driscoll had a lot to lose by expressing his opinions for the record about his newspaper. Yet he did so. "It's run by opportunists, career-minded people," he said. "They couldn't care less what the actual facts were in the Fazzano case or with the bridge inspectors, or anything else. They don't care. Their minds are elsewhere. That is 'the story.' And that's what people have to be concerned about."

The public already was concerned, though it generally had to make judgments without any inside information. Public confidence in the media (as measured by the annual Harris Surveys) declined significantly in the 1980s from levels of the early 1970s. By contrast, confidence in virtually every other institution had risen. The media have created many of their own problems by pretending to occupy high moral ground while pursuing commercial interests. The hypocrisy of it galls people. A shrill insistence on First Amendment "rights" in inappropriate situations has been a common scenario. It frightens me when I think that only since the 1960s have many of these free speech and free press privileges been firmly established. They could easily be removed in a judicial backlash sustained with popular support.

One such sign was the 1986 appointment to the Supreme Court of Antonin Scalia, described by the conservative *New York Times* columnist William Safire as "the worst enemy of free speech in America today." Another sign was the sex-life exposés in 1987 that destroyed the careers of politician Gary Hart and PTL Minister Jim Bakker. Especially among supporters of the targeted men, the stories were certain to foster lingering suspicion over the motives and tactics of big-time media. Ironically, such pressures were growing just as the nation was gearing up to celebrate the two hundredth anniversary of the creation of the Constitution, whose Bill of Rights protects the press.

Better self-policing is necessary to protect legitimate reporting from intrusive control by the courts in an escalating spiral of libel verdicts. A workable standard was articulated at a seminar by an editor of the *Washington Post*. "Imagine that you get caught, at the most sensitive part of the investigation," she told other writers and editors. "Can you explain it to a reasonable person? So they can say, 'Yeah, I can see that'?"

Most journalists I've encountered are well-intentioned people working under difficult conditions. But there are those who deserve much more scrutiny. Are they getting it? Spencer Klaw, the editor of the *Columbia Journalism Review*, insisted that the *Courant*'s experiences were not worth a story because it was just one paper, not much different than many others. And Pulitzer Administrator Robert Christopher told me that chain control ensures that the strengths and weaknesses of each newspaper become well-known throughout the profession. "Obviously," he said, "the top people at Knight-Ridder know down to a gnat's eyebrow what every one of their top editors have been doing." Yet the *Hartford Courant*'s trauma occurred with virtually no public disclosure. In fact, there was a chorus of outside acclaim.

Can I link every single recent abuse, without question, to the paper's form of ownership? Of course not, though I suggest that the pattern is persuasive. In its overall outline, the transformation fits the nationwide scenario described by such commentators as Ben Bagdikian, Berkeley's journalism school dean. The *Courant*'s upheavals were doubtless more dramatic than those at most other places, in part because many employees and subscribers cared deeply about the institution. Yet the changes were not unique. Accounts of newspaper sales in other cities have pointed to many of the same problems.

It's difficult if not impossible for a single independent researcher to a create satisfactory methodology for describing all of the country's varied news organizations. For better or worse, I have tried to unravel a complex situation by focusing on events in one region that I know intimately and where many people trusted me with sensitive information. The limitations of analysis by totally disinterested observers are apparent from the other writers who, from time to time, have reported upon the *Hartford Courant*'s transformation by Times Mirror. Usually, they have cited Ned Coll's turnaround and the bridge inspection awards as evidence that things worked out well for the new owners and for the community.

During the 1970s, former *Courant* President Edmund Downes predicted in general terms that a chain would have inherent problems in serving the public. Many of us at his paper did not know enough to believe him then. Times Mirror itself recognized from the Murphy regime that it could not rotate in executives who pursued their vision of journalism without sensitivity to the locale. As of the mid-1980s, the chain was learning a more pleasant lesson from the Davies stewardship: that adept public relations could hide vastly more serious shortcomings. Pacification. Profits. Prizes. It was an effective combination.

Reflecting persistent unhappiness with the monopoly in Hartford, a group of investors announced plans to raise funds for a new daily and Sunday newspaper to compete with the *Courant*. Yet the plan was totally impractical. In the long run, Times Mirror could afford to co-opt whatever editorial improvements a rival might make, then strangle it financially. What alternatives are feasible in such a situation? I have two simple recommendations.

The first is to encourage more investigative reporting about the media. The "Afghanistan Theory" must be eroded to create more accountability. Sydney Schanberg, the former *New York Times* columnist who found a new forum writing for *Newsday*, advocated such an innovation in the wake of Hart's downfall in 1987. "If we were to begin reporting on the press energetically, I think one thing could be predicted with certainty. People would read it," he wrote. "The problem is that, like all other large and powerful institutions, our newspapers and networks won't get off their backsides and move towards change unless they are compelled to—by, say, unpleasant publicity."

My second suggestion is that owners of newspapers—whether

they be chains or independent—should mix new managers with old hands who have self-confidence and genuine loyalty to their communities.

The *Courant* never had a proper blend during my years there. Downes and his editors cared about putting out an honest, traditional, journal of record. But profits, innovations and image are also important in the newspaper business. And because the old management was so ingrown, it did not incorporate improved techniques as well as it should have.

A newspaper is made up of many sections. Some became stronger under Times Mirror. Some weaker. "The sadness I have," concluded former *Courant* business writer David Wessel of the *Wall Street Journal*, "is how happy we all were that it was Times Mirror that was buying the *Courant*. I really believed the *Courant* had a lot of potential that it wasn't realizing, and the *L.A. Times* would help us."

"I guess I was wrong," he said slowly. "And that's a sad commentary on one of the giants of journalism in America."

Wessel had a solemn tone when he spoke. Who can blame him? Yet as I write these last words, I feel buoyant with the belief that improvements will occur because of my disclosures. As hopefully as the *Courant*'s first printer-editor and as shamelessly as any cub reporter, I believe in the power of the printed word—whether in a paper of record or, if all else fails, in my own record on paper.

NOTES AND SOURCES

This book is based on more than four hundred interviews. Additional background comes from two hundred others undertaken for magazine articles published from 1985 through 1987 on related topics. In a sense, however, I have been preparing the book ever since I began at the *Courant* in 1970.

My dual motivations, as a historian and as a whistleblower, pulled the manuscript in separate directions. To resolve the literary problem, I rigorously attributed sources like a historian, but kept the final manuscript contemporary by laying aside most of my research on the *Courant*'s early history and on other newspapers.

During the interviews, I tried to maintain a detached attitude so I could obtain the maximum amount of information, including the views of those who did not share my concerns. During the writing, I tried to move beyond my years of training as a reporter and put my own feelings on paper.

NOTES AND SOURCES

PREFACE

"A *Times* column,"... "Press Clips" by Geoffrey Stokes, *Village Voice*, Aug. 27, 1985. Lifetime security encouraged dull writing, Stokes went on to write. "But it has also meant freedom—and besides, no one has ever accused Schanberg of being dull."

The *Times'* metropolitan... "Cajun Flies and Westway" by Sydney Schanberg, *New York Times*, July 27, 1985. Besides Westway, the column also criticized the New York papers' front-page treatment of the difficulties of New Orleans chef Paul Prudhomme in opening a New York restaurant. "This is big news?" Schanberg asked.

The plan was to... Westway was ultimately blocked in the fall of 1985 by a federal court order and lack of support in Congress.

"Our newspapers, oddly... The *Times* had carried a number of news and opinion pieces about Westway through the years. Schanberg's criticism was over the degree of coverage. Through an aide, he commented to the author in 1987 that he believed the Westway column was not the sole reason for his demise, only "the final straw" after such things as his support of a colleague in litigation against the newspaper. Discussions of Schanberg's departure, including official comments from the *Times*, appeared in: *Columbia Journalism Review*, November/December 1985; *Washington Post*, Sept. 26, 1985; and *Editor & Publisher*, Aug. 24 and Oct. 5, 1985. Schanberg was offered a job on the *Times* magazine but unsuccessfully insisted on restoration of his column.

The newspaper's three-sentence... *New York Times*, Aug. 20, 1985.

When Schanberg finally... *Hartford Courant*, Sept. 27, 1985.

"Newspapers write about... *The Press* by A.J. Liebling (Pantheon) 1981, p.36.

"In 1971, fifty percent... Newspaper Advertising Bureau Vice President Charles Kinsolving, *Editor & Publisher*, Aug. 3, 1985.

His prediction seems... *The Buying and Selling of America's Newspapers* edited by Loren Ghiglione (Berg) 1984. From the editor's introduction, p. xi: "At the current rate, there will be no single, family-owned dailies by the year 2000. And, as groups buy groups, the American press of tomorrow may begin to look like the Canadian press of today—two groups, Thomson and Southam, control about half the nation's circulation, and ten groups control 80 percent."

It and Knight-Ridder... Interviews with Ben Bagdikian, Norman Isaacs, Jay Shaw and Keith McGlade, all in 1986.

The advertisements in... See Finding Number One, *The People & The Press*, Times Mirror, 1986. This handsome, eighty-page booklet was prepared with the assistance of Professor Michael Robinson of George Washington University and the American Enterprise Institute.

Press critic Ben... Speech to the American Society of Newspaper Editors, April 11, 1986. Bagdikian amplified three of his four points as follows:

> 1) Profit-squeezing. "In most chains, this pressure is greater than in most independent papers. Now in order to justify a lot of these

changes, some major speakers for the chains have enunciated the dogma that the public is not really interested in serious news and that what counts is graphics and so forth. And that's contrary to the best evidence [as developed by industry polls]... Chain papers carry twenty-three percent less local and national news than independent papers. I think the reason for that is that local news is more expensive than syndicated matter."

2) Conflicts of interest. "A survey of editors published in 1980 showed that a third of chain editors said they would not feel free to publish stories damaging to the interests of their paper's parent firm."

3) Too much concentrated power. "We distrust big government because of the inherent danger of stultifying bureaucracy, insensitivity and the arrogance of excessive power. We don't do that because we believe that all governmental leaders are crooks or incompetents or power-hungry demagogues... The same applies to large newspaper chains."

He boasted... *UnderCurrents* (an internal newsletter of the *Courant*), Dec. 6, 1985.

It boggles the mind... John Tarpey interview, 1984.

The transformation of... Maureen Croteau interview, 1985.

In *The Media Monopoly*... *The Media Monopoly* by Ben Bagdikian (Beacon) 1983.

Critics writing in the... *New York Times Book Review*, June 26, 1983; *Columbia Journalism Review*, May/June 1983. Andrew Hacker is the critic quoted from the *Times Book Review*.

I was one of the 106... The figure comes from a list maintained by *Courant* reporters Jon Sandberg, Howard Sherman, Leonard Bernstein, Paul Frisman, Susan Howard and John Hyland.

"Takeovers," argued Acting Antitrust... *Kansas City Star*, June 23, 1985.

In commenting on... George Seldes interviews, 1987. During the interviews in rural Vermont, Seldes was preparing for publication of his twenty-first book, *Witness to a Century* (Ballantine) 1987.

Finally, I thank the... I also appreciate the help of Investigative Reporters and Editors and the Freedom of Information Center (both located at the University of Missouri School of Journalism) and the Columbia University Graduate School of Journalism, especially its Pulitzer Prize staff.

DISASTER (Chapter 1)

In the early morning... Much of this account of the Pace family's ordeal is derived from my *Connecticut Magazine* article of January 1986, "After the Fall."

"Then I told her... These quotations are from a broadcast interview by Andrew Houlding of WTNH-TV in New Haven, who broke the story of the litigation impasse June 28, 1985.

It would be well... *Courant*, Oct. 8, 1985.

Probably, it was . . . Michael Davies' strong views are apparent in his columns: "When Money Makes Lawyers and the Courts Go Round, We All Pay," *Courant*, Feb. 9, 1986; "Connecticut Can Become a National Leader in Civil Justice Reform," *Courant*, March 30, 1986; and "The Strange Case of the Rogue Telephone and a $7.47 Million Jury Award," *Courant*, Feb. 15, 1987.

After one of the . . . *Courant*, June 24 to July 1, 1984.

John Reitemeyer . . . *Courant*, April 29, 1979.

"If you change a . . . *Wall Street Journal*, Oct. 11, 1985.

AMERICA'S OLDEST NEWSPAPER (Chapter 2)

"Was it not for the Prefs . . . *Courant*, Oct. 29, 1764.

Green published his . . . Part of this early history is derived from two earlier accounts of the paper: *Older Than the Nation* by John Bard McNulty (Pequot) 1964 and *One Hundred Years of Hartford's Courant* by J. Eugene Smith (Yale) 1949. Supreme Court spokeswoman Toni House and the eminent constitutional historian Leonard Levy of Claremont Graduate School confirmed my suspicions that *Hudson and Goodwin* was the first press freedom case to reach the high court. "Remember, though," Levy wrote me, "that the Justices of the Supreme Court rode circuit and presided over the Sedition Act trials (singly, with a district judge, not en banc)." Levy also emphasized that the specific question before the justices involved common law jurisdiction.

When a printer . . . *Encyclopedia of American History* edited by Richard B. Morris (Harper & Row) 1976, pp. 940-42. What is reputed to be the original press is on public display at the *Courant*.

As one of four . . . *Chronological Tables of American Newspapers* Compiled by Edward C. Lathen, (American Antiquarian Society) 1972, p. 9.

The paper boasted of . . . *Older Than the Nation*, p. 19.

The newspaper's success . . . Webster's first appearance in print was in a 1780 edition of the *Courant*. He provided a response to Benedict Arnold's explanatory essay on his wartime treason. Webster went on to become a lawyer; the architect of the nation's first copyright laws; a New York magazine and newspaper editor; and a dictionary, American history and medical encyclopedia author.

Until well into . . . *Isaac Asimov's Book of Facts*, (Bell) 1981, p. 310. Asimov describes it as "the best-seller of all American books," with "well over 100 million copies." (Presumably he's not counting the Bible on the best-seller list.)

Webster simplified the American . . . *Noah Webster* by John Morgan (Mason/Charter) 1975, p. 46.

"New England's speech . . . *Noah Webster*, p. 53.

The *Courant* told its . . . *Courant*, April 16, 1806. The story originally appeared in a New York newspaper, the *Utica Patriot*.

Jefferson's administration was . . . For a full account of the motives behind the prosecution, see *Politics and the Constitution in the History of the United States Vol. II*, by William Winslow Crosskey and William Jeffrey, Jr. (University of Chicago) 1953, pp. 766-784.

NOTES AND SOURCES

A Supreme Court . . . *United States v. Hudson & Goodwin*, 7 Cranch 32 (1812). One of the companion prosecutions was against Tapping Reeve, founder of America's first law school, the Litchfield Law School. For an account of that case, see 57 *Connecticut Bar Journal* 196.

The decision terminated . . . For a discussion of the American development of free expression rights until the World War II era, see *Political and Civil Rights in the United States*, edited by Norman Dorsen, Paul Bender and Burt Neuborne (Little, Brown) 1976, pp. 19 to 36.

Bit by bit, the Supreme . . . The Supreme Court gradually protected free speech and press freedom by interpreting the Bill of Rights in two ways:

> First, the court said that prosecutions for political opinion can occur only when the advocates pose an *imminent* danger to public peace. That interpretation first arose in dissenting Supreme Court opinions in *Schenck v. United States*, 249 U.S. 47 (1919) and *Whitney v. California*, 274 U.S. 357 (1927). It did not become the clear majority view until the 1969 decision, *Brandenburg v. Ohio*, 395 U.S. 444. Second, the court's famous libel decision *New York Times v. Sullivan*, 376 U.S. 254 (1964) drastically limited press liability for criticism of the performance of government officials.

Peter Parley, a best-selling . . . Peter Parley was the pen name for Samuel Goodrich (1793-1860) and several authors employed by him to write books for juveniles. The books sold about seven million copies from 1827-60. See *The Encyclopedia of American History*, p. 857.

A firm then known . . . Samuel Goodrich (Peter Parley), as cited in *Older Than the Nation*, p. 38.

For example, it defended the . . . *Courant*, Nov. 11, 1952.

When a local theater . . . Reitemeyer testimony before Connecticut's General Assembly. *Courant*, April 16, 1953.

Nonetheless, the paper . . . Richard Ahles and Robert Waters interviews, 1985 and 1986. Ahles, a former *Courant* reporter, was vice president for news at Connecticut's biggest broadcast news organization, WFSB-TV. Waters was the *Courant*'s former Washington correspondent.

"The Hartford papers . . . *Washington Expose* by Jack Anderson (Public Affairs) 1967, p. 38.

Neither of the paper's . . . The two were the late Washington correspondent Robert Byrne and Hartford political columnist Jack Zaiman.

"I believe," explained . . . *Courant*, July 15, 1979. The quotation is from Jack Zaiman's general remarks upon retirement.

"It's much harder . . . Ralph Nader interview, 1985.

But many of us . . . Richard Ahles interview, 1986. "Chains, in most instances, have to be more bottom-line oriented, They have to—how shall I put it?—homogenize the news business. I know that's something television stations are frequently accused of. But newspapers do it, too. A newspaper is the only news medium that can cover local communities adequately. In an hour and a half of news, we cannot cover every local meeting. Radio is becoming deregulated. So they're going to do less and less, too."

By late October 1970... *Courant*, Nov. 8, 1970 and Nov. 18, 1985.

"Pretty good" was... Ralph Nader interview, 1985.

Washington columnist Jack... *The Anderson Papers* by Jack Anderson with George Clifford (Ballantine) 1974, pp. 84-89. Anderson received vital assistance from his associate Brit Hume, who later became an ABC-TV newscaster.

The House found... *New York Times*, July 20, 1974.

"*The Hartford Times*... *Evaluating the Press*, edited by Loren Ghiglione (New England Daily Newspaper Survey) 1973, p. 52. Among the evaluators for the project were Ben Bagdikian, then of the *Columbia Journalism Review*, and Edwin Diamond, media critic of Post-Newsweek Stations of Washington, D.C.

The book described... *Evaluating the Press*, p. 45.

PLAYING MONOPOLY (Chapter 3)

During the 1970s, nationwide chains... These figures come from "Newspaper Groups," a 1982 study by the Rand Corp. for the U.S. Small Business Administration. Scale efficiences such as bulk purchases of paper, the study concluded, "are not empirically significant" in explaining chain expansion. Rand instead pointed to federal tax policies.

As part of this process... The initial approach by Times Mirror is documented in subsequent litigation before Connecticut's Department of Public Utility Control (DPUC). See Dec. 7, 1979, legal brief submitted by Consumer Counsel Barry Zitser in Docket No. 791003.

The paper had long... Some employees snapped up the shares. Photo Editor Phillip Acquaviva, for example, regularly invested under a company-sponsored loan program set up to encourage employee ownership. He started at the paper in 1936 at $15 dollars a week. At his retirement in 1975, he owned more than one percent of the company's stock. Phillip Acquaviva interview, 1985.

Other journalists and... Kenneth Hooker interview, 1984. Hooker, business editor of the *Courant* from 1976 to 1980, covered the paper's sale. He went to Boston to become editor of *New England Business*. His view is worth quotation at some length:

> It's fair to say that I wrote a number of things as [*Courant*] business editor which did not go down well with the Establishment. There was no significant effort to stop this. I can think of one instance when Dick Mooney thought a Sunday column I wrote was too strong, the language personally insulting. I can think of more instances when he came and accused me of pulling the punch: "Hey, let's get out and say it, there's a certain amount of rascality here."

Hooker's view is generally confirmed by others, including his former assistant, David Wessel, later of the *Wall Street Journal*.

"One of the weaknesses . . . Olcott Smith interview, 1985.

One of these was . . . Michael Sudarsky interview, 1985.

Pryor, an Ohioan . . . Millard Pryor interview, 1985.

Pryor found the paper . . . Millard Pryor interview, 1985. Pryor had superintended the growth of Lydall sales from $16 million in 1973 to $109 million in 1984. Accustomed to such financial success, he remembered thinking, "This paper was being run very, very, very badly."

The 1976 death . . . Kenneth Hooker interview, 1984.

"An hour after . . . Kenneth Hooker interview, 1984.

Among these, "Cap Cities" . . . Of all Fortune 500 companies in 1985, Capital Cities ranked thirty-third in its ten-year record for earnings-per-share growth. By contrast, the newspaper chain Gannett was eighty-ninth and Times Mirror was ninety-third. In net income as a percent of sales, Cap Cities ranked seventh of the 500 companies. *Fortune* April 29, 1985. See also, "Capital Cities' Capital Coup," *Fortune*, April 15, 1985.

To cooperate, the newspaper . . . The deceased editor was William Foote. Overall, some 32,000 out of outstanding 527,770 shares were sold on this closed market for the $33 price. Some 10,500 shares shortly afterwards went for $36 apiece. (Other stock had accumulated besides that from the Foote estate.) See *Prospectus* of the Hartford Courant Company, Aug. 23, 1978.

"Why are you willing . . . Michael Sudarsky interview, 1985. All his comments come from that interview.

Olcott Smith had a theory . . . Olcott Smith interview, 1985.

The seven directors . . . "Position Paper on the Proposal of Capital Cities Communications, Inc. to Acquire the Company," (1978).

Downes and his allies . . . The directors sought guidance from a non-binding poll of shareholders in October 1978. Some forty-two percent of the polled shareholders said the paper should be sold if its executives could negotiate a sufficiently attractive offer. To far-sighted industry analysts, this vote suggested that the *Courant* was, in effect, for sale.

In recommending sale . . . Edmund Downes letter to employees, July 10, 1979. "In the judgment of management, there is no newspaper company with which the *Courant* could be associated that has as much to offer the employees of the *Courant* and the community as does Times Mirror. They enjoy an excellent reputation for maintaining high standards of journalistic excellence, local editorial independence and enlightened employee relations."

TINSELTOWN AND TELEVISION (Chapter 4)

"Its power and reach . . . *The Powers That Be* by David Halberstam (Knopf) 1979, p. 94.

"Otis's first desire . . . *Thinking Big* by Irene Wolt and Robert Gottlieb, (Putnam) 1977, p. 325.

"The track record was uneven . . . Robert Gottlieb interview, 1985.

Even working in the . . . The lecturer was Stuart Robinowitz.

Later, I was startled . . . The classmate was Jacqueline Sharkey, a former *Washington Post* writer and editor. She went on to become a professor of journalism at the University of Arizona and win national awards for her investigative reporting in *Common Cause Magazine*.

In 1977, it spent . . . Jay Shaw interview, 1986. Shaw was Times Mirror's first publisher of the two papers.

In the 1977 decision . . . *Home Box Office, Inc. v. Federal Communications Commission*, 567 F.2d 9 (1977).

"Wright went crazy when . . . Stuart Robinowitz lecture, March 23, 1983. I audited all of Robinowitz's classes.

"I would say, in general . . . Ralph Swett testimony, July 6, 1978. Swett was later promoted to a Times Mirror vice presidency.

In explaining their rationale . . . DPUC decision, July 13, 1978.

Robert Erburu, president of . . . Robert Erburu testimony, Oct. 30, 1979.

"Advertising is the lifeblood . . . Barry Zitser interview, 1985.

In Times Mirror's testimony . . . Oct. 30, 1979, DPUC hearing.

"A parent company," the . . . March 7, 1980, decision by DPUC, p. 13. The sixteen-page decision is a concise summary of the issues of the litigation and the views of regulators.

Connecticut's Supreme Court . . . *Times Mirror Co. v. Division of Public Utility Control*, 192 Conn. 506 (1984). This was a unanimous decision written by Chief Justice Ellen Peters. It overturned an earlier decision favoring Times Mirror written by Superior Court Judge David Borden.

"Certainly, unsparing criticism . . . March 7, 1980, DPUC decision.

Yet the paper did . . . The newspaper did run two op-ed essays, "Should One Firm Own the Local Newspaper and Cable Franchise?" by Elliot Gerson and Michael Dorfsman, *Courant*, Feb. 19, 1984.

The secret negotiations . . . *Courant*, Dec. 8, 1979.

THE BEACH BOYS (Chapter 5)

Although he'd never . . . This apt description of Vetrano was coined in a column by John Lacy, *Courant*, July 24, 1981.

"My observation is . . . Phillip Acquaviva interview, 1985. He retired as photo editor a decade previously.

The paper's single . . . "What Really Happened to Miss Donaghue" by Joel Lang, *Northeast*, March 21 and 28, 1982, is a superb summary of the case until that time. My June 1985 article ("Power of Attorneys" in *Connecticut Magazine*) also covered the scandal, with a special focus on Connecticut's inadequate disciplinary procedures for lawyers. WFSB-TV reporter Les Coleman narrowly beat the *Courant* in breaking the story in 1981. But the newspaper stories following immediately afterward were much more extensive and had more impact.

One burly servant . . . Mark Stillman interview, 1986, confirmed in interviews with two other witnesses.

The *Courant* provided... *Courant*, Jan. 23, 1981.

It might have interested... "Ed Asner [star of "Lou Grant"] spent a month studying Mark Murphy's operation." Jay Shaw interview, 1986.

Three veterans at the... The three were Magazine Editor Joel Lang, Capitol Bureau Chief Robert Murphy and reporter Jon Sandberg, who became city hall bureau chief in mid-1981. Their quotations are from 1984 and 1985 interviews confirming accounts I had originally heard shortly after Mark Murphy's 1981 arrival.

His appointment as... *Thinking Big*, p. 457.

Because I had... I put out six issues of the magazine before the arrival of the new editor, then stayed on for four more months as an acting assistant editor.

"We want to put... "What Have They Done to My Newspaper?" by Dick Davies, *Connecticut Magazine*, October 1981. See also, the *West Hartford News*, March 19, 1981.

Barnes said the feedback... Dick Barnes interview, 1985.

THE FALL (Chapter 6)

In an interview with... *Washington Journalism Review*, April 1982.

He told one reporter... Carol Giacomo interview, 1985.

One time was in... "What Have They Done to My Newspaper?" by Dick Davies, *Connecticut Magazine*, October 1981.

Murphy and his... Keith McGlade interview, 1986.

"It was Murdoch journalism... Millard Pryor interview, 1985.

The story said... *Courant*, April 5, 1982.

Hartford's State's Attorney... John Bailey interview, 1985.

"The paper became... Theodore Driscoll interviews, 1985 and 1986.

"I was earning more... Joseph Fazzano made the remark to me in a courthouse corridor in 1977 or 1978. His reference was to his overall income at the turn of the decade, not to fees in the ITT case.

A front-page diagram... *Courant*, May 3, 1983.

"No search warrant... Bernard Sullivan press conference and printed statement, May 5, 1983, amplified in 1985 interview.

An Englehart cartoon... The cartoonist graciously allowed use of his illustration in this book. But that does not show agreement with this critique of the Fazzano news coverage. He continued to believe that police had proceeded in a bumbling, delayed-filled manner deferential to the police union attorney. As befits a deft caricaturist, Englehart values diversity of opinion. "If we dish it out," he said, speaking generally of the press, "we should be able to take it." Bob Englehart discussion with author, 1987.

"From the start... Managing Editor Reid MacCluggage, as quoted in "The Violent Death of Jeanette Ortiz" by Joel Lang and Robin Finn, *Northeast*, July 17, 1983.

"I was assigned to go... Theodore Driscoll interview, 1985. The other quotations are from Driscoll interviews.

He was told..."I just don't have any recollection of sitting on it [the story]," responded Dick Barnes in a 1987 interview. He added, "It sounds like something I'd say, that it didn't have a news peg. That's a concern I'd have, that it didn't just drop out of the ether." Concerning Driscoll's other claims, Barnes said, "I just can't get into this thing with Driscoll. It's a personnel matter. He and I have a long history."

Not because he . . . Fazzano ultimately was given a suspended sentence, but forbidden to practice law for four months. Instead, he had to donate his services full-time for charity during that period, and one day a week for fourteen months thereafter.

THE KANSAS CITY CHIEF (Chapter 7)

"I don't ever want . . . *Courant*, Aug. 30, 1983.

Murphy had been caught . . . This account was confirmed in 1985 correspondence with David Laventhol.

Looking back, Davies said . . . Michael Davies interview, 1985.

The changes that took place . . . David Laventhol interview, 1985.

When you assign . . . Laventhol's nursing coverage example apparently was hypothetical. *Courant* files revealed no such story published during the Murphy era.

The Davies family . . . Michael Davies interview, 1986. Much of the subsequent information in this biographical section comes from the same interview, *Who's Who* and applications for Pulitzer Prizes.

He impressed a visiting speaker . . . Norman Isaacs interview, 1986.

As it turns out . . . Richard Kirschten interview, 1984.

"He's a very bright guy . . . Robert Clark interview, 1985.

Davies walked into . . . This assessment came from, among others, former *Kansas City Star* Projects Editor Roger Moore in 1984.

. . . AND THE REST OF THE TRIBE (Chapter 8)

But finally, at one of . . . Michael Davies speech at staff meeting, May 1984.

In late August 1983 . . . *Northeast*, Aug. 28, 1983.

Kirkup's story twitting . . . *Northeast*, Sept. 11, 1983.

The closing of the . . . In confirming the account, the magazine editor emphasized that *Northeast* was essentially at the break-even point by 1987, "a rarity in the Sunday magazine field." Lary Bloom interview, 1987.

An advertising executive . . . The account that follows is from Joe Kirkup interviews in 1984 and 1987, with salient details confirmed by other sources. However, Editor Lary Bloom said he could not remember any protest from the paper's advertising director. He said the magazine would operate independent of such pressures anyway, though he conceded that "common sense" indicated the anti-trapping article would not go in the same issue as special fur advertising.

It ran the edited . . . *Northeast*, Oct. 30, 1983. In a 1987 interview, Bloom said he wanted Kirkup's piece softened and moved to inside pages because its quality was disappointing.

However, all but one . . . The top-level departures included: 1) Editor Mark Murphy; 2) Managing Editor Reid MacCluggage; 3) Assistant Managing Editors Don Thornton and 4) Steve Rice; 5) Metro Editor Dick Barnes; 6) News Editor John Keane; 7) Sports Editor Jim Smith; 8) Business Editor Tom Bush; and 9) Washington Bureau Chief Bill Stall. There were two other top supervisory editors: Assistant Managing Editor Denis Horgan and Assistant Managing Editor for Features Henry McNulty. Both gave up staff management but retained titles. Horgan, who had replaced his departed predecessor just three weeks before Davies' arrival, held his title of assistant managing editor for two and a half years, by far the longest tenure of the top Murphy news editors. But during that time he gradually lost a great deal of supervisory control. He did assumed the duties of "writing coach" and general trouble-shooter. He ultimately became a columnist. McNulty in early 1984 was named the paper's ombudsman and an associate editor. Another associate editor, Irving Kravsow, wrote a column and performed a variety of community relations functions.

She had, the publisher . . . Michael Davies speeches in staff meetings, 1984.

He conceded, however . . . Michael Davies interview, 1985.

Petty's undergraduate classmates . . . The school data was provided by the alumni office of the University of Missouri.

"Missouri is a good school . . . Michael Davies interview, 1986.

The situation created . . . "Reporters and correspondents" held about 51,000 jobs in 1982. Source: *Occupational Outlook Handbook*, 1984-85 edition, U.S. Department of Labor, p. 157. Because the distinction between reporters and broadcasters in radio is somewhat vague, another useful statistic comes from the *U.S. Handbook of Labor Statistic*, which is another Labor Department publication. Its 1985 edition (p. 50) cited 204,000 jobs as editors and reporters (including those in magazines and publishing) and 157,000 public relations workers.

One former reporter . . . Linda Howell interview, 1985.

The front page news story . . . *Courant*, March 17, 1984.

That same week . . . The author heard of the incident at the time and later confirmed the janitor's recollections in a telephone inquiry to him.

On a staff of just . . . The figure comes from a list maintained by reporters at the paper.

"They keep coming . . . David Laventhol interview, 1985.

"Davies is basically . . . Keith McGlade interview, 1986.

PR AND PACIFICATION (Chapter 9)

"The complaints were . . . Pulitzer Prize application by Marty Petty, Jan. 31, 1985.

Davies also began . . . *Courant*, Feb. 16, 1986.

Maintaining that his . . . Henry McNulty interview, 1985.

He thereby attracted . . . William Cockerham and Barbara French interviews, 1984 and 1985.

James Napoli, the paper's . . . James Napoli interview, 1985.

Returning from the meeting . . . Jack Kadden interview, 1984, confirmed by another source.

The assignment was . . . The reporter was Deborah Pinckney, an intern who had a master's degree from the University of Chicago and who had several years experience teaching school.

"Not having daily competition . . . *Courant*, June 24, 1984.

"One of the priorities . . . *UnderCurrents*, July 19, 1985. For an example of how the strategy worked, see *Editor & Publisher*, April 19, 1986.

"Any time the . . . Richard Ahles interview, 1985.

A major turning point . . . *Courant*, May 6, 1984.

"The Davies column . . . John Tarpey interview, 1984.

In his column . . . *Courant*, May 20, 1984.

Dissenting from Davies . . . David Wessel interview, 1984.

In late 1984, Davies . . . John Filer interview, 1984. Gerald Demeusy interviews, 1985 and 1986. A former *Courant* reporter, Demeusy was a friend of Filer's who assisted in the negotiations.

As an inducement . . . In a 1987 interview with the author, Bloom vigorously denied that Filer had been given any special treatment. Bloom urged the author to seek corroboration from Demeusy. But Demeusy then recalled Bloom as telling Filer, "Don't worry about it. The way you write it is the way it's going to appear." Demeusy added, "I'd tell him [Bloom] that to his face because I was there when he said it."

There was considerable . . . While much of the speculation was just word of mouth, a *New England Business* story entitled "Aetna Is Rethinking Its Diversification Binge" appeared the week before Filer's resignation.

In his magazine story . . . "Hartford Reflections" by John Filer, *Northeast*, March 17, 1985.

New England Monthly . . . "Secrets: The Hidden World of Harry Gray" by Jonathan Harr, *New England Monthly*, October 1985.

To publish a blistering . . . *Courant*, *Business Weekly*, Sept. 23, 1985.

"I have the subconscious . . . Robert Murphy interview in *Wall Street Journal*, Oct. 11, 1985. Other writers spoke privately to the author about similar feelings.

Among newspaper executives . . . "Doonesbury" also placed second in the category "least favorite" in the reader poll, which received 2,747 responses. *Courant*, March 24, 1985.

"THE DOONESBURY GANG . . . *Courant*, June 30, 1985.

"I consider it an enormous . . . *Courant*, Aug. 10, 1985.

"Whom are you protecting . . . *Courant*, June 23, 1985.

NOTES AND SOURCES

A MIRROR OF THE TIMES? (Chapter 10)

Even during the . . . The subsequent section is largely based on 1984 interviews with Jack Kadden. Moore never followed through on seeking AP or UPI help. In a 1987 interview, he stressed his support of strong local coverage.

Davies told his . . . Michael Davies staff meeting, 1984.

"I don't think . . . David Laventhol interview, 1985.

Yet his boss . . . Otis Chandler interview with KABC-TV in Los Angeles Oct. 18 to 29, 1979, as quoted in *The Media Monopoly* by Ben Bagdikian, p. 118. Chandler made a similar comment to the *Washington Post*, July 24, 1977, as quoted in *The Media Monopoly*, p. 118. See also, "Learning Cashbox Journalism" by Ron Dorfman, *Quill*, July/August 1986.

One married editor . . . Interviews with confidential newsroom sources, included the two women quoted, 1984-87.

They had only their . . . Interviews with William Cockerham, Theodore Driscoll, Ann Garvin, Vivian Martin, Miriam Silver, and numerous others. Silver had been a confidante of an editor with considerable influence over hiring and assignments.

Another thing was . . . *Ronald Winter v. Hartford Courant* Workers' Compensation Case No. E-3397, First District of Connecticut. The newspaper went on record as opposing the reporter's claims.

But according to . . . Interviews with sources. In an interview, the editor denied any improper conduct, or knowledge of Winter's settlement.

In mid-1987, the State . . . Lena Ferguson interview, 1987. She was spokeswoman for the state commission.

By publicizing her . . . *Courant*, July 12, 1986. WFSB-TV reported Apple's case the day of filing, July 6.

With considerable fanfare . . . "Revised Ethics Code Sets Rules on Gifts, Conflicts, Nepotism" by Michael Davies, *Courant*, Aug. 3, 1986.

Indeed, he helped preside . . . The *Courant* never published a story on the rival newspaper, though it did investigate the matter. For a discussion of the probe of the judge, see Chapter 17.

Yet his own . . . William Cox interview, 1987, supported by other sources.

The name developed . . . For an enlightening discussion of whether character issues should be reported, see "Kennedy's Woman Problem/Women's Kennedy Problem" by Suzannah Lessard, *Washington Monthly*, December 1979. The *New Republic* originally commissioned the piece. But the magazine's owner forbade publication. Editor Michael Kinsley resigned over the decision, then returned. His memorable account, "Yes, We Have No Bananas," appeared in the magazine Nov. 24, 1979.

In his Sunday column . . . "A Sloppy Story Rushed Into Print" by Michael Davies, *Courant*, May 10, 1987.

Davies' 1986 lawsuit . . . *Michael J. Davies v. Carol M. Davies*, Hartford Superior Court, No. 0317841S.

One day early . . . William Cockerham interviews, 1985.

He ambled over . . . Cockerham's account was confirmed by another reporter who asked for anonymity. Carole Rich, deputy metro editor, also confirmed the account, except that she remembered the cluster of journalists as being only three or four.

"I don't want ever want . . . *UnderCurrents*, Dec. 6, 1985.

THE SPIKE (Chapter 11)

We also had . . . Insurers' $7.1 billion in profits on workers' compensation (after dividends to stockholders) from 1978 through 1983 were tailing off sharply in the early 1980s. See *Best's Insurance Management Reports*, Oct. 24, 1983.

Albert was intrigued . . . One area of vigorous debate concerned the relative performances of private and state-operated funds. See "Comparing Comp Systems" by Barry Martin, *Business Insurance*, Jan. 18, 1982.

"There's virtually no . . . Peter Barth interview, 1983.

When Murphy encouraged . . . The squad's document researcher, Leah Segal, conducted a systematic library search for previous investigations in this field, but she found nothing so comprehensive. The closest things were newspaper probes of: carcinogens by the *Bergen* (N.J.) *Record* in 1976; farming health hazards by the *Des Moines Tribune* in 1979; brown lung disease by the *Charlotte Observer* in 1980; and the workers' disability system by the *Boston Globe* in 1981.

Year after year . . . See U.S. Dept. of Labor, Annual Evaluation Reports, Conn.-OSHA Plan, 1979-83.

Despite the extra premium . . . The discussion of the silicosis cases is primarily based on reporting by Larry Williams and Claude Albert. I reviewed the legal records and the transcripts of interviews with claimants.

Cancer cases averaged . . . *Workers' Compensation and Work-Related Illnesses and Diseases* by Peter Barth with Allan Hunt (MIT) 1982 (paperbound), p. 145, "Average cost per compensated case closed, New York, 1973." The average award almost certainly increased since the time since the study. Still, no one had bothered to conduct a more recent one despite the importance of the topic.

An insider's opinion . . . Edward Bernacki interview, 1983.

Adding support to this . . . Arnold Rilance interview by Larry Williams, 1983.

John Antonakes, Liberty . . . John Antonakes interview, 1983.

Charles Bergin of . . . Charles Bergin interview, 1983.

"When you don't . . . Albert Henderson interview, 1983.

Late Sunday, May 6 . . . *Courant*, May 7, 1984.

I resigned in July . . . I broke the sexual harassment story in "Secrets from His Honor's Chambers" in the *Hartford Advocate* (Nov. 21, 1984) and amplified the disclosures in "Dishonorable Intentions," *Connecticut Magazine* (April 1985). The judge resigned his lifetime appointment April 30, 1985.

All five stories . . . The stories were published as follows:

In *Occupational Health and Safety News:*

"Funding of Occupational Ignites Controversy in Connecticut" (December 1984);

"Future of Health Hazard Litigation Calls for Fair Levels of Compensation" (October 1985);

"Missing Persons" (June 1986);

In the *Hartford Advocate:*

"UTC Goes Shopping for a Clinic" (March 20, 1985)

In *Connecticut Magazine:*

"Burden of Proof" (May 1985)

Additionally, research for the *Courant* project was the basis for "UTC Medical Director Says Doctors Need More OH Training," *Occupational Health & Safety News* (January 1986), and "A Doctor's Job," *Hartford Advocate* (April 3, 1985). Also, it laid groundwork for *Connecticut Magazine* articles (June 1986) on problems with civil liability and insurance systems, "Nuts, We Ain't Payin'," as well as my year-long assignment as the Bureau of National Affairs special correspondent for Connecticut.

"You probably don't... Larry Williams interview, 1985.

"Thirty or forty years... Ben Bagdikian interview, 1986.

"There you had... Michael Davies interview (taped), 1985.

Hallmark had 19,000... *Dun's Business Rankings* (1986), p. 486. *Dun*'s listed 19,000 Hallmark employees nationwide, including 5,500 at the firm's Kansas City, Mo. headquarters.

Connecticut-based insurance... Joseph Martin interview, 1986. Martin was spokesman for the Insurance Association of Connecticut.

They were gearing up... " 'Nuts, We Ain't Paying" by Andrew Kreig, *Connecticut Magazine*, June 1986.

He liked to say... Keith McGlade interview, 1986; Bob Davis interview, 1986. Davis was a *Wall Street Journal* reporter.

A *Wall Street Journal*... Bob Davis and Tom Condon interviews, 1986.

BUSINESS "REALITIES" (Chapter 12)

The company picked... The description of the format of the sessions comes from author's interviews with participants.

The results showed... 1985 interview with management source who saw the results but preferred to remain unidentified.

The results shocked... 1985 interview with a different source, who had a close working relationship with top executives.

"She's been a problem... The account of the meetings comes from several sources present, including former Sports Editor Al Simonds and writer Sherwood Anderson.

It quoted Metro Editor... *UnderCurrents*, April 5, 1985.

Executives today are... "Editors Who Become Publishers" by Andrew Radolf, *Editor & Publisher*, April 19, 1986.

One area of controversy... "Advertising in Disguise," *Consumer Reports*, March 1986.

Television and direct mail . . . Craig Standen, speaking on "Business Realities" at 1985 ASNE convention.

A full-page . . . The figures come from a semi-annual trade publication, *Standard Rate & Data Service.* It is published by a firm of that name located in Wilmette, Ill.

THE PUNDITS (Chapter 13)

Soon after his . . . Davies also allocated new space (usually two extra pages on Sundays) for opinion by creating a "Commentary" section that provided more space for community viewpoints.

Davies wrote a Sunday . . . *Courant*, Oct. 14, 1984.

These essays were . . . *Courant*, Oct. 28, 1984.

Davies used the . . . This particular ombudsman's memo was authored by a designated news reporter in Henry McNulty's absence.

The *Hartford Advocate . . . Hartford Advocate*, Nov. 7, 1984.

Davies attention deflected . . . *Face the State*, WFSB-TV Hartford, Nov. 24, 1985.

Disclosure of the . . . *Courant*, Nov. 4, 1984.

A Polman column . . . *Courant*, Jan. 21, 1984.

But when Davies . . . Dick Polman interview, 1984. The matter was confirmed by knowledgeable *Inquirer* executive who asked for anonymity.

Davies, for his part . . . Michael Davies interview, 1985.

Davies, for example . . . The anecdote was provided to me by a *Los Angeles Times* editor with first-hand involvement in the in-house investigation that cleared the editor, James Hill. Hill confirmed the story in a 1985 interview. "My feeling," he said, "was I had given truthful testimony. He [Davies] tends to make vendettas." Because I had already obtained details of the anecdote and confirmed them with Hill before he requested I not use it, I did not feel bound by his request.

When a reporter resigned . . . David Lesher interview, 1985; confirmed by other newsroom sources.

Condon made the best . . . See, for example, *Courant*, May 13, 1984.

Fire Me . . . . . And I'll Sue! A Manager's Survival Guide to Employee Rights (Alexander Hamilton Institute) 1984; "Procedures That Safeguard Your Right to Fire" by Thomas Condon and Richard Wolff, *Harvard Business Review*, November-December 1985.

Following the company-sponsored . . . Tom Condon interview, 1987.

"We've been looking . . . Tom Condon interviews, 1984 and 1985.

He took the job . . . Tom Condon, Al Simonds and Henry Scott interviews, 1986. Condon was read by 77 percent of readers responding in the poll, followed closely by humor writer Colin McEnroe's 76 percent.

But he believed . . . Tom Condon interviews, 1985, 1986 and 1987.

NOTES AND SOURCES

PRIZE HUNTING (Chapter 14)

"It's like money . . . Robert Christopher interview, 1986. All of his quotations here are from that interview.

He told me . . . William Cockerham interview, 1985.

"All of us march . . . "Marching to an Inner Drum," June 1977 speech to Investigative Reporters and Editors by Seymour Hersh.

Answers came from . . . Geoffrey Hazard interview, 1985.

First Amendment principles . . . *Groping for Ethics in Journalism* by Eugene Goodman (Iowa State) 1983, p. 24.

Before *Washington Post* . . . *Groping for Ethics in Journalism*, pp. 161-64.

After that, only . . . Robin Kuzen, Bud Kliment and Robert Christopher interviews, 1985 and 1986.

"I keep waiting . . . An excellent critique of the process was provided by David Shaw in a series published in the *Los Angeles Times*, Jan. 6 through Jan. 9, 1980. Also, he wrote "Due Process for the Pulitzer Prizes," *Washington Journalism Review*, June 1981. See also, "Proliferating Prizes" by Tom McNichol, *Washington Journalism Review*, July, 1986.

INSPECTING THE INSPECTORS (Chapter 15)

Shortly after he . . . James Napoli interview, 1985.

And we've seen . . . "SAFETY, CLEAN AIR TAKE BACK SEAT IN STATE AUTO TESTS," *Courant*, Aug. 18, 1985. This copyrighted exposé concerned flaws in the state's auto emissions testing program.

A reader was . . . Letter to the editor by James Carroll, *Courant*, July 4, 1984.

The bridge fell . . . I researched the *Courant*'s coverage of this early history for a piece entitled "After the Fall" for the January 1986 issue of *Connecticut Magazine*.

Authorities and the news . . . In 1986, a jury rejected Connecticut's $25 million negligence suit against the New York bridge designers. *Courant*, Aug. 15, 1986.

The story published . . . *Kansas City Star*, Jan. 30, 1983.

In December 1983 . . . *Kansas City Times*, Dec. 10, 1983.

Metro Editor Dick . . . Carol Giacomo interview, 1986. Her knowledge was based on Davies' remarks to her two years previous.

By then, the . . . The statistics come from correspondence between the state and interested parties. See letter Aug. 3, 1984 from DOT Commissioner William Burns to William Olds, executive director of the Connecticut Civil Liberties Union.

Bowman later said . . . Bowman several times talked with members of the paper's investigations team in my presence about the progress of the bridge probe.

"Hand radios were . . . "Watch and Report" by Craig Baggott, *IRE Journal*, spring 1985.

"If people'd spend . . . I witnessed the argument.

The day of publication . . . *Courant*, June 24, 1984.

In Kansas City . . . *Kansas City Star*, Jan. 30, 1983.

Yet Davies' role . . . Mark Stillman interview, 1986. Ron Gallagher interview, 1986. Gallagher could not recall a discussion of "Fraud" but said Davies wanted the headline bigger.

"The *Courant* refused . . . Michael Davies column, *Courant*, July 1, 1984.

"We have even . . . Michael Davies column, *Courant*, July 1, 1984.

"There is not . . . Press release by DOT Commissioner William Burns, July 18, 1984.

SWORN EVIDENCE (Chapter 16)

"As we anticipated . . . *Editor & Publisher*, July 28, 1984.

The account ran virtually . . . Interviews with confidential source, 1985.

McGuigan reasoned that . . . Austin McGuigan interview, 1985.

"We go after . . . Austin McGuigan and Dick Lehr interviews, 1985.

The grand jury . . . Grand jury report by Superior Court Judge Francis Hennessy, released March 7, 1985.

The *Courant* accused . . . *Courant*, March 10, 1985.

This finding of . . . The firing of the two divers was upheld in a labor arbitrator's report July 16, 1986. The arbitrator ruled that the divers had dived on two of the six disputed days. Connecticut OLR File Nos. 06-2878 and 06-2879.

"The *Courant* followed . . . Theodore Driscoll interview, 1985.

The newspaper never . . . March 1984 report to state by Engineers Fay, Spofford & Thorndike of Lexington, Mass.

Yet the paper . . . The *Courant*'s probe focused so narrowly on the predetermined theme that the reporters never described a sharp curve at the bridge that constituted a far more serious hazard than the possibility of collapse. Thirty-six traffic accidents there between 1980 and 1983 injured nine people and killed two others.

Icy water, rats and . . . Charles Banky testimony, Dec. 7, 1984.

Grand jury testimony . . . James Cavanaugh testimony, Aug. 29, 1984.

"I think we assumed . . . Mark Stillman interview, 1986.

They found essentially . . . William Burns press release March 7, 1985; Austin McGuigan interview, 1985.

"I remember giving . . . Russell Lucy testimony, Sept. 6, 1984.

"His report conclusively . . . Austin McGuigan interview, 1985.

Stillman: I had them . . . Mark Stillman testimony before state Department of Transportation inquiry board ("DOT Board," hereafter), June 28, 1984.

Bowman testified that . . . Christopher Bowman testimony before DOT Board, June 28, 1984.

The divers Jones . . . See, for instance, Charles Banky testimony, Dec. 7, 1984, pp. 75-77.

The newspaper assumed . . . This issue of whether "partial" inspections were occurring was never addressed either in the grand jury report or in the newspaper stories.

Instead, the editorial board . . . *Courant*, March 10, 1985.

"Mike resented me . . . Austin McGuigan interview, 1985.

"We gave it . . . I provided Klaw with some suggestions, but did not go into my suspicions at great length. At that time, I was not far enough along in my own research.

He had worked . . . "For me," said Christopher Bowman in a 1986 interview after he'd moved on to a much better job at the *Sacramento Bee*, "the *Courant* was like going to Heaven's Gate. And I felt that way until the day I left. They emphasized doing the big-picture story, writing well, perspective—the kind of things I felt I had the instinct and talent to do."

"Davies' column has . . . Marty Petty letter to Pulitzer Board, Jan. 30, 1985. A *Courant* reader study, however, showed that the publisher's column had one of the lowest readerships of any staff-written column in the paper, just fifty-one percent. Henry Scott interview, 1986.

"It was my lot . . . *Courant*, March 16, 1986.

Davies also gave . . . *UnderCurrents*, Dec. 6, 1985.

The publisher led . . . *Courant*, April 4, 1985; *UnderCurrents*, April 5, 1985.

A book published . . . *The Investigative Journalist's Morgue* Edited by Steve Weinberg and Jan Colbert (Investigative Reporters and Editors) 1985, pp. 19 and 92.

WHAT'S NEWS? (Chapter 17)

"While it is . . . *The Media Monopoly* by Ben Bagdikian, p. xvi.

Davies, for his part . . . Michael Davies interview, 1985.

Because of Hart's . . . Michael Davies column, *Courant*, May 10, 1987. The editorial board sounded similar themes in editorials May 8 and May 10, 1987.

"But its stories are . . . Daniel Schaefer interview, 1986.

"Stories are being written . . . Charles F.J. Morse remark to author, 1985. Many others made similar comments.

"Reporters took a car . . . Michael Davies letter, Jan. 27, 1986. All of Davies' quotations are from the letter.

The newspaper's massive, copyrighted . . . *Courant*, Aug. 18, 1985.

The experts essentially said . . . See, for example, *Courant*, Nov. 1, 1985.

As a reaction . . . See U.S. Environmental Protection Agency internal memorandum from investigator Richard Wilson to Air Management Division Director Louis Gitto, Oct. 30, 1985. "The results reinforce our earlier findings that the accuracy of the testing equipment in Connecticut is outstanding . . . ." See also Gitto's letter to Connecticut, Nov. 5, 1985: "Other states operating similar systems could look to Connecticut for an example of an excellent quality control program."

Four more reporters . . . An anonymous description of the second investigation was mailed to several Connecticut news organizations in late 1986. It was so detailed that it appeared to have been prepared by an insider. The author learned of the whistleblower's report in early 1987 and confirmed its details and interpretation with state and *Courant* sources. Former reporter Susan Howard, for example, said she believed that the second round of tests exonerated the state's testing system from the original claim of unreliability. Another reporter speaking on a not-for-attribution basis was extremely disturbed that some legislators had called for an end of all emissions testing because of the newspaper's stories.

Yet buried some . . . *Courant*, June 20, 1985.

"The governor demanded . . . Michael Davies letter, Jan. 22, 1986.

Indeed, the *Courant* . . . 1986 interviews with confidential sources in newsroom and on editorial board.

Chief State's Attorney . . . Most of the following account is drawn from the more than eighty interviews I conducted for my December 1985 *Connecticut Magazine* article, "The Undoing of Austin McGuigan."

"I thought the . . . James Napoli interview, 1985.

Rick Hornung, the . . . Rick Hornung interview, 1985.

The Hartford daily's . . . The reporter, who was godmother to Hornung's child, called the assignment "outrageous." Miriam Silver interview, 1987.

The paper typically . . . *Courant*, Feb. 16, 1986.

My own review . . . Another allegation against McGuigan was that he had delayed for many months in undertaking a thorough investigation of a semi-independent subordinate suspected (and ultimately convicted) of taking small-time bribes. No persuasive evidence of a McGuigan cover-up ever surfaced. Indeed, McGuigan initiated the grand jury probe. A judicial inquiry later found his conduct blameless. See opinion by Superior Court Judge Martin McKeever, Feb. 8, 1985.

"Austin McGuigan was . . . Lincoln Millstein interview, 1985.

In one column . . . *Courant*, March 30, 1986.

As it happened . . . Connecticut and its insurer settled the lawsuits by the six Mianus victims and their heirs for $7.7 million nearly three years after the bridge collapse. Aetna, the state's insurer, was liable for only the first million dollars, with the state paying the rest. *Courant*, May 17 and May 22, 1986.

Connecticut Attorney Gen. . . . Joseph Lieberman interview, 1986.

Only one feature . . . *Courant*, Sept. 6, 1984.

"The technique was . . . Arthur Anderson interview, 1984.

One thing made Anderson's . . . Tom Condon, Theodore Driscoll and Vivian Martin interviews, 1984, 1985 and 1986. Two other reporters concurred on a not-for-attribution basis. Neither Marty Petty nor Michael Jenner, her successor as managing editor, responded to written requests for interviews. Roger Moore was interviewed immediately after he gave a speech at the 1987 IRE national convention in Phoenix that praised investigative efforts at the *Courant*. He said he knew of no problems with its investigative stories. For example, he denied knowledge that a grand jury had followed up the bridge probe. Moore said that the second emissions story was not published because the state's complaints and "requirements" made a sound methodology impossible. At the time of the interview, Moore had left the *Courant* and was a finalist for an editing job at the parent *Los Angeles Times.*

CONCLUSION (Chapter 18)

"The very purpose . . . Edward Jay Epstein remark during panel discussion at Yale Law School, Oct. 25, 1986.

Davies played a key . . . For a full account of Davies' retaliation against the public television network, see "Power Play" by Andrew Kreig, *Connecticut Magazine*, June 1987. "Public TV is supposed to be in the quality game, not the ratings game," responded the publisher after his efforts were exposed. "We went way out of our way last year to cooperate with Public TV people in all sorts of ways. Since it's not reciprocated, then probably it's not something that's in our best interests." After publication of the article Davies withdrew cooperation from the book and threatened the author with a lawsuit if the book were not fair and accurate.

"There is no credibility . . . "The People and the Press," Times Mirror booklet, January 1986. While Times Mirror's Gallup survey did not find the public had a "believability" problem with the media, "Majorities think the press is excessively influenced by the 'establishment' and special interests."

Their scientific poll . . . Michael Davies commented on the poll in a 1986 interview. "It's one of the most positive surveys I've ever seen in my years in the business in terms of dramatic change in reader acceptance," Davies said. "In a sense, that was one stamp of validation on the efforts." Davies and Henry Scott declined to allow the author to read the survey. "They [executives] don't want it to get out," commented columnist Tom Condon in another 1986 interview, "because it upsets their whole theory of what they're doing." Yet Scott, apparently reading from the poll in a later interview, reported a variety of findings, including the statistics on readers' perceptions of unfair reporting.

A former Kansas City . . . Confidential source interview, 1986.

"I could fill up . . . Steven Seligman interview, 1986.

In fact, the poll . . . Henry Scott interview, 1986.

Times Mirror, acknowledging . . . *New York Times*, June 27, 1986.

"If you look at . . . Keith McGlade interview, 1986. Jay Shaw, Times Mirror's first publisher in Connecticut (at the Stamford and Greenwich newspapers from 1978 to 1983), concurred with Keith McGlade's assessments in a 1986 interview.

Laventhol, in effect . . . Erburu's 1976 operation to combat cancer was reputed to have been successful. *Wall Street Journal*, March 4, 1986.

"This is really . . . *Courant*, March 7, 1986.

In keeping with . . . *Courant*, May 22, 1986. The story said there were 311 reporters and editors, leaving the implication that there may have been even more. Yet Astrid Garcia, an attorney in the paper's Human Resources Department in charge of the count, gave a much lower figure. "I came up with 266 in the professional workforce," she said in an interview, adding that she had carefully hand-counted the May 29 total from written documents.

Of all our media . . . "The leadership of a vigorous paper is stronger than any other force in a community," said former *Boston Globe* editor Thomas Winship. "It can be a force for evil or for good, but always the strongest force." See "The 'Useful Agenda' of Thomas Winship" by Terry Fiedler, *New England Business*, May 18, 1987.

The trend was aptly . . . "Network News Today: Which Counts More—Journalism or Profits?" by John Weisman, *TV Guide*, Oct. 26, 1985. See also, "The Literary-Industrial Complex: How the Corporate Mentality Has Undermined the Profession of Publishing" by Ted Solotaroff, *New Republic*, June 8, 1987.

After receiving favorable . . . Ned Coll interview, 1984; *Wall Street Journal*, Oct. 11, 1985.

Businessman Millard Pryor . . . Millard Pryor interview, 1985.

"The bottom line . . . Theodore Driscoll interview, 1985.

One such sign . . . "El Nino's Current" by William Safire, *New York Times*, June 20, 1986.

Ironically, such pressures . . . The first ten Amendments were ratified in 1791, two years after the main part of the Constitution.

Better self-policing . . . An important libel case in the mid-1980s threatened legitimate investigative reporting. It involved a federal appeals court decision reinstating a two million dollar jury verdict against the *Washington Post* in a suit brought by the former president of the Mobil Oil Co. Judge Skelly Wright was in the 2-1 minority of *Tavoulareas v. Washington Post Co.*, 759 F.2nd 90 (1985). He wrote, "If this excessive jury verdict on these mundane, flimsy facts is upheld, the effect on freedom of expression will be incalculable. The message to the media will be unmistakeable—steer clear of unpleasant news stories and comments about interests like Mobil or pay the price." The full appeals court upheld the *Post*'s position in 1987.

"Imagine that you . . . Laura Stepp speech, IRE 1985 national convention in Chicago.

The editor of . . . Spencer Klaw discussion, 1985.

"If we were to . . . "In Covering Itself, Press Fails the Test" by Sydney Schanberg, *Baltimore Evening Sun*, May 28, 1987.

Accounts of newspapers . . . See, for example, "A Times Mirror Headache" by Alex Jones, *New York Times*, Feb. 19, 1984, "Invasion of the Gannettoids" by Philip Weiss, *New Republic*, Feb. 2, 1987, and *The Buying and Selling of America's Newspapers*, op. cit. A more general survey of such problems nationwide was provided by *The News at Any Cost: How Journalists Compromise Their Ethics to Shape the News* by Tom Goldstein (Simon & Schuster) 1986.

Reflecting persistent unhappiness . . . *Courant*, Oct. 25, 1985.

"The sadness I have . . . David Wessel interview, 1984.

Appendix

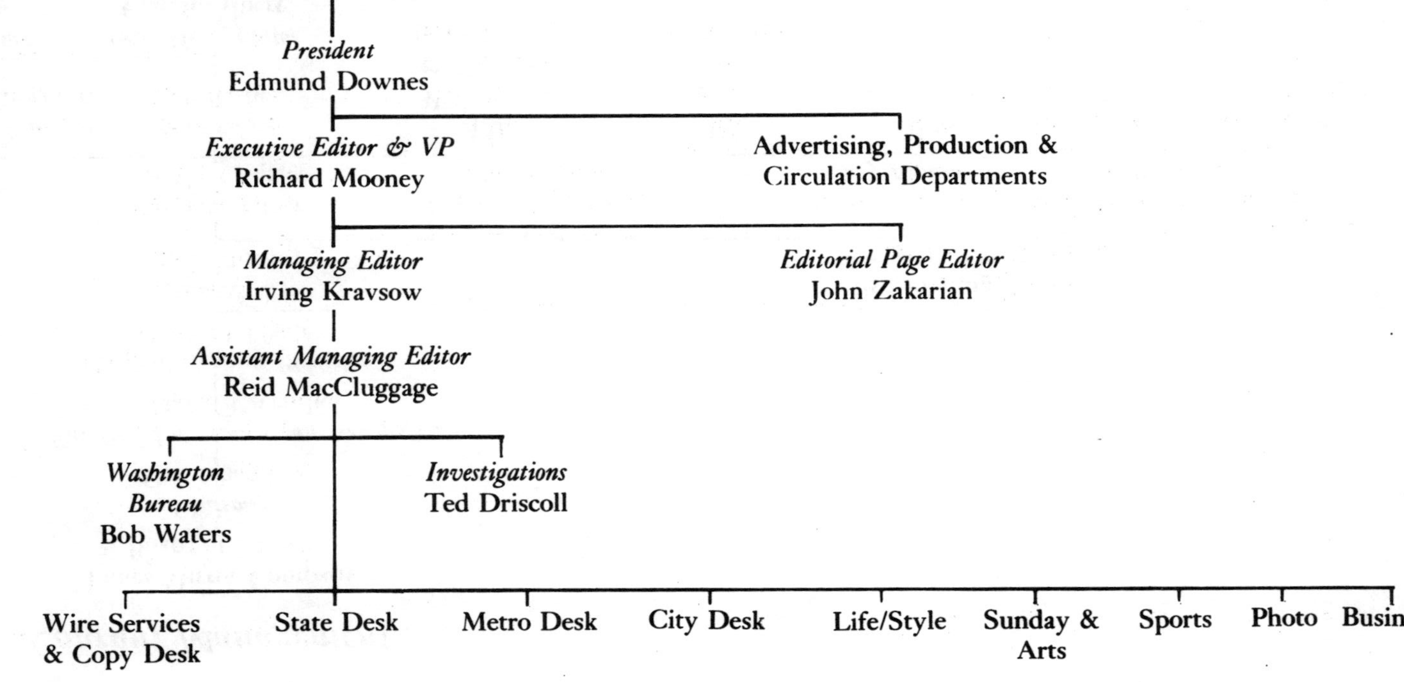
1979—Courant Management
Local stockholders (who had no voting control)
& Board of Directors
President
Edmund Downes
Executive Editor & VP
Richard Mooney
Advertising, Production &
Circulation Departments
Managing Editor
Irving Kravsow
Editorial Page Editor
John Zakarian
Assistant Managing Editor
Reid MacCluggage
Washington
Bureau
Bob Waters
Investigations
Ted Driscoll
Wire Services
& Copy Desk
State Desk
Metro Desk
City Desk
Life/Style
Sunday &
Arts
Sports
Photo
Business

1982—Courant Management

Times Mirror Company
& Board of Directors

Chairman
Otis Chandler

Vice President, East Coast Newspapers
David Laventhol

Hartford Courant Publisher
Keith McGlade

Editor & VP
Mark Murphy

Advertising, Production
& Circulation Departments

Managing Editor
Reid MacCluggage

Editorial Page Editor
John Zakarian

Magazine Editor
Lary Bloom

Associate Editor (columnist)
Irving Kravsow

AME National*
Don Thornton

Metro Editor
Dick Barnes

AME
Wire Services
& Copy Desk
Irene Driscoll

AME
Features
& Arts
Henry McNulty

Sports
Jim Smith

AME Photos
Steve Rice

Business Ed.
L. Millstein

Washington
Bureau
Bill Stall

Dep. Metro Editor
Claude Albert

Assistant Metro Editors

State — City — Sunday — Gen. Assignment & Courts — Politics — Specialities — Investigations

* Assistant Managing Editor (AME)

1986—Courant Management

Times Mirror Company
& Board of Directors

Chairman
Robert Erburu

President—designate
David Laventhol

Hartford Courant Publisher, Editor and CEO
Michael Davies*

Executive Editor & Vice President
Michael Waller*

Advertising, Production
& Circulation

Deputy Executive Editor & Vice President
Marty Petty*

Managing Editor
Michael Jenner*

Editorial Page Editor
John Zakarian

Magazine Editor
Lary Bloom

Assoc. Editor
(columnist)
Irving Kravsow

Assoc. Editor
(ombudsman)
Henry McNulty

Assistant Managing Editor (AME)
Roger Moore*

AME
Brian Meehan
(night supervisor)

AME
Randy Cox*
(photos and graphics)

National
J. MacDonald

Chief Deputy
Metro Editor
J. Stebbins*

Features
& Arts
S. Summers*

Sports
J. Pessah

Business
S. Woodward*

* University of Missouri and/or Kansas City *Star* background

THE KANSAS CITY STAR.

★ Sunday morning, January 30, 1983, Main Edition, 26 sections, including STAR magazine 75¢

Taxpayers lose as inspectors cheat

Buildings often unchecked; workers falsify records, loaf

By Richard M. Johnson and David Hayes
staff writers
© 1983, The Kansas City Star and Times

Many city inspectors responsible for ensuring the safety of buildings in Kansas City regularly lie about their working hours, loaf at home or in bars and restaurants when they are supposed to be on the job and steal tax money by falsifying work and mileage records, a two-month investigation shows.

The inspectors' dawdling and their falsifying of daily mileage and time sheets were documented during a surveillance and records check conducted by *The Kansas City Times* and *The Kansas City Star*, which lasted from late November to last week.

During the probe reporters observed 18 of the city's 46 code inspectors from the Public Works Department, including two key building inspectors who were assigned to the 43-story Hyatt Regency hotel during its construction as well as the primary inspector of the Vista International Hotel now under construction.

None of the inspectors followed was found to be honestly reporting the work he did. Instead, each was found to have falsified his work sheets to inflate the amount of time spent checking construction sites for compliance with city codes.

(The editor of *The Star* and *The Times* comments on the betrayal of the public's trust. Page 6F.)

Kansas City has been the site of two of the worst structural failures in the nation's history—the collapse of the Kemper Arena roof in 1979 and the collapse of the Hyatt sky walks in 1981. After the Hyatt tragedy, city officials announced a new effort to ensure safety in its buildings.

But the lies on reports and the sporadic work habits discovered during the recent investigation raise serious questions about that effort.

When the investigation concluded last week, reporters had on multiple occasions followed each of the city's eight general building inspectors—who check construction jobs ranging from the Vista, at 200 W. 12th St., to home remodeling jobs. The surveillance also included five other inspectors, who check new home construction, their supervisor and four other randomly selected inspectors whose responsibilities range from plumbing checks to elevator inspections.

The reporters found that all but one of the inspectors observed spent time in restaurants or bars, repaired their cars or simply went home when they were supposed to be working. The exception was an inspector who also falsified his time sheets but who could not be followed for an entire day.

Some of the inspectors also were observed running personal errands or strolling through stores at shopping malls. Also found was a city elevator ins-

See Inspectors, pg. 9A, col. 1

MELVIN W. BREGG, building inspector **Monday Jan. 10, 1983**

Mr. Bregg approaches his car after an hour and a half in Waid's Restaurant, 10:14 a.m.

Mr. Bregg prepares to leave the Vista International Hotel site, 1:07 p.m. He claimed 15 cents for parking but did not park near a meter.

Arriving home early for the day, Mr. Bregg backs down his driveway toward the garage, 1:35 p.m.

DAILY REPORT vs. ACTUAL ACTIVITIES

The following is a log of activities of Melvin W. Bregg, a building inspector assigned to major Downtown construction, from surveillance on Monday Jan. 10:

7:31 a.m.: Mr. Bregg arrived at work at the city inspection office, 3410 Troost Ave.

8:38 a.m.: Leaving the office, Mr. Bregg drove north and west to Waid's Restaurant, 3063 Southwest Boulevard.

8:46 a.m.: Mr. Bregg entered Waid's and sat in a booth.

9:05 a.m.: Lawrence L. Rieder, a building inspector, and Joel L. Eastwood, a supervisor, arrived and joined Mr. Bregg in a booth.

10:09 a.m.: Mr. Rieder and Mr. Eastwood left Waid's.

10:16 a.m.: Mr. Bregg drove out of the restaurant.

10:23 a.m.: Parking at One Pershing Square, Mr. Bregg went into the office building. He did not list an inspection at that location.

10:38 a.m.: Mr. Bregg came out and drove north.

10:46 a.m.: The inspector arrived at a service station at 10th Avenue and Burlington Street, North Kansas City, and made a purchase inside.

10:52 a.m.: He drove north to a service station at 12th Avenue and Burlington Street, where he bought gas.

10:56 a.m.: Mr. Bregg left and headed south to Downtown Kansas City.

11:08 a.m.: The inspector stopped at Howard Johnson's Downtown, 6th and Main Streets, where his log says he delivered city smoke detector sheets.

11:15 a.m.: Mr. Bregg left the motel.

11:19 a.m.: He arrived at the Mercantile Bank Garage, 1112 Grand Ave., and drove into the now-vacant parking structure, which is being renovated.

12:30 p.m.: Mr. Bregg left the garage.

12:35 p.m.: The inspector arrived at the Vista International Hotel, parked next to the contractor's trailer at 11th and Central Streets and walked in.

1:10 p.m.: Mr. Bregg drove away from the Vista site, out of Downtown and toward South Kansas City.

1:35 p.m.: The inspector arrived home at 9607 Holmes Rd., turned around and backed down his driveway into the garage.

NOTE: Mr. Bregg did not leave home between 1:35 p.m. and 4:00 p.m. He listed nine inspections at locations he did not visit during this workday.

Assigning reporters to spy on government inspectors was one of Michael Davies' favorite story ideas in Kansas City. On Jan. 30, 1983, this Sunday front page story presented the findings of a surveillance upon building inspectors.

The Hartford Courant

ESTABLISHED 1764, DAILY EDITION, VOL. CXLVII NO. 176 SUNDAY, JUNE 24, 1984—16 SECTIONS FINAL $1.00 PER COPY

Bridge Inspection: After Mianus

Fraud, Laxity Mar DOT Program

Probe Shows Wasted Time, False Records

· The Hartford Courant / 1984

This story was reported and written by Courant staff writers Christopher J. Bowman, Craig W. Baggott and Clifford Teutsch. Photography was by Tony Bacewicz.

One year after three people died in the Mianus River bridge collapse, Connecticut's revamped bridge inspection program is marred by falsified records, wasted time, inconsistent performance and poor supervision, a three-month investigation by The Courant has found.

Some inspectors faked underwater inspections, collecting double pay for dives they didn't make. Others — warned earlier this year to "put in your time on each bridge like lives depend on it" — sometimes spent as little as 15 minutes examining a bridge.

Following in inspectors' footsteps led reporters to story. Page B3.

The investigation revealed dramatic differences between how state officials say inspections should be done and how they actually are done despite a bridge safety budget that was expanded to about $1.7 million this year.

There is no direct evidence that the safety of Connecticut's bridges is being compromised. In fact, an engineer hired by The Courant to spot-check state bridge inspections found no significant omissions. But the wide range of performance found by The Courant raises serious questions about the reliability of a program designed to ensure safety.

The Courant investigation, which included 65 days' surveillance of inspectors, an examination of records and a series of interviews, revealed:

- Nineteen of the 54 bridge inspections observed by The Courant were done in less than 30 minutes, the minimum time expected by state Department of

See A System, Page A6

MONDAY: A year after the Mianus River bridge collapse, Connecticut taxpayers are about to start paying higher gas taxes and motor vehicle fees to finance a $5.5 billion transportation repair program. But the federal government and other states have done little but talk about their decaying roads and bridges.

Hartford Courant Photos / Copyright, 1984

Bridge inspectors Keith W. DeBishop, left, and Leonard J. Maloney pause atop a bridge on Winsted Road, Torrington, at 9:57 a.m. on May 1, 1984. (Numerals at bottom right indicate date and time of picture.) Picture at right shows the deterioration of the bridge supports. DeBishop and Maloney took 12 minutes to inspect this bridge.

Two Frogmen Find Treasure-Trove in Connecticut Coffers

To hear Stanley C. Jones tell it, his state underwater inspection team dives almost every day, checking bridges across the state for anything that might make them unsafe. State records show the same thing.

But the fact is the team doesn't do much work.

They are responsible for ensuring the underwater safety of about 300 bridges across Connecticut, including most of the longest, highest and most heavily traveled. But during 77 hours of surveillance Jones, the team leader, dived 11 minutes and his partner, Charles A. Banky, did not dive at all.

Although Jones, an ex-Navy diver, said in an interview June 13 there is no way his team can check underwater piers and foundations without diving, he and Banky filed inspection reports without diving and collected bonus pay as if they had.

Each man collected more than $420 in bonus pay after reporting on his biweekly time sheets that he had dived April 24, April 25, May 1, May 10, May 18 and June 4.

But The Courant watched them on those days, and they made no dives.

Under state law, someone collecting unearned pay could be charged with larceny.

"It must be a mistake," Jones said, when told of the Courant's findings Friday.

"I don't have any comment. I can't even recollect the situation," Banky said.

When a reporter said larceny might be involved, Jones interrupted and said, "We don't do that."

Then he said abruptly, "Why don't we terminate this interview."

The state awards bonus pay for

See Frogmen, Page A8

State underwater bridge inspectors Charles A. Banky, left, and Stanley C. Jones, right, stopped at this bridge over the Naugatuck River in Ansonia for 11 minutes on May 16. They didn't dive, but each collected double pay for that day as if he had, according to their time sheets. Jones' is shown at right. The photograph was taken at 12:32 p.m. as noted in the bottom right corner.

In Connecticut, Davies revived the "inspecting the inspectors" story idea in a series that began June 24, 1984. Yet there were major problems with it. For example, the newspaper showcased a deteriorated bridge in Torrington, Conn. The caption for the copyrighted photos on the front page said that inspectors "took 12 minutes to inspect this bridge." The newspaper did not mention that state-hired engineers had already analyzed the bridge's condition thoroughly in a twenty-nine-page report that included numerous photos.

APPENDIX

STATE OF CONNECTICUT
DEPARTMENT OF TRANSPORTATION
EMERGENCY BRIDGE PROGRAM

BRIDGE NO. 00614
ROUTE 800
OVER ABANDONED RAILROAD
TORRINGTON, CONNECTICUT

March, 1984

Fay, Spofford & Thorndike, Inc.
Engineers
191 Spring Street, P.O. Box 802
Lexington, Massachusetts 02173

APPENDIX

BRIDGE INSPECTION
UNDERWATER PORTIONS
BR 22 NEW 6/83

Off System

STATE OF CONNECTICUT
DEPARTMENT OF TRANSPORTATION
BUREAU OF HIGHWAYS

SHEET NO. 1
INSPECTION DATE 25 APRIL 1984
SUBMITTED BY: JONES

TOWN WILLINGTON BRIDGE NO. 04809
ROUTE-STREET DALEVILLE SCHOOL RD.
OVER FENTON RV. TYPE RLD BEAM

(1) Class of Inspection BIENNIAL	(8) Marine Growth NONE
(2) Divers BANKY & JONES	(9) Underwater Visibility 3'
(3) date of Previous Inspection NONE	(10) Condition of Rip Rap INADEQUATE
(4) Tide or River Stage NORMAL	(11) Scour AS NOTED.
(5) Current Strength 1/4 KNOT	(12) Obstructions NONE
(6) Weather CLEAR	(13) Channel CLEAR
(7) River Bed Composition MUD/SAND/GRAV.	(14) Remarks RLD BEAM / REBUILT

PIERS DNA NUMBERED SOUTH TO NORTH/WEST TO EAST DNA ABUTMENTS W/E

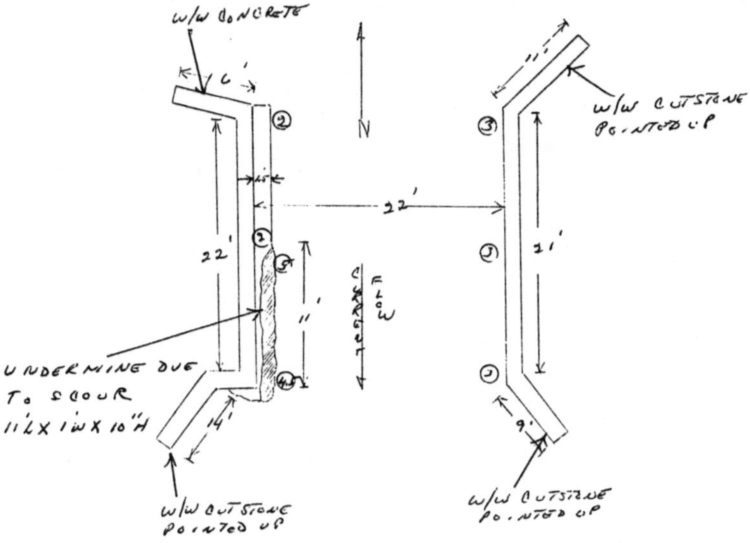

W/W CONCRETE
6'
1.5'
22'
22'
11'
N
FLOW
CURRENT
21'
11'
9'
14'
W/W CUTSTONE POINTED UP
UNDERMINE DUE TO SCOUR 11'L X 1'W X 10"H
W/W CUTSTONE POINTED UP
W/W CUTSTONE POINTED UP

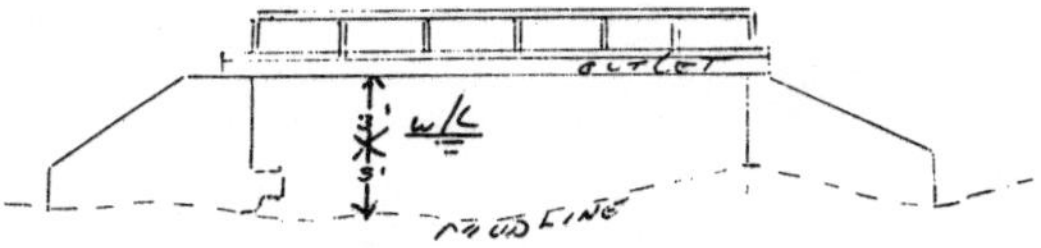

OUTLET
W/L
3'
MUDLINE

ABUTMENTS & FOOTING CONSTRUCTED OF CONCRETE.
WEST ABUTMENT UNDERMINED 11'L X 1'W X 10"H
UNDER WATER PORTIONS OF THIS STRUCTURE ARE IN GOOD CONDITION OTHER THAN AREA NOTED

This bridge inspection report helped convince Chief State's Attorney Austin McGuigan that the *Courant* was wrong in saying divers did not make a diving inspection April 25, 1984. As indicated by the lower diagram, Diver Stanley Jones noted scouring several feet below the waterline ("W/L" in diagram.).

APPENDIX

The Hartford Courant

MARTY PETTY
MANAGING EDITOR

Sunday, June 24

TO: The Bridge Inspection Team, Editor, Photographers, Artists... Hell, the whole staff - everyone

Somehow writing a note does not seem an appropriate way to recognize the - to quote a local newscast - "incredible" project which we gave our readers this morning. It was FIRST RATE!

Better yet, it is a Courant project! It took 150% from everyone. I think like most folks who were involved up to the final moments before press time, one cannot really believe the impact of such a story. And the impact of that "special" effort was really driven home Saturday night when that first tearsheet was placed in front of me.

Hope everyone's as proud!

Great job --

Marty

c: Davies

ESTABLISHED 1764 THE OLDEST CONTINUOUSLY PUBLISHED NEWSPAPER IN AMERICA
HARTFORD, CONNECTICUT 06115 ■ (203) 241-6780

The newspaper's editors never wavered from their original insistence that the bridge surveillance was flawless. In a speech at the national convention of Investigative Reporters and Editors June 20, 1987, Roger Moore encouraged reporters elsewhere to emulate the *Courant*'s bridge and auto emissions projects.

Do you believe what's in the news?

MODERATOR

Don Noel
Political Columnist
The Hartford Courant
Hartford

PANELISTS

Walt Dibble
News Director
WTIC AM-FM
Hartford

Eugene Martin
Executive Editor
The Waterbury Republican and American
Waterbury

Mildred McNeill
Vice President, News and Public Affairs
WVIT-TV, Channel 30
New Britain

Marty Petty
Vice President and Deputy Executive Editor
The Hartford Courant
Hartford

Michael Sechrist
News Director
WTNH-TV, Channel 8
New Haven

Donald Sharpe
Editor and Vice President
The Jackson Newspapers
New Haven

Pat Sheehan
News Anchor
WFSB-TV, Channel 3
Hartford

If you're like most Americans, you trust news organizations more than you trust President Reagan. That's just one of the surprises to come out of a recent investigation of public attitudes toward the press.

And on June 19th you'll be able to express your views and know that they've been heard.

To help area residents, business people, and public officials understand the news media and public reaction to it, a free public forum will be held on Thursday, June 19 in the University of Hartford's Lincoln Theater. The People & The Press: A Public Forum will reveal the results of a recent study conducted by The Gallup Organization for The Times Mirror Company. With media experts also present — representing Connecticut newspapers, radio stations and television stations — you'll have a chance to express your views, and ask questions, too.

Join us for this examination of the news media, when an informative and interesting dialogue will help us all learn a little bit more about the people and the press.

A PUBLIC FORUM

Thursday, June 19
8:00 p.m.

Lincoln Theater
University of Hartford,
West Hartford

Admission is free.

Sponsored by

The Hartford Courant

Times Mirror

with the cooperation of
Connecticut Daily Newspaper Association
Connecticut Associated Press Broadcasters Association.

The *Courant* made extensive public relations efforts to win the loyalty of subscribers. This advertisement was part of the chain's "People & the Press" national ad campaign.

APPENDIX

STATE OF CONNECTICUT

★ Thank You for Sharing Your Idea. ★

Please send your ideas to: *Employees' Suggestion Awards Program, 165 Capitol Ave., Hartford, 06115.*

Interdepartment Message

STO-201 REV. 11/81 STATE OF CONNECTICUT
(Stock No. 6938-051-01)

SAVE TIME: *Handwritten messages are acceptable.*
Use carbon if you really need a copy. If typewritten, ignore faint lines.

	NAME	TITLE	DATE
To	The Honorable William A O'Neill	Governor of Connecticut	August 23, 1985
	AGENCY	ADDRESS	
	NAME	TITLE	TELEPHONE
From	Benjamin A. Muzio	Commissioner	2240
	AGENCY: Department of Motor Vehicles	ADDRESS	

SUBJECT SERIES OF ARTICLES IN THE HARTFORD COURANT REGARDING CONNECTICUT'S EMISSIONS INSPECTION PROGRAM

The Hartford Courant, on July 17, engaged the services of a paid consultant, Schaller Honda of New Britain, a dealer licensed by the Connecticut Department of Motor Vehicles, to "adjust the test vehicle where it should consistently have failed to meet state hydrocarbon standards."

The stated purpose of these adjustments was to test the accuracy of the testing equipment in the State's Auto Emissions Program.

During the period from July 23 to August 7, this maladjusted vehicle was tested at all of the 18 Auto Emissions Inspection Stations, failing at five and passing at 13 stations with varying degrees of readings.

The equipment used by the contractor, Hamilton Test Systems (HTS), in the 44 test lanes at 18 stations is subjected to the following procedures, all of which are designed to assure consistently accurate readings:

1. Electronic calibration before each and every test: The electronic calibration resets the zero and span (full scale) settings to a true constant value.

2. Gas Calibration: A known valve of gas is fed into the analyzer at least twice a week and the machine response is checked for conformity to the known value.

3. All analyzers are checked for leaks twice a day.

4. Random, unannounced checks of HTS equipment (similar to what the Courant attempted to achieve) are performed at least once every two weeks by DMV quality audit teams.

The quality assurance methods and test procedures in Connecticut also have been audited by the U.S. EPA and were described as excellant and a model for all programs.

The tampering performed by the mechanic (making the PCV valve inoperative) is specifically cited in Chilton's repair manual for Honda vehicles as a source of deterioration and lack of consistency in a vehicle's performance and emissions levels.

SAVE TIME: *If convenient, handwrite reply to sender on this same sheet.*

Connecticut Department of Motor Vehicles Commissioner Benjamin Muzio issued a three-page report finding serious problems with 1985 *Courant* allegations of problems in Connecticut's emissions control testing program.

APPENDIX

SERIES OF ARTICLES IN THE HARTFORD COURANT REGARDING CONNECTICUT'S EMISSIONS INSPECTION PROGRAM

According to Jim Burke, Senior Engineer for American Honda Motor Co., Inc., disconnecting vacuum hoses in the PCV System could cause erratic emissions readings.

Mr. Burke also said that maladjusting the carburetor idle mixture (either too lean or too rich) could also cause erratic emissions readings especially if the idle speed is increased to compensate for the maladjustment thus causing "pullover."

The DMV's automotive engineering consultant, Harry Gough, said the adjustments "created unpredictable engine operating conditions and produced unpredictable results. The methodology used by The Courant was quite unscientific, unreliable and flawed."

The Courant reporter, saying his editors would not allow him to divulge information, refused to provide DMV the name of the dealer who tampered with the vehicle or provide any invoices. This information was requested by DMV in order to learn the specific adjustments made to the test vehicle and, thereby, to evaluate properly the significance of the test results.

The Auto Emissions staff, through other sources, determined where the vehicle had been maladjusted and, unknown to the Courant, arranged a meeting with Schaller Honda service personnel. DMV learned:

* The service manager, Roland Cormier, admitted the vehicle was tampered with.

* He indicated the carburetor was maladjusted to a <u>borderline pass/fail condition.</u>

* He admitted tampering with the pollution control devices by disconnecting a vacuum hose from the PCV system.

* He also admitted that the analyzer used to check the vehicle was malfunctioning at that time. It was later repaired at a cost of $464. A second analyzer used to back up this first test was found by a Quality Audit team on August 15 to be malfunctioning with a 19% leak.

* He also stated that he had advised The Courant reporter that the vehicle, as adjusted, would produce a borderline emissions reading and <u>could cause a variation of readings</u>.

* He produced copies of work orders that were denied the Department by The Courant relating to the vehicle and the analyzer.

With this information, I then directed Bill Ferris and Don Byers of my staff, along with representatives of HTS, to meet with The Courant editors prior to publication of the article, to explain, in detail, the false assumptions and flawed analysis. The editors chose to ignore the facts as presented.

THE HONORABLE WILLIAM A. O'NEILL - page three - August 23, 1985

SERIES OF ARTICLES IN THE HARTFORD COURANT REGARDING CONNECTICUT'S EMISSIONS INSPECTION PROGRAM

The methodology employed by the Courant reporter was unscientific and inaccurate.

The DMV stands behind its previous offer to assist The Courant in performing a scientific and accurate evaluation of the program, by having the vehicle set to manufacturer's specifications and then be tested.

In May, 1984, the U.S. EPA visited Connecticut to perform a field audit of its test procedures and quality assurance provisions. In its followup report, the EPA said, "In general, we found the inspection and quality control aspects of the (Connecticut) program are excellant. Overall, Connecticut's inspection station network is well designed and efficiently operated. The audit revealed that Hamilton Test Systems does a thorough job of quality control at the inspection lanes and that the Department of Motor Vehicles monitors the HTS operation effectively, paying particular attention to quality assurance of the analyzers."

I am convinced the testing equipment used by HTS is accurate and the quality audit procedures are more than adequate to detect any failings in the system.

I will ask the technical personnel from EPA in Ann Arbor, Michigan, to return and perform a complete audit of the equipment in Connecticut's Auto Emissions Program.

Respectfully submitted,

Benjamin A. Muzio
Commissioner

BAM/jw

APPENDIX

The Hartford Courant

MICHAEL J. DAVIES
EDITOR, PUBLISHER and
CHIEF EXECUTIVE OFFICER

January 27, 1986

Robert C. Christopher
Secretary, The Pulitzer Prize Board
702 Journalism
Columbia University
New York, NY 10027

Judges of the Pulitzer Prize Committee:

Connecticut residents have long complained about the state Department of Motor Vehicles' emissions testing and safety inspections programs, saying that the tests are inconsistent and unfair. The Courant set out to discover if there was any basis for those complaints. Reporters took a car through all 16 safety inspection stations and all 18 emissions testing stations. The car had been adjusted so that it should have failed the emissions tests, and sidelights from the oar were removed, a failure the safety inspectors should have caught.

Reporter John Mura found that safety inspections were perfunctory at best and no more guaranteed the safety of a vehicle than did a carwash. The average inspections lasted one minute, 40 seconds, and critical items such as brakes and steering were rarely checked. None of the inspectors noticed the missing sidelights. Even though it had been adjusted to fail the emissions tests, the car passed at 13 of the 18 testing stations with readings all over the scale.

The ramifications of the story are still being felt. The governor and legislature both have called for reorganization of the DMV. Legislative leaders are forming a committee to study whether a private corporation could do a better job of running the department.

We are proud to submit this effort for your consideration.

Sincerely,

MJD:ls

ESTABLISHED 1764 THE OLDEST CONTINUOUSLY PUBLISHED NEWSPAPER IN AMERICA
HARTFORD, CONNECTICUT 06115 ■ (203) 241-6478

Courant Editor and Publisher Michael Davies sought a Pulitzer Prize in 1986 for the emissions story. Davies was himself a Pulitzer juror in 1986 and 1987.

APPENDIX

UNITED STATES ENVIRONMENTAL PROTECTION AGENCY
REGION I
J. F. KENNEDY FEDERAL BUILDING, BOSTON, MASSACHUSETTS 02203

RECEIVED
NOV 05 1985
AUTO EMISSIONS DIVISION

Benjamin A. Muzio, Commissioner
Department of Motor Vehicles
60 State Street
Whethersfield, CT

Dear Commissioner Muzio:

Per your request of August 29, 1985 an EPA Audit Team consisting of Region I and headquarters personnel conducted a two day unannounced audit of the Connecticut Motor Vehicle Inspection Program on September 17 and 18, 1985. The results of this audit were excellent. All of the analyzers checked were within the audit limits specified by EPA. This is quite an accomplishment in that we would normally expect a small percentage of the analyzers to be outside these limits. The quality control procedures used by your Department and Hamilton Test Systems are well designed and conscientiously implemented resulting in consistent accuracy throughout the system. Other states operating similar systems could look to Connecticut for an example of an excellent quality control program.

The accuracy of the testing is providing a significant air quality benefit to the citizens of Connecticut. The testing system is identifying a high percentage of those vehicles which are emitting pollutants significantly above the EPA standards. The reduction in emissions due to the repair of these vehicles is providing cleaner air throughout the state.

I have enclosed the official audit report from our Office of Mobile Sources. Please let me know if we can be of further assistance.

Sincerely yours,

Louis F. Gitto, Director
Air Management Division

cc: Stanley Pac, Commissioner, DEP
Michael R. Deland, Regional Administrator
Richard Wilson, Director, Office of Mobile Source

The U.S. Environmental Protection Agency found Connecticut's emissions testing program to be working well in 1985.

APPENDIX

UNITED STATES ENVIRONMENTAL PROTECTION AGENCY
WASHINGTON, D.C. 20460

OCT 30 1985

OFFICE OF
AIR, NOISE AND RADIATION

MEMORANDUM

SUBJECT: Connecticut Inspection/Maintenance Program

FROM: Richard D. Wilson, Director
for Office of Mobile Sources

TO: Louis F. Gitto, Director
Air Management Division, Region I

In response to Commissioner Muzio's request of August 29, 1985, representatives of my office and yours conducted a system audit of the Connecticut vehicle inspection/maintenance (I/M) program on September 17 and 18, 1985. The purpose of this audit was to investigate whether the emission testing equipment and quality assurance procedures used by both the I/M contractor, Hamilton Test Systems, and the State Department of Motor Vehicles (DMV) are adequate to provide accurate testing.

The detailed analysis of the data collected in the audit is attached. The results reinforce our earlier findings that the accuracy of the testing equipment in Connecticut is outstanding due to the considerable attention that is given to quality control by the testing contractor and by the State DMV. We feel that this is very important, since it ensures that Connecticut citizens are getting fair, accurate tests regardless of the test station they choose.

When you transmit this information to Commissioner Muzio, please convey our willingness to provide any additional technical assistance that may be needed from this office. If we can be of further assistance, please feel free to contact me at FTS 382-7645 or Charles Gray in Ann Arbor at FTS 374-8404.

Attachment

ACKNOWLEDGMENTS

I am deeply grateful to those who provided their counsel and encouragement during the manuscript's early stages. Foremost among those outside the daily newspaper industry were my friend Geoffrey Waldau, a Washington, D.C. economist; my two agents, Lewis Chambers of the Bethel Agencies and Peter Shepherd of Harold Ober Associates; Barry Hildebrandt, president of the Peregrine Press; Katherine States, former executive editor of the *American Lawyer*; and Howard Bray, former executive director of the Fund for Investigative Journalism. My Fund grant came from a special bequest set up in memory of Albert Kihn, a cameraman at KRON-TV in San Francisco who was killed on assignment.

Others who provided expert advice, welcome support or courageous assistance were: Deane Avery; William Cockerham; Tom Condon; John Donohue; Irene Driscoll; Theodore Driscoll; Carol Giacomo; Helen Kicin; Lincoln Millstein; Cheyney Ryan; Al Simonds; Robert F.X. Sillerman; Joseph Steinberg; Kathi Van Brunt; and Jean Viallet. Any themes or conclusions in the book, however, are entirely my own.

INDEX

INDEX

INDEX

INDEX

INDEX

NOTE ON THE AUTHOR

A student newspaper editor, rowing team member and heavyweight boxing champion at Cornell University, Andrew Kreig received perfect grades in earning an MSL degree as a Ford Foundation Fellow at Yale Law School. He worked 14 years for the *Hartford Courant* in Connecticut before becoming a magazine writer in 1984. His efforts have helped force two unethical judges off the federal bench and jail two hoodlums who assaulted him at his home. He is a member of the American Society of Journalists and Authors, Investigative Reporters and Editors and the national ethics committee of the Society of Professional Journalists (SDX). SPIKED was assisted by a research grant from the Fund for Investigative Journalism in Washington, D.C.